Population Health

An Implementation Guide to Improve
Outcomes and Lower Costs

Population Health

An Implementation Guide to Improve Outcomes and Lower Costs

George Mayzell, MD, MBA

CRC Press
Taylor & Francis Group
Boca Raton London New York

CRC Press is an imprint of the
Taylor & Francis Group, an **informa** business

A PRODUCTIVITY PRESS BOOK

CRC Press
Taylor & Francis Group
6000 Broken Sound Parkway NW, Suite 300
Boca Raton, FL 33487-2742

First issued in paperback 2021

© 2016 by George Mayzell
CRC Press is an imprint of Taylor & Francis Group, an Informa business

No claim to original U.S. Government works

Version Date: 20150831

ISBN 13: 978-1-03-209823-4 (pbk)
ISBN 13: 978-1-4987-0555-4 (hbk)

Visit the Taylor & Francis Web site at
http://www.taylorandfrancis.com

and the CRC Press Web site at
http://www.crcpress.com

Special thanks to
Cheryl Trantham

Contents

Author

George Mayzell, MD, MBA is currently a principal with Rx Health Partners LLC, a healthcare consulting company. He was most recently the senior vice president, chief medical officer, and chief clinical integration officer of AMITA Health, the joint operating company formed in February 2015 by Adventist Midwest Health, based in Hinsdale, Illinois, and Alexian Brothers Health System, based in Arlington Heights, Illinois.

AMITA Health encompasses nine hospitals and an extensive physician provider network of more than 3000 physicians. Dr. Mayzell, who joined the organization in January 2013, worked with hospitals, payers, and providers in unique partnership models to build accountable care organizations, population health programs, and care management models of the future.

Dr. Mayzell previously served as CEO of Health Choice and senior vice president of Methodist Le Bonheur Healthcare in Memphis, Tennessee.

Per Dr. Mayzell, "AMITA Health is an organization committed to change and to adopting new healthcare delivery models that will be critical in what promises to be challenging economic times."

Dr. Mayzell has more than 30 years of experience in medicine and is a board-certified internist and geriatrician. He earned his medical degree from the University of Medicine and Dentistry of New Jersey and his MBA from Jacksonville University.

He previously served as senior medical director of managed care for the University of Florida and Shands Hospital. He spent more than 10 years with

Blue Cross Blue Shield of Florida, working as regional medical director for care and quality and corporate managing medical director for pharmacy and care. Additionally, he has more than 10 years of practice experience.

Dr. Mayzell has coauthored seven books, including *Leveraging Lean in Healthcare* and *Physician Alignment: Constructing Viable Roadmaps for the Future.*

Contributors

Kevin S. Attride is the director of clinical integration for Adventist Midwest Health, where he revamped the quality program for the clinically integrated network and implemented new HIT tools to improve the network's cost efficiency and outcomes performance. He also serves as the leader for the organization's Medicare Shared Savings Program and Cigna ACO, which continue to enhance the network's value-based care delivery system.

Attride previously worked for Adventist Health System in Orlando, Florida, and was enrolled in a multiyear leadership development fellowship program where he was afforded the opportunity to receive training under seasoned executives of Florida Hospital, one of the most successful integrated delivery networks in the country.

He earned his MBA from the University of Central Florida and baccalaureate from Southern Adventist University. As a lifelong learner, he continually seeks opportunities to advance the delivery of healthcare and improve patient care through whole-person health.

David J. Ballard was appointed on October 1, 2013 as a chief quality officer of Baylor Scott & White Health (BSWH), the largest not-for-profit healthcare system in Texas, which includes 43 hospitals, 500 patient care sites, 6000 affiliated physicians, 34,000 employees, and the Scott & White health plan. A board-certified internist, he trained at the Mayo Graduate School of Medicine following his completion of degrees in chemistry, economics, epidemiology, and medicine at the University of North Carolina (UNC), where he was a Morehead Scholar, North Carolina Fellow, and junior year Phi Beta Kappa inductee. Dr. Ballard held progressive academic appointments as assistant and then associate professor at the Mayo Medical School, as associate professor with tenure at the University of Virginia School of Medicine, as professor of medicine with tenure at the Emory University School of Medicine, and professor of epidemiology in The Rollins School of Public Health of Emory University. He joined the Baylor Health Care System (BHCS) in 1999 as its first chief quality officer. He serves on the board of managers of The Heart Hospital Baylor Plano and of the BHCS-Kessler/Select rehabilitation and long-term care joint venture. In July 2011, Dr. Ballard was appointed president of the BHCS, now BSWH, Safe, Timely, Effective, Efficient, Equitable, Patient-Centered (STEEEP) Global Institute to provide healthcare performance improvement solutions to healthcare organizations throughout the world. In 2012, he was selected as chair of the newly formed BHCS STEEEP Governance Council to set strategy and direction for operational functions related to STEEEP care across BHCS, which is now scaled across BSWH under his leadership.

Dr. Ballard serves on the editorial boards of *Health Services Research*, *The Journal of Comparative Effectiveness Research*, and *The Mayo Clinic Proceedings* (as health policy section editor). He is a 1995 recipient of the Academy Health New Investigator Award (given annually to an outstanding health services research scholar in the United States less than 40 years of age) and a 2012 recipient of the John M. Eisenberg Article-of-the-Year in *Health Services Research*. His book, *Achieving STEEEP Healthcare*, published in 2013, received the Shingo Research Award for its contributions to operational excellence and was followed by the publication in 2014 of its companion book, *Guide to Achieving STEEEP Healthcare*. He is a 2014–2017 member of AHRQ's National Advisory Council. Dr. Ballard serves on the UNC School of Public Health Foundation Board and is a past member of the Board of Trustees of The Lawrenceville School and of the Texas Hospital Association. In 2008 he earned the Distinguished Medical Alumnus Award of the UNC School of Medicine.

Bryan N. Becker is currently the associate dean for clinical affairs and vice president for clinical integration at the University of Chicago Medicine. He earned his AB degree in English from Dartmouth College and MD from the University of Kansas. He then went on to train in internal medicine at Duke University Medical Center and nephrology at Vanderbilt University Medical Center. Subsequently, Dr. Becker took on a variety of roles at the University of Wisconsin, heading up the nephrology section, developing a new community-based practice, and ultimately overseeing the clinical activities of the Department of Medicine across academic and community-based sites, all while practicing clinically. He then led the faculty practice plan at the University of Illinois and progressively moved through various roles, including chief medical officer and CEO for the University of Illinois Hospital and Clinics, before transitioning to his present position at the University of Chicago Medicine. He has served as president and as a member of the board of the National Kidney Foundation, and as a board member for a number of organizations, including WWT, a revenue cycle management company, and Forward Health Group, a cutting-edge population health management and healthcare measurement company.

Katie Carow has more than 20 years of experience in strategic and physician resource planning, mergers and acquisitions, business development, marketing, and operations. She specializes in developing business strategies based on data-driven evidence. She initiated and led clinical and senior leadership teams to identify growth opportunities based on financial performance and market advantages. Carow has managed 3- to 5-year planning processes, as well as annual tactical plans, and developed aligned physician growth strategies. She identified physician specialty and group targets for recruitment, succession planning, and retention.

Carow has provided planning, analytical, and marketing direction for academic, community, and pediatric hospitals and systems, as well as nonprofit and government organizations. She developed business plans, analyzed major markets, facilitated retreats, and led the patient satisfaction improvement process. In prior positions, Carow oversaw the planning department, PHO marketing, physician referral call functions, and integrated operations of a $20M PHO with a 500-member multispecialty group. She is also very familiar with CON regulations and the filing process, having worked with a team to obtain approval for a $280M inpatient tower.

Carow is an adjunct professor at the University of Illinois. She earned her master's degree in business administration with a concentration in international business from Clemson University, South Carolina, and studied in Italy. She is a fellow of the American College of Healthcare Executives, member of the Society for Healthcare Strategy and Market Development, and chaired the Education and Networking Committee as a board member of the Chicago Healthcare Executives Forum.

Kathleen M. Ferket is currently the vice president of the Care Continuum at Amita Health Enterprise, a nine-hospital system in metropolitan Chicago. She is responsible for overseeing care management across the continuum. Prior to joining Adventist Midwest Health, Ferket served in a variety of leadership roles, including as executive director for nursing services, executive director for Women's and Children's services, as well as relationship management for strategic physician and community relationships. She is on the board of the Illinois Organization of Nurse Leaders and served as chairperson for the policy and advocacy and continuum of care committees. She participated in the 2012–2014 strategic planning process for the American Organization of Nurse Executives. She is a board-certified nurse practitioner and has presented nationally at AONE and Magnet conferences, as well as local conferences and events. She was recognized as the Nursing Spectrum 2008 winner for Advancing Nursing Practice, a 2011 UIC Pinnacle Leader, and received the Ron Lee lifetime achievement award from the Illinois Department of Public Health. She volunteers for the Illinois Multiple Sclerosis Foundation and serves on the board for the Infant Welfare Society. As a registered leadership coach, Ferket mentors leaders in navigating change, workplace conflict, and purposeful communication.

Neil S. Fleming is the vice president of quantitative sciences in the Center for Clinical Effectiveness/Office of the Chief Quality Officer, Baylor Scott & White Health in Dallas, Texas. He oversees the biostatistics and health economics groups with direct responsibilities that include evaluating clinical and financial outcomes related to quality interventions, such as implementation of health information technology and the patient-centered medical home model that occur throughout the system. He is also clinical professor of health services research at the Robbins Institute for Health Policy and Leadership in the Hankamer School of Business, Baylor University in Waco. He previously served as vice president and chief operating officer of the Baylor Health Care System STEEEP Global Institute, and as BHCS vice president for Healthcare Research.

Cliff T. Fullerton is the chief medical officer for Baylor Scott & White Quality Alliance and chief population health officer for Baylor Scott & White Health (BSWH) in Dallas, Texas. Dr. Fullerton is a practicing board-certified family physician and past president of Family Medical Center at Garland/North Garland located in Garland, Texas. He earned his MD and completed his internship at the University of Texas Southwestern Medical School/Parkland Memorial Hospital in Dallas, before going on to a residency in family medicine at the University of Oklahoma Health Science Center in Oklahoma City. He earned his master's of science in healthcare management from the University of Texas at Dallas. Dr. Fullerton previously served as the chief quality officer for HealthTexas Provider Network (HTPN), the BSWH-affiliated medical group practice in North Texas, within which he led the Patient-Centered Medical Home (PCMH) initiative and the establishment of a Care Coordination resource to support patient transitions between acute and ambulatory care, and between primary and specialty care. He has also been active in the broader medical community, serving as a board member of the Texas Academy of Family Physicians Foundation, a member of the Dallas–Fort Worth Business Group on Health Diabetes Committee, a clinical advocate with the Texas Medical Foundation, and a physician champion for Texas DOQ-IT. He is a current member of the Texas Medical Association Quality Council and Management Services Organization Task Force.

Briget da Graca is a senior medical writer within the Office of the Chief Quality Officer for Baylor Scott & White Health (BSWH) in Dallas, Texas. She earned degrees in biochemistry and science and technology journalism from Texas A&M University, and in 2012 earned her JD summa cum laude from the Southern Methodist University Dedman School of Law. She has worked with health services researchers within BSWH for more than 10 years, examining a variety of topics related to the effectiveness and efficiency of care, and in 2015 was a presidential scholar for the Academy Health Institute on Advocacy and Public Policy.

Edward M. Rafalski is currently the chief strategy and marketing officer for BayCare Health System in Clearwater, Florida. In this role he is responsible for developing and executing strategic planning; reframing pressing strategic and marketing issues; and creating a common vocabulary for discussing strategy, marketing, and communications issues across BayCare, including in service excellence and the patient experience. Prior to BayCare, he was the senior vice president of strategic planning and marketing for Methodist Le Bonheur Healthcare, Memphis, Tennessee, and the vice president of marketing for Alexian Brothers Hospital Network, Arlington Heights, Illinois. Dr. Rafalski has an extensive background in strategic planning, data analytics, decision support, GIS, business development, marketing, public relations, group purchasing, and managed care contracting. He has also served as an executive liaison for emergency departments and children's hospital operations.

After graduating from the University of Chicago with a bachelor's degree in public policy studies, Dr. Rafalski earned a master's degree in public health from Yale University School of Medicine. He earned his PhD in public health sciences from the Division of Health Policy and Administration at the University of Illinois, School of Public Health, where he has taught as a clinical assistant professor. His health services research and teaching interests include the effects of market economics on healthcare services, healthcare decision support, quantitative methods, health disparities, marketing, and strategic management. He recently joined the faculty of the University of Tennessee Health Science Center at the College of Medicine in the Department of Preventive Medicine as an adjunct associate professor and the University of Memphis School of Public Health as an affiliate research professor, where he teaches managerial epidemiology. Dr. Rafalski is a fellow of the American College of Healthcare Executives, Six Sigma Black Belt, and member of the 2014 TNCPE Board of Examiners, trained in the Baldrige Criteria for Performance Excellence.

 **Pam Williams** is currently working as a consultant on clinical integration network development for several organizations nationally. Prior to that, Williams was the CEO of Adventist Health Partners and Adventist Midwest Management Services, a health system–owned physician group and management services organization in the western suburbs of Chicago. As the founding executive of these two organizations in the mid-1990s, she has worked to develop and modify physician compensation formulas throughout her healthcare career.

After initially training and working as an occupational therapist, Williams began her healthcare management work as the administrator of a large multidisciplinary behavioral health group from 1982 to 1990. She then joined Adventist Health System in 1991 and her early work with Adventist was focused on the development of the practice that is now Adventist Health Partners, initially a primary care and now multispecialty group serving three counties and nearly 200,000 patients.

Also during her tenure with Adventist, Williams was the founding executive for Adventist Health Network, a clinically integrated physician hospital organization serving four hospitals and more than 800 physicians. The time spent developing this clinically integrated network allowed her to assist in the development of evidence-based guidelines, physician incentive programs, and quality reporting systems.

With the current imperative to find ways to incent physicians and care teams to be both productive and provide value to their patients, Williams has worked to utilize her experience and the experience of others to continuously improve the compensation models used at Adventist.

Introduction

Most healthcare companies are now talking about population health. They talk about it either as it is here now and they have to move toward the model, or alternatively, like it is never coming and things will never change.

Population health is built on the premise of taking better care of patients earlier in the disease process and therefore lowering their ultimate cost. We are not just dealing with the "rising risk" population, but also with preventive care and "wellness." For these programs to be effective, there is often a multiyear wait.

We all agree that our current model of healthcare is fractured and does not provide quality healthcare for many average Americans. While most agree that today's American healthcare is high quality, it is not uniformly delivered to all Americans. Healthcare is also too expensive, and relative to other international countries, we are not getting the value of healthcare for the money that we put into it.

Our current model cannot continue indefinitely, although in many parts of the country, it feels like fee-for-service reimbursement models are here to stay. Many agree that we will move toward different payment models and different delivery models. The argument is more about how quickly this will happen and how completely it will happen rather than whether or not it will happen. Many hospital systems and delivery models are convinced this metamorphosis will be many years away and its fee-for-service or pay-for-click will never completely stop.

We are already starting to see a move toward value-based payment in Medicare and beginning in the commercial space. It is still very much a transitional model since it only affects a fraction of the payment. I believe that we are now on the journey to population health. This is an evolutionary process that may not proceed in the linear fashion we might have originally thought.

Population health is about being responsible, both clinically and financially, for a population of patients. This requires a payment model that supports global payment such as full risk, but even more importantly, requires a thoughtful review of what care is delivered when and where, as well as the identification of a discrete population, which is still quite a challenge.

Identifying a patient population can be challenging in itself. In order for us as caregivers to be sure we are improving the health of our patients, we need to know whom we are accountable for, and we need to be reimbursed with a longer perspective in mind. While Medicare can identify these patients, care delivery for these groups can be geographically challenging.

Another issue is the time frame used to deliver population health. This is a challenge in our current insurance and payment model since many patients are only tied to an insurer for one year at a time. In order to invest the resources in preventive health, the population or individual patient must be tied to the one responsible for the clinical and financial outcomes for many years. There is no easy setup in our current insurance model to accomplish this. One theory is that this might be tied at the employer level since many employees tend to stay at a company longer than they stay at a single insurer. This is still a large leap of faith at the employer level.

With this in mind, it makes more sense to look at this as a journey, where ultimate true population health may be many years away. However, some or many of the tenets of population health may happen much sooner. Thus we are back to the move to value-based payment that is a major foundation of population health. We consider this as a move from the first curve of healthcare, which is simply volume and cost, to the second curve of healthcare, which is cost, outcomes, and value.

It is quite possible that this move to the second curve and value-based payment may accelerate more quickly than we think. Centers for Medicare and Medicaid Services (CMS) is already committed to moving to value-based payment models over the next few years. The focus is on Medicare Advantage, ACOs, and bundled payment programs. Commercial payers have also committed to being right behind Medicare in this change. As we move from volume to value, the delivery model must change as the payment model shifts. This would mean paying for outcomes and some form of full risk payment. Under this model, physicians must be aligned with payments and the rest of the delivery system in a partnership collaboration. This will require data and data evaluation in a more robust fashion. This will also require patient engagement and commitment to their own health needs.

This engagement will shift the model from healthcare delivery to a "health" model. While health is defined as "a feeling and state of mind as well as freedom of disease," it can also be defined in a more functional manner. It is more than simply preventing disease or wellness. To be a successful population health organization, we will need to move from the current delivery model to a more health-driven model where we are depending on the delivery system, public health, commitment, and engagement of the customers, and perhaps their employer.

I am optimistic about the new delivery model on "health," and rather than being concerned about the changes ahead, I look forward to creating and building a new healthcare model that better serves the patient, our communities, physicians, and the health delivery system.

David L. Crane
Executive Vice President/Chief Operating Officer
AMITA Health

Chapter 1

What Is Population Health?

George Mayzell

Contents

The current health delivery system in the United States is not only broken, but also unsustainable! The system in the United States is not so much a health system as it is a "sickness system." Arguably, the United States does a pretty good job taking care of patients when they are ill and particularly if they are well insured and from certain socioeconomic groups.

Despite the commitment of almost 17% of our gross domestic product (GDP) to healthcare, the United States performs poorly compared to other developed countries in many critical healthcare determinants, including life expectancy, one of the most cited healthcare measurements. The U.S. healthcare system consistently underperforms when compared to other nations, including Austria, Canada, and France. Comparing the United States to 11 other countries in the Commonwealth Fund report,[1] the United

States ranks last in the areas of quality of care, access to care, care efficiency, care equity, and healthy lives.

U.S. International Ranking

In our current system of healthcare delivery, most of the stakeholders have an economic incentive to deal with illness. Thus, many of the individuals who make the majority of decisions for a healthcare delivery model, despite personal moralities, are financially incentivized to treat sick patients. The system is in fact designed for sick care and not preventive care. In most cases there is no emphasis for payment for wellness or prevention. If there is return, it is often many years later in the future; therefore, there is little direct return on investment (ROI) on prevention and wellness in the short run for payers or employers.

In only four categories, effective care, safe care, coordinated care, and patient-centered care, the United States ranked fifth.[2] There are also disparities in the quality and access to care based on not having insurance, where a person lives, and other socioeconomic indicators. The U.S. health system has made some strides in quality of life and life expectancy in certain groups and demographics. Unfortunately, there are still significant opportunities with disparity (Figure 1.1).

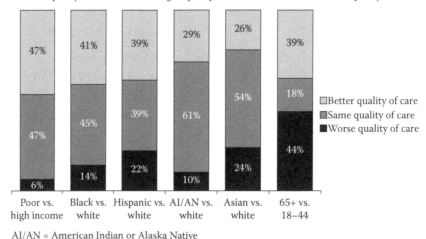

Disparities in Quality of Care for Selected Groups

Percent of quality measures for which groups experienced worse, same, or better quality of care:

AI/AN = American Indian or Alaska Native

Figure 1.1 Disparity chart. (Adapted from AHRQ, National Healthcare Disparities Report, 2011, http://www.ahrq.gov/qual/qrdr11.htm.)

The current system of healthcare delivery is clearly unsustainable as more and more of our GDP is used to treat illness. There is increasing financial pressure on Medicare, expansion of Medicaid, while a large portion of the country still remains uninsured. In addition, there is increasing transparency in our delivery model, which exerts pressure on the system to change its paradigm.

Population Health versus Public Health

Population health is all about what happens outside of our current healthcare delivery model. It is all about what happens outside the four walls of the physician's office, hospital, or diagnostic center. What we have learned is that simply managing the delivery of healthcare is not enough to provide "health" (well-being) at the patient level. There is 85% of "health" or quality of life that is not about healthcare delivery, but about other environmental, behavioral, and socioeconomic factors that contribute to what we call quality of life. We can no longer wait till people get sick to intervene. By the time people get ill, the medical costs and treatment costs are large and will continue to destabilize the U.S. economy. By modifying risk factors, or eliminating them, we can control society's long-term medical costs as well as improve productivity.

There are important differentiators between population health and public health, although there are many similarities. Public health is often thought of as government directed and traditionally has focused on disease survival, and dealing with communicable diseases and environmental factors, such as water supply, clean air, and similar problems. Public health traditionally has focused on public good items such as drinking water safety, etc., relating to the entire population. The term public health is slowly being replaced by population health. Population health is a much broader term that covers not only activities but also a policy-driven approach to health and wellness. Population health is about healthcare of a group of individuals and invariably drills down to the individual level, looking at improvement of both health and healthcare. Population health also focuses on individual and societal risk factors for disease and tends to be more proactive than a traditional public health model.

The current sickness model will have to move toward a health model and preventive care model. Health has many different definitions, but it is not simply the absence of disease. Health is also wellness or a state of well-being. Healthcare delivery is only a small component of health.

Much of this new focus will most likely be driven by corporations, large employers, and governmental payers. These employers will no longer focus only on their own healthcare costs; they need to start focusing on the total cost of the employee to the corporation. These costs include things like presenteeism and absenteeism. These are factors that lead to a productive workforce and will be critical for the long-term success of any company. These factors are often more expensive to any company in the long run than the actual financial costs of healthcare. The costs of absenteeism and presenteeism have long been underestimated and have not been part of the healthcare equation in the past. An active and productive workforce is critical for a competitive U.S. business.

Definition of Population Health

One solution to this unsustainable paradigm of healthcare delivery is to embrace the concept of population health. There are several different definitions of population health; and there is no clear agreement on one definition. However, all of the definitions essentially get you to the same place. Here are the three following definitions.

Definition One

The distribution of health outcomes within a population to help determine the influence, distribution policies, and interventions that affect the determinants.[3]

Definition Two

A sophisticated care-delivery model that involves a systemic effort to assess the health needs of the target population and to proactively provide services to maintain and improve the health of that population.

Definition Three

The Canadian Federal Advisory Committee used the following definition: "Population health refers to health of a population as measured by health status indicators as influenced by social, economic, and physical environments; person health practices; individual capacity and coping skills; human biology; early childhood development; and health services."[28]

Essentially, population health is the identification of a population and the responsibility for both the health and healthcare of the population. To achieve this, one must focus not only on the healthcare delivery model, but also on the health and well-being of the population. This requires a focus on wellness, preventive care, and controlling chronic diseases.

Health versus Healthcare Delivery

It is important that we differentiate between healthcare and health. One definition of health can be controversial and is often a negative in that it is described as the "absence of disease." With population health definitions, health is a positive and includes wellness, prevention, and a sense of well-being. In addition, as we measure our current definition of health, it tends to focus on things like disease rates, illness burdens, and medical cost. In a population health world, the focus is also on well-being, quality of life, and productivity. One of the challenges is to develop metrics that can measure health and wellness accurately. We are used to measuring total cost of healthcare in specific outcomes of the disease process. We must now look to measuring quality of life, productivity, and other "health" metrics.

> The primary determinants of disease are mainly economic and social, and therefore its remedies must also be economic and social.
>
> **So Michael G. Marmont 2001**
> *Professor, Epidemiology and Public Health*
> *University College London*

The health of a population can be measured by health status indicators and is influenced by social, economic, physical, environmental, and personal health practices; individual capacity and coping skills; human biology; early childhood development; and health services and procedures.[1] These are often called healthcare determinants.

It is often hard to differentiate between risk factors and healthcare determinants. Determinants focus on environmental exposures, including physical and social, while risk factors are often based on lifestyle decisions. Healthcare determinants can be defined as any factor or characteristic that brings a change in one's health condition. See examples of classic risk factors in Figure 1.2. Some of the different categories of determinants include

- Social determinants—including education, economic stability, health and healthcare, social and community context, and neighborhood environment
- Physical and environmental determinants
- Healthcare determinants
- Genetic determinants
- Behavioral determinants
- Biological determinants

Populations can be defined by conditions, geography, political factors, or physical boundaries. They can be defined as a population's philosophy, cultural conditions, or a payer source. They can also be defined by a country or ethnicity, religion, or any other group that has defining characteristics. Thus far, in the United States, it has usually been a payer source from the standpoint of practicality. This is probably the easiest way of identifying a population that can be monitored and measured. Accountable Care Organization (ACO) can potentially be seen as a prodrome of a population health model. This model will have to shift as we move to more holistic populations.

One of the most critical things to understand about population health is that it is a very different concept from that of healthcare. When we talk about health in the United States, we generally think about healthcare and healthcare delivery models. We talk about a sickness model, and we talk about the functioning of our hospitals, physicians, and integration of these parts of the delivery system.

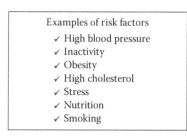

Examples of risk factors
✓ High blood pressure
✓ Inactivity
✓ Obesity
✓ High cholesterol
✓ Stress
✓ Nutrition
✓ Smoking

Figure 1.2 Risk factors of health.

As we move to population health, the concepts are very different. We are really talking about health. This is a much broader concept than healthcare delivery. Healthcare delivery is clearly an important part of health; however, it is a relatively small component. In fact, healthcare delivery is only thought to be ~10%–15% of the determinants of health.[4]

In Figure 1.3, we can see that healthcare delivery is really only a small part of what is important. We can see that genetics plays a significant role at 20%, and, at least until recently, this has been something that had been impossible to affect. New technologies may put this in a different light. Environmental causes are an additional 20%, and these fit into some of the classic public health entities of water, air, and toxins. Finally, the most significant effect on health is healthy (or unhealthy) behaviors.

Over recent years we have been spending time and energy on healthy behaviors, but we have rarely focused on a public health venue in any coordinated fashion. Smoking has been an exception, with major public health focused on education and taxation. More recently, obesity and sedentary lifestyle have gotten significant attention.

If you look at where we spend time, energy, and resources, we spend most of our resources on medical services and very little on healthy behavior (see Figure 1.4). One of the major challenges is the cost of these unhealthy behaviors and additional negative determinants of health to

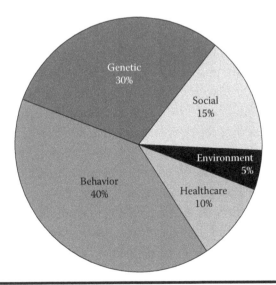

Figure 1.3   The leading determinants of health. (Adapted from McGinnis JM, Williams-Russo P, Knickman JR. *Health Affairs*, 2002; 21(2): 79–93. Available at http://www.healthaffairs.org.)

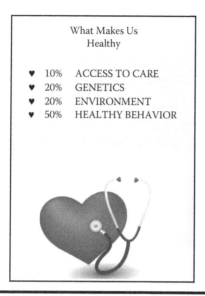
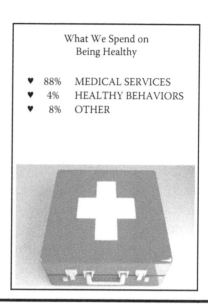

What Makes Us Healthy		What We Spend on Being Healthy	
♥ 10%	ACCESS TO CARE	♥ 88%	MEDICAL SERVICES
♥ 20%	GENETICS	♥ 4%	HEALTHY BEHAVIORS
♥ 20%	ENVIRONMENT	♥ 8%	OTHER
♥ 50%	HEALTHY BEHAVIOR		

Figure 1.4 Health versus healthcare: What makes us healthy? (Adapted from the Bipartison Policy Center and Boston Foundation/New England Healthcare Institute, June 5, 2012.)

society in general. Healthcare costs are rapidly rising out of control, and as we try to get a handle on its drivers, we realize that we cannot do this through a classic health delivery model. We must start focusing on these determinants of health. We cannot control the rising cost of healthcare unless we promote well-being and "health."

As we look at Figure 1.5, a high-level view of population health, we can see a broad view of population health. Healthcare delivery is where we spend most of our resources, which can be broken down into access and quality/outcomes. These also include things like cost of care, geographic availability of clinics, insurance coverage, and others. Quality-based care looks at evidence-based care, preventive care, and disease management.

On the health side, we have items such as genetics and individual behaviors. These include obesity, smoking, seatbelts, alcohol, and other personal choice items. In addition, we also have on the side of health, the classic public health factors that are environmental. These include environmental exposures; social and economic issues, including healthcare disparity; as well as things like communicable diseases, water, air, and toxins.

A population health delivery model broadens the traditional medical delivery system (Figure 1.6). It includes items and processes of integration that are not often part of our current healthcare delivery model. These items

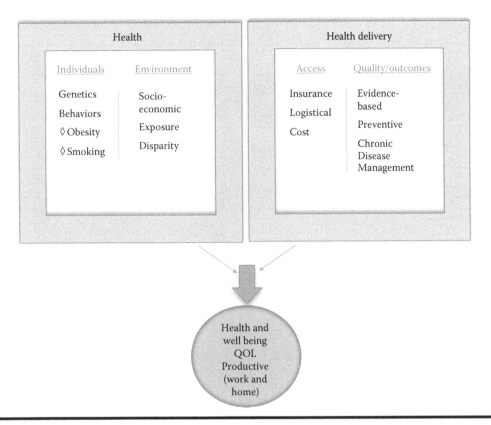

Figure 1.5   A high-level view of population health.

and processes include a focus on prevention, wellness, and the population that typically does not seek healthcare resources. The following items will be further delineated in future chapters.

■ Team-based care models
■ Care coordination, inpatient, and outpatient
■ Integration of behavioral health
■ Health risk assessments and their integration into care models
■ Palliative and end-of-life planning
■ A primary care network with focus on patient-centered medical homes and attributes of care
■ Patient engagement
■ Health prevention and wellness infrastructure
■ A metric system that focuses on performance productivity quality life as well as medical outcomes measurements

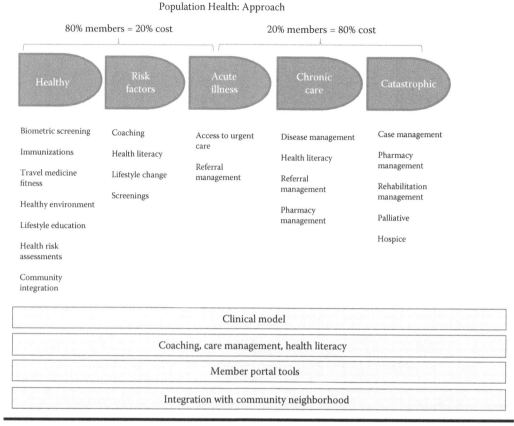

Population Health: Approach

80% members = 20% cost   20% members = 80% cost

Healthy	Risk factors	Acute illness	Chronic care	Catastrophic
Biometric screening	Coaching	Access to urgent care	Disease management	Case management
Immunizations	Health literacy		Health literacy	Pharmacy management
Travel medicine fitness	Lifestyle change	Referral management	Referral management	Rehabilitation management
Healthy environment	Screenings		Pharmacy management	Palliative
Lifestyle education				Hospice
Health risk assessments				
Community integration				

Clinical model
Coaching, care management, health literacy
Member portal tools
Integration with community neighborhood

Figure 1.6   Population Health. (Adapted from the Fabius population health model. Courtesy of Ray Fabius.)

■ Predictive modeling
■ Electronic medical records that link to all providers (health information exchanges), and connect to mobile health, personal health records, patient portals, and telehealth/virtual visit technologies

Building a Population Health Model

If you look carefully at where healthcare resources are expended, they are focused on healthcare delivery and not on health. We spend inordinate amounts of money on caring for the sick and focusing on access to the delivery of highly technical and high-quality healthcare. However, very little is spent preventing disease and slowing the progression of disease. As we look at ourselves compared to other countries, we see that we spend more than every other developing country on healthcare expenditures as a percentage of the GDP. At the same time, we spend much less on the social determinants of health, that is, behaviors and prevention, as a percentage of the GDP (Figure 1.7). Population health will shift this resource utilization to focus on preventing the need for high-dollar expenditures on healthcare delivery. Admittedly, this is not a quick fix and will take years, if not decades, to fully change the paradigm. What is clear is that the current model is unsustainable and the current healthcare trends cannot last. We must change the way in which we focus on health and healthcare. This will be difficult and challenging.

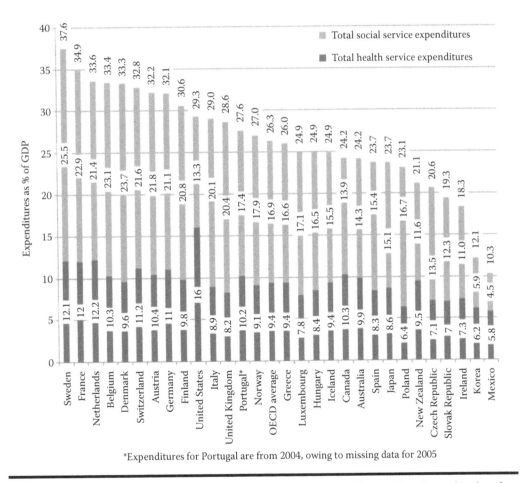

*Expenditures for Portugal are from 2004, owing to missing data for 2005

Figure 1.7   Total health-service and social-services expenditures for Organization for Economic Cooperation and Development (OECD) countries, 2005. (Reproduced from Average Health and Social Services Expenditures: Associations with Health Outcomes. With permission from BMJ Publishing Group Ltd.)

Currently, the payment model does not support preventive health and population health. As the payment model evolves and our metrics for population health become clarified, we will move toward this new model of delivery. In the interim, we will need to deliver healthcare under both models of healthcare. This would include our current volume delivery model and our future value delivery model. It is this middle time period that will be increasingly challenging over the next many years.

Bibliography

1. Commonwealth Fund Report 2014. US health system ranks last among 11 countries on measure of access, equity, quality, efficiency, and healthy lives. Commonwealth Report June 2014. Available at: www.commonwealth fund.org.
2. www.beckershealthcarereview.com/quality. Accessed on January 7, 2015.
3. Highest rates of obesity, diabetes in the South, Appalachia, and some tribal lands: Estimates of obesity now available for all U.S. counties [news release]. Atlanta, GA: Centers for Disease Control and Prevention, 2009. Available at http://www.cdc.gov/media/pressrel/2009//r09119c.htm. Accessed on December 18, 2009.
4. McGinnis JM, Williams-Russo P, Knickman JR. The case for more active policy attention to health promotion. *Health Affairs*, 2002; 21(2): 79–93. Available at http://www.health affairs.org. Accessed on January 7, 2015.
5. Dunn JR, Hayes MV. Toward a lexicon of population health. *Canadian Journal of Public Health*, 1999; 90(Suppl 1): S7–S10.
6. Centers for Disease Control and Prevention. Heart disease facts: America's heart disease burden. Available at http://www.cdc.gov/heartdisease/facts.htm. Accessed on December 18, 2009.
7. Kindig D, Stoddart G. Models for population health. Peer reviewed. *American Journal of Public* Health, 2003; 93(3): 380–383.
8. Association for Community Health Improvement, 2013. Trends in Hospital-Based Population Health Infrastructure: Results from an Association for Community Health Improvement and American Hospital Association survey. Chicago: Health Research & Educational Trust. December 2013, pp. 380–383. Available at www.healthycommunities.org.
9. Kindig DA. Understanding population health terminology. *The Millbank Quarterly.* 2007; 85(1): 139–161.
10. Nash DB, Reifsnyder J, Fabius RJ, Pracilio VP. *Population Health Creating a Culture of Wellness.* Sudbury, MA: Jones & Bartlett Learning, 2011. Available at www.jblearning.com. Accessed on January 7, 2015.
11. Punke H. US healthcare system ranks last among 10 peers, *Beckers Hospital Review.* June 17, 2014.

12. Nash DB. Game changers for population health. Available at http://tinyurl. com/Nash-interview. Accessed on January 7, 2015.
13. www.beckershealthcarereview.com/quality.
14. The Advisory Board Company, Health Care Advisory Board. The Scalable Population Health Enterprise. *Generating Clinical and Financial Returns from Cost-Effective Care Management,* April 9, 2014.
15. Growth and Performance, Resetting Priorities: The Path from Volume to Value, Sg2's Annual Business and Technology Forecast, 2011.
16. The Advisory Board Company. Health Care Advisory Board, Care Transformation Center, The Scalable Population Health Enterprise. Generating Clinical and Financial Returns from Cost-Effective Care Management, April 2014.
17. A governance institute white paper, GovernanceInstitute.com. Moving Forward. Winter 2013. Executive Summary. Building Authentic Population Management through Innovative Payer Relationships.
18. Huynh TM, Cohen D. Innovators and early adopters of population health in healthcare: Real and present opportunities for healthcare—Public health collaboration. *Healthcare Papers,* 2013; 13(3): 53–57. Doi: 10.12927/ hcpap.2014.23683.
19. Shannon D. Effective physician-to-physician communication: An essential ingredient for care coordination. *Physician Executive Journal,* January– February, 2012.
20. Burns J. Do we overspend on health care, underspend on social needs? *Managed Care,* OECD Publishing, September 2014.
21. Burton R. Health policy brief: Care transitions. *Health Affairs,* 2012. Available at http://www.healthaffairs.org/healthpolicybriefs/brief.php?brief_id=76. Accessed on January 7, 2015.
22. Bodenheimer T. Coordinating care—A perilous journey through the health care system. *The New England Journal of Medicine,* March 2008; 358: 1064– 1071. DOI: 10.1056/NEJMhpr0706165.
23. AHRQ National Healthcare Disparities Report 2011. www.ahrq.gov/qual/ardr11. htm.
24. Riegelman R. *Public Health 101: Healthy People-Healthy Populations,* Sadbury, MA: Jones and Bartlett, 2010.
25. Larkin H. Population Health, Lessons for Hospitals Transitioning to Population Health Management, H&HN/December 2014; 30–31.
26. Hodach R. *Provider-Led Population Health Management.* Bloomington, IN: AuthorHouse, 2014.
27. McAlearney AS. *Population Health Management: Strategies to Improve Outcomes.* American College of Healthcare Exec, Chicago, IL: Health Administration Press, 2003.
28. Association for Community Health Improvement, 2013. Trends in Hospital-Based Population Health Infrastructure. Results from an Association for Community Health Improvement and American Hospital Association survey. Chicago: Health Research & Educational Trust. December 2013. Accessed at www.healthycommunities.org.

Chapter 2

Why Population Health Now?

George Mayzell

Contents

The healthcare environment has been changing rapidly over the last 20 years. Certainly the good old days have been replaced with a constant change in a complex environment. It is worthwhile to take a step back and assess how we got from there to here and why we are here. While the theoretical and societal values of population health have not changed and can be easily articulated, it is only recently that the financial model has made these more profitable.

There were dramatic changes in healthcare in the twentieth century, with life expectancy improving dramatically. Since the 1900s, life expectancy has increased by more than 30 years, with most of the improvement attributable to public health. The 10 greatest public health improvements from 1900 to 1999 were as follows:

■ Vaccination
■ Motor vehicle safety
■ Safety in the workplace
■ Control of infectious diseases
■ Decrease in coronary disease and stroke
■ Healthy foods
■ Maternal and child healthcare
■ Family planning
■ Drinking water fluorination
■ Recognition of the hazards of tobacco and healthcare education

CDC Works Out Morbidity and Mortality Weekly[1]

These public health advances led to major improvements in healthcare. One can see the importance of the healthcare environment as well as individual behaviors.

The old days, as some of us who have been around for a while call them, were very different. Healthcare costs were under control, we thought. Healthcare information systems were rudimentary and patients felt financially accountable. We will not take you back to the days before health insurance or explain why health insurance came into being, but we will start with a time when costs were under control and patients typically had a 20% coinsurance. There was no such thing as copays or health maintenance organizations (HMOs), and those who were uninsured would get care at the emergency room. This was a time when patients would pay their bills when leaving the physician's office, or, many times, the physician's office would simply bill the patient for care. That was also a time when the fee structures were "usual and customary." There used to be controversy on who would file an insurance form, the patient or the practice; in many practices, the office would simply provide a super bill and ask for cash payment. Patients would then be expected to file their own claims. I know that for some this seems implausible.

Rising Healthcare Costs

As we move along the healthcare timeline, healthcare services become increasingly more expensive, and the idea of a "network" of providers takes shape. This is the PPO (preferred provider organization) era. Physicians and hospitals would agree to take a lower fee in exchange for getting increasing patient volume. Healthcare costs were still increasing but more modestly, and insurers were able to compensate by raising premiums. Labor costs were increasing, there was a shortage of nurses, and new technologies were on the boom. Thus, even though medical costs were rising, there was no outcry from the employers who were footing most of this bill.

As cost increasingly became a problem, HMOs were born through national legislation. The concept of HMOs was reasonable. HMOs would focus on preventive care and maintenance of care to slow down the progression of disease and control medical costs. This process was managed by payers. At this time, there was a lot of focus on what were called the three rules of managed care: costs, quality, and access. The challenge was balancing these three fundamentals in the right proportion. It was difficult to achieve the best in class in all three of the fundamentals at the same time, so trade-offs had to be made. One of the major trade-offs was limiting access through smaller networks and utilization review. This resulted in significant public-sector concerns. HMOs built systems to help control costs and built limited networks to manage cost and quality. It was the limited networks, with the general public's perception of limiting care, which ultimately led to the demise of HMOs. In many cases, the public actively rebelled at some of these perceived and actual limitations.

It was also during this HMO era when the concepts of capitation and shifting risk were started. Capitation is simply paying physicians (usually in advance) on a per patient or per head basis. It is usually reimbursed as per member (or per patient) per month (PMPM). This payment caused a dramatic change in how physicians practiced medicine and a major disconnect in the functionality of practices. Part of this process was about shifting the financial risk of the patients to the providers. This was the fundamental start of major changes in healthcare.

Managed care was being increasingly vilified and insurers and employers were moving back closer to a PPO model, which often included very high copays. Healthcare costs were continuing to rise. These high copay plans were euphemistically called consumer-directed healthcare, focusing on the fact that the consumer now had first dollar payment for up to several thousand dollars and, therefore, was more engaged in healthcare decision making. These plans exist today and are continuing to grow.

More recently the Affordable Care Act, or ACA, was introduced, more commonly called Obamacare. The design of this was supposedly to help out-of-control costs, expand access and availability to healthcare, place limits on insurers by adding consistency, and pushing accountability down to the provider level. As it turned out, this federal legislation has caused much controversy about its intent and its success. The legal wrangling continues on even at the time of this writing. Many feel that it has had much benefit especially, on the insurance side and access side; however, most feel it has done little to help long-term medical costs (see Figure 2.1).

Another powerful driver for a change in healthcare delivery is changing demographics. The "silver tsumini," or age wave as it has been called, is supercharging the need for a new healthcare delivery model. We will be taking care of more elderly, who are living longer, and have more chronic diseases. This has also been called the compression of morbidity as these elderly folks absorb a disproportionate amount of healthcare resources during a shorter period of time. Adding to this challenge is the fact that, at least in the public programs (Medicare), there will be fewer and fewer individuals working on a percentage basis to financially support this baby boom generation. As the population gradually ages, there will be fewer working people to pay the Medicare tax that ultimately funds this program. The current healthcare system was not designed for this demographic shift (Figure 2.2).

Financial Drivers

Few would disagree that care in this country is actually incredibly fragmented. Much of this is because of the financial fragmentation that misaligns our system. An example of this is that, after your discharge from the hospital, you often get bills from 10 to 15 different entities. You get bills from everything from lab, radiologists, pathologist, the hospital, and each physician. Financial incentives are usually misaligned between the physicians and the hospital with the physicians getting paid for each visit and the hospital getting one fixed payment (DRG) for each visit. Financial drivers misaligned the care coordination and are a major source of rising healthcare costs.

When managed care came on the scene, the focus was on managing the cost of healthcare via a number of routes, including narrow networks, utilization review, and aggressive contracting. One of the main goals was to

Critical ACA Initiatives

2010	2011	2012	2013	2014	2015
Children for 26 years can stay on their parents' policies	Medical loss ratio: Rebates must be offered to beneficiaries	Accountable care, hospital readmission, and hospital value-based purchasing program in place	First open enrollment via the state and federal marketplaces	Standard benefit package	High-cost insurance plans (premiums >$10,200 for individual and >$27,500 for families) will have a 40% excise tax
Small business tax credits	Medicare beneficiaries in the part D "donut hole" receive 50% discounts		Expansion of Medicaid preventive services options	Tiered plans on the marketplace (bronze, silver, gold, platinum, and catastrophic) with different levels of premium and cost	
Temporary pre-existing condition insurance	Voluntary long-term care insurance program			Insurers cannot restrict coverage or base premiums on health status or gender	
New insurance rules that ban rescinding coverage when people get sick and ban lifetime caps on coverage	Employers must disclose the value of benefits on employees' W2			Premium and cost-sharing subsidies available for families	
Children with preexisting conditions cannot be denied coverage				The individual mandate kicks in: was delayed to 2016 for small employers; large employers will be subjected to the mandate starting in 2015	
Preventive care for certain services					
Health insurers must submit justification for "unreasonable" premium increases and report share of premium spent				In states that choose this option, Medicaid eligibility was expanded to legal residents	

Figure 2.1   ACA timeline. (Adapted from The Commonwealth Fund's Health Reform Resources Center, http://www. commonwealthfund.org/interactives-and-data/health-reform-resources-center, accessed September 6, 2014.)

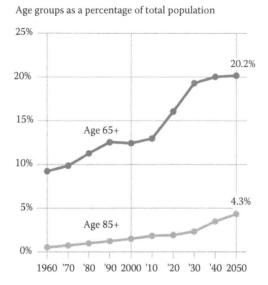

Age groups as a percentage of total population

Figure 2.2   Long-term care financing crisis, Diane Calmus, February 6, 2013. Older population is projected to grow rapidly. (Data for 1960–2000: Frank Hobbs and Nicole Stoops, "Demographic Trends in the 20th Century," U.S. Census Bureau, Census 2000 Special Reports, CENSR-4, Table 5, November 2002, http://www.census.gov/prod/2002pubs/censr-4.pdf [accessed August 17, 2012]. Data for 2010–2050: U.S. Census Bureau, National Population Projection, NP2008-T12, http://www.census.gov/population/www/projections/summarytables.html [accessed August 17, 2012].)

focus on the high-cost patient. This is usually the top 10% of patients of the population, who account for anywhere from 30% to 50% of healthcare cost, depending on the population. These patients were often hospitalized, which is the most expensive part of healthcare delivery. Managed care spent much time and resources looking at these patients in terms of length of stay, limiting admissions, and preventing readmissions. In addition, other high-risk patients were moved into case management or care coordination models to help smooth these transitions of care and control costs while improving the quality of this population.

Initially this model was fairly successful in controlling some of the major costs. One of the challenges in this model is that it was very hard to know who was going to spend healthcare dollars in advance. The challenges that the patients have to spend healthcare dollars this year are not necessarily the ones who are going to have high healthcare expenditures next year. This is where predictive analytics play a role. Our models are slowly getting better at predicting who will spend healthcare dollars in the future. One challenge of a predictive model is that even though we can adequately statistically predict whose going to spend healthcare dollars, it does not necessarily lead to any obvious intervention. Sometimes the risk factors and statistical models are very confusing and the underlying medical etiologies are hard to sort out. For example, you can statistically predict that the patient will have high expenses in the next couple of years. But what we often do not know is if it will be next year or in 2 or 3 years, and we often do not know exactly what those expenses will be. Therefore, it makes it difficult to intervene in a preventive fashion to limit those future healthcare costs. We can be much more accurate in predicting and preventing healthcare expenditures in looking at large populations; it is more difficult when focused at the individual patient.

To combat some of these issues, managed care started focusing on managing the patient's disease state. This was mostly focused on disease management of diabetes, asthma, depression, and other conditions. This helped to manage this group of patients, but arguably did not dramatically shift the overall cost curves. There was also the complexity of many of these patients having multiple diseases, and, thus, it was complicated to manage all these comorbid conditions.

Another group of patients that was a focus point is the "rising-risk" patients. These are the patients with risk factors for disease. These are patients that have underlying risk factors, such as hypertension, obesity, smoking, or others. We are not spending an appreciable number of healthcare dollars currently, but over the next several years. As these risks turn into disease processes, healthcare expenditures will become significant.

Just Managing the "Sick" Doesn't Work

There are also other patients who do not have current risk factors but still have behavioral traits or genetic traits that will lead to risk factors in the future. (Changing behaviors early in these patients will have a large effect on long-term healthcare costs.) What we have learned is that focusing only on the sick patients and patients with risk factors will not control medical costs in the long run. We must focus on the entire population, which includes all groups of patients. The main group that has traditionally not been attended to is the group of healthy patients who need preventive care, they should be focused on to prevent future preventable diseases. It is only by focusing on these patients as well as the others that we can actually control long-term healthcare costs. This is a basic tenet of population-based health.

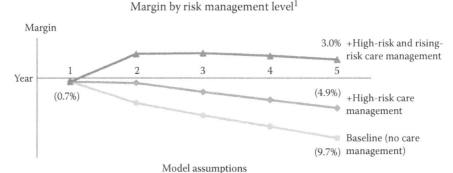

Financial analysis indicates necessity of rising-risk patient management

Margin by risk management level[1]

Metric	Initial	After high-risk care management	After high-risk and rising-risk care mangement
Inital cost reduction	0%	10%	10%
Cost growth rate	5%	4%	4%
Rising-risk moving to high-risk	18%	18%	12%

(1) Patient population segmented between high-risk 5%, rising-risk 20%, and low-risk 75%.

Figure 2.3   Care management and margin, *Playbook for Population Health.* **(From The Advisory Board Company.** *Prioritizing Population Health Interventions from Data Aggregation to Actionable Insights.* **© 2013. All rights reserved. With permission.)**

From the example in chart (Figure 2.3), one can see that a population health program without care management yields a −9.7% margin. Obviously, a population health program without care management is ineffective, but what is interesting is that with the addition of interventions with high-risk care management patients, the margin only improves to −4.9%. It is only by adding interventions with rising-risk patients that the program becomes effective with a margin of 3%. Simply managing the high-risk patients will not significantly deflect the trend lines. Approximately 18% of the rising-risk patients rise to the high-risk category each year. The challenge is that it is difficult, if not impossible, to know which 18% will rise. If you only manage the high risk, you still end up with negative margins. With no care management, the margins are almost −10%. If you manage just the high-risk and medium-risk cases, the margins are approximately −5%. It is only when you manage the high-risk and the rising-risk patients that you can get positive margins at your 5-year time frame.

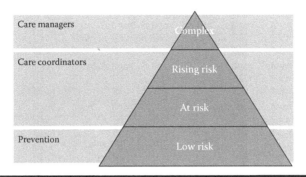

Figure 2.4 Risk pyramid.

The data is showing us that simply business as usual with the short-term view of high-risk and chronic-disease patients will not "knuckle" the healthcare-cost curves. The critical pieces of this puzzle are getting better data on all patients so that appropriate risk stratification can be done with more robust predictive modeling programs. We need to have better technologies and engagement strategies and focus on the transitions of care. And these transitions of care will lead to higher quality and less costly healthcare delivery by focusing on better care coordination (Figure 2.4).

Changing from Volume to Value

So now we have established that simply managing the sick and the sickest of the sick will not get us to either consistent quality outcomes nor will it control the rising cost of healthcare. One of the major impediments to making the necessary changes in healthcare is the fact that the payment model does not support alignment of healthcare resources or payment for good outcomes. Thus, one of the other major transitions of healthcare is the movement from volume-based reimbursement to value-based reimbursement.

This can be done in several stages, but it is different than classic population health. Figure 2.5 highlights some of the changes that need to occur in a value-based healthcare delivery model. In the early stages, this is really still a refinement of our current healthcare delivery model and not really a new delivery system. As this evolves, it will surely have to take on the latter. One of the critical pieces of this transition will have to be a change in the payment model. Right now the rewards are for paying for each visit or activity. A critical piece of this new model is starting to pay

Figure 2.5 Volume to value. (From HRET, Transforming Healthcare through Research and Education, http://www.hret.org/. With permission.)

for outcomes, or at least processes of care, that are evidence based. This new model will need to be team based, often utilizing the patient-centered medical home model and will need increased patient engagement. Future healthcare will not just be focused on the physician delivering care but on a whole team of medical providers all working at the top of the license to deliver great healthcare and "health." The patient's health literacy will be a critical piece of this model. The patient will become a partner and will influence medical care and have access to his or her medical records. Scale will become increasingly important since the average patient panel will shift from its current 2000–3000 members in a primary care practice to 3000–4500 patients in a practice. This will require a different type of care model, particularly as it focuses on care of the entire population, including preventive and wellness care. Physician extenders and other team-based initiatives will be a critical piece of this new model. The new focus will be on outpatient care, where 60% of the care takes place, rather than on the much more expensive and resource-intensive inpatient care. The new model focuses on delivery systems and not just on hospitals and physician practices.

Six Separate Components of This Transition

The current healthcare model has supported itself through many reinforcing elements. It is organized by medical specialties with separate, independent practice physicians. It functions on a fee-for-service, or volume-based, platform. There is significant cross-subsidization of low-paying units. Duplicate services abound with little integration. Fragmentation of patient populations and care processes are prevalent. IT systems are isolated and disconnected from each other. Quality is often focused on activities and processes rather than outcomes.

This transition from volume to value will be very difficult. Right now, healthcare is paid for based on how much is done, not how well you do it. The system of payments is based on treating the sick, not keeping the healthy well. This new model will be akin to keeping one foot in one canoe and the other foot in another canoe as providers try to balance service and value-based payments. There will also have to be a major focus on quality metrics and quality outcomes. This will require a vertical blending of the delivery model with a blurring of the margins between the payers, insurers, and providers. Scale will be critical in that there will be huge economies of scale creating integrated delivery systems, and especially in the healthcare informatics space. Most people believe that this move from volume to value will happen over the next 3–5 years, but no one knows for sure.

One thing is clear, we are not getting great value for healthcare expenditures. It is estimated that there is at least $750 billion in healthcare waste. An article by Barbara Starfield documents where some of the waste is believed to be lurking.

Healthcare is also getting much more complex according to CMS data. Medicare beneficiaries have multiple conditions, multiple positions, multiple prescriptions, and suffer from disconnected and uncoordinated care. Complexity in healthcare makes it extremely important that the coordination of care is seamless in an integrated healthcare informatics system (Figure 2.6).

As we look at our economy in the current challenge of the national debt, it is important to consider how important health is in this equation. The health of a population is directly linked to its successful economy when one takes into account the importance of productivity both at work and at home.

We are spending nearly 18% of our gross domestic product on healthcare. We are spending one-eighth as much on education. It seems obvious that an improvement of education would be directly linked to productivity. This appears to be a vicious circle. Most of the increases in the cost of healthcare have been related to the increasing burden of chronic illness, increasing unit costs, and higher utilization cost.[26,27] The United States spends much more on healthcare delivery than other developed nations.

14% of Medicare patients have 6+ chronic conditions
Of these,

➤ 2/3 are hospitalized each year
➤ 16% had 3 or more hospitalizations per year
➤ 49% had at least 1 post-acute visit
➤ 25% were readmitted within 30 days
➤ Had an average spend of $32,658 per year
➤ Represented 46% of total Medicare spend

Figure 2.6 Chronic diseases drive utilization. (Adapted from *Chronic Conditions among Medicare Beneficiaries*, Chartbook, 2012 edition, Baltimore, MD, 2012.)

Six Requirements to Change to Value-Based Care

To move this new value-driven platform requires a number of different steps according to Porter et al.[2] The first one is organized around the customer, with the patient-centered approach. In an article in the *Harvard Business Review* this approach has been dubbed as an "integrated practice unit" or IPU. In these units, the focus is directed at the patient, his or her conditions, complications, and circumstances and is not an isolated focus on a disease or multiple disease processes.

Another transitional point is that care delivered by a team of clinicians should be in a multidisciplinary approach. Thus, it is not just about the physician delivering care; it is also important to note that this team-based care model is similar to the patient-centered medical home model that we see today.

Another requirement is that providers see themselves as part of the organizational team. This means that they function not only as a team inside the practice but also as a broader team in the delivery model. Another term for this might be the "medical neighborhood." The team also takes responsibility for the full cycle of care encompassing outpatient, inpatient, and everything in between. This unit must also have easy access and patient availability.

The next transition point is to measure outcomes and cost for every patient. This requires not only a patient-focused approach but also a relentless push toward quality and outcomes. We must also move to either bundled payment or some formal global payment system that aligns incentives across the various physicians and others provider, and it all must take place in an integrated delivery model. In addition, all stakeholders must share common medical information systems.

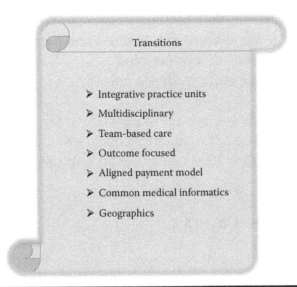

Figure 2.7 Transitions to value based care. (Adapted from Porter ME et al., *Harvard Business Review,* **October 2013; 50.)**

Geographic reach must be beyond the local medical delivery system. This is often a hub-and-spoke model, with referals into the hub from distant sites.

The last item is one of the most important items. The information delivery model must have a common IT platform so that information can be accessed from any site by any provider (Figure 2.7).

Employers' Care

While healthcare is important, health is even more important. We look at the workplace and the issues of productivity as they relate to the concepts of absenteeism and those present. At the workplace, besides paying direct healthcare costs, there is also the indirect cost of long-term and short-term disability. On top of this is absenteeism.

When one looks at absenteeism, it is not just about the individual health of the worker but also the health of the worker's family. How many times has a parent stayed home for a sick child or to take the child to the hospital or physician's office? Thus, the health or wellness of all the members of the family is a critical aspect of the work environment.

As businesses enter the new global environment, the cost of healthcare becomes a defining competitive disadvantage. When these costs are added to the cost of poor health, they become staggering. When we add the direct cost of healthcare to the indirect cost of short- and long-term disability and absenteeism, the numbers are eye popping.

Employers on average suffer with absenteeism:

- 115 hours per employee per year lost productivity as a result of illness
- Over 10 days per year per person secondary to chronic illness
- 400 days per year per 1000 employees that are avoidable sick days[15]

Engagement of the Payers

As we move to the next era of population health, each healthcare provider will take on new and different roles in the healthcare continuum. Moving into the space called a healthcare neighborhood will include an integrated delivery model of all healthcare providers, as well as a strong base of community services. Added to this would be incentives at the individual level focusing on patient engagement and behavior change. Health literacy and patient engagement will be central to this new model of care. The payer's role will also change as will the patient's role.

Payers will be working with providers and benefits managers to engage consumers in their own healthcare. In addition, they will create incentives to steer patients to the most efficient providers with good outcomes. They will also have transparent pricing on the cost of healthcare and will work with companies and benefit managers to set up structures that encourage appropriate patient and physician behaviors.

It Is Really Different This Time?

Why do we expect to be successful this time when we were not successful in the past: what's different about this in the past? Many people equate the current movement to the HMO movement in the 1980s. There are several differences. A major one is the urgency to change. The national debt is at record levels; employers are forced to compete on an international level and must cut their benefit costs. We now have better data and better knowledge of what drives healthcare. High deductible plans and the shift to defined contribution by employers are getting patients involved. In addition, the

	It's new and improved	
	Old managed care	New population health
Patient	Limited access	Engaged focus on "health"
Employer	Employee benefit	Manage costs Absenteeism Presenteeism
Payment	Decreased unit costs Increased volume	Aligned payment models Rewards value
Information systems	Immature	Being developed

Figure 2.8   Managed care moving to population health.

physician culture is changing. Physicians leaving training now have different expectations and different goals of employment and work-life balance. Physician leadership must drive this change (Figure 2.8).

Migration to Population Health

The journey or migration to population health is very difficult. The two biggest challenges are that one will have to live in both worlds of fee-for-service and value-based payment for several years. These are two very different delivery models and very difficult to balance in the same delivery system. Also, this is a cultural change that will take some time.

The second major challenge is that the economics do not support a fast move to population-based healthcare. Currently there is limited payment for "value" and, therefore, getting too far ahead of the delivery system can cause economic hardships. Currently the healthcare system is still paid for volume, and often there is a misalignment of payment models among the various healthcare payers.

There are four stages in the migration to population health: preparation, transformation, operational, and growth. The first stage is mostly about assessing your delivery system and teaching and training your delivery system on the nuances of population health. The second stage is actually building the model of population health. Cost efficiency, and clinical integration are valued on both the fee-for-service side and the value-based payment side, and, therefore, in this stage, it makes sense to work on things that create value in both payment models. These include such things as patient-centered medical homes, team-based care, clinical information and information sharing, inpatient and outpatient care management, and network development, including physician alignment and employment models. In addition, there is the criticality of information systems. Health information exchanges and other shared data is mission critical. Cost management and clinical variation to improve outcomes and decrease costs are foundational.

Next up is operationalizing the population-health model. This includes identifying key populations, usually through collaboration with payers. This is where understanding attribution models and attaching specific providers to your delivery system is important. Understanding the payment model and setting up the right payment infrastructure with critical alignment of these financial incentives are critical to long-term success.

When implementing these plans, future growth in the marketplace is critical. This means looking at the payment models of Medicare, Medicaid, and commercial insurers. Programs can be started as a pilot program and then expanded.

Final Word

Overall, I am optimistic about the future of healthcare. Both our technology and our training mean that we have some of the best healthcare in the world. As our economic model changes we will move to more patient-focused, team-based delivery of healthcare. I am optimistic about the future. Healthcare delivery and accountability will shift down to the providers who are best suited to balance quality, costs, access, and outcomes. It will be a bumpy road for many years; however, I believe we will have a better healthcare system.

Bibliography

1. CDC works out morbidity and mortality weekly review April 2, 1999/48/12:241–243.
2. Porter ME et al. The strategy that will fix healthcare. *Harvard Business Review*, October 2013; 50.

3. The Commonwealth Fund's Health Reform Resource Center: http://www. commonwealthfund.org/interactives-and-data/health-reform-resource-center (Accessed on September 6, 2014).

4. Starfield B. Is US health really the best in the world? *(Reprinted) Journal of American Medical Association*, 2000; 284(4), 483–485.

5. Watson Wyatt/National Business Group on Health. *International Journal of Workplace Health Management*. The Value of Population Health Management Strategies, 2007/2008.

6. U.S. Department of Health and Human Services, 2005.

7. Care Coordination. A strategic priority in the shift to accountability. Sg2 Report.

8. Burton R. Health policy brief: Improving care transitions. *Health Affairs*, 2012.

9. Bodenheimer T. *New England Journal of Medicine*, 2008; 358: 1064–1071.

10. Shaddon D. *Physician Executive,* 2012; 38(16): 21.

11. Morbidity and Mortality Weekly Report (MMWR), published by Centers for Disease Control (CDC), Identified ten great public health achievements in the United States during 1900–1999. Box 1.3. Public Health Achievements of the Twentieth Century and Challenges for the Twenty-first.

12. Mokdad AH, Marks JS, Stroup DF, Gerberding JL. Actual causes of death in the United States, 2000. *Journal of American Medical Association,* 2004; 291: 1238–1245. [Errata, *Journal of American Medical Association,* 2005; 293: 4, 298.]

13. Kue Young T. *Population Health Concepts and Methods.* 2nd edition. Oxford: Oxford University Press, 2005, pp. 392.

14. *Health Care Transformation: First Curve to Second Curve Markets.* HRET

15. The Advisory Board Company. *Prioritizing Population Health Interventions from Data Aggregation to Actionable Insights,* 2013. The Advisory Board Company. Advisory.com

16. OECD. *Health at a Glance 2009.* OECD Publishing.

17. Burns J. (ed.) Do we overspend on health care, underspend on social needs? *Managed Care*, September 2014. MultiMedia USA.

18. Serxner SA, Gold DB, Bultman KK. The impact of behavioral health risks on worker absenteeism. *Journal of Occupational and Environmental Medicine,* 2001; 43(4): 347–354.

19. HRET. Trends in Hospital-Based Population Health Infrastructure, December 2013.

20. Riegelman R. *Public Health 101: Health People—Healthy Populations,* 2009, Jones & Bartlett Publishers.

21. McAlearney AS. *Population Health Management: Strategies to Improve Outcomes.* Chicago, IL: Health Administration Press; 2003.

22. Moving Forward. Winter 2013. Executive Summary.

23. Better, Smarter, Healthier: In historic announcement, HHS sets clear goals and timeline for shifting Medicare reimbursements from volume to value. hhs.gov/news, January 26, 2015.

24. HRET. Trends in hospital-based population health infrastructure: Results from an Association for Community Health Improvement and American Hospital Association Survey, December 2013.

25. Vox.com. January 20, 2015. 8 facts that explain what's wrong with American health care. Updated by Sarah Kliff.

26. Thorpe KE. Trends: The impact of obesity on rising medical spending. *Health Affairs*, 2004, *Supplemental Web Exclusives*, W4: 480–486. DOI: 10.1377/hlthaff. w4.480.

27. Thorpe et al. The rise in healthcare spending and what to do about it. *Health Affairs*, 2005; 24(6): 1436–1445. DOI: 10.1377/hlthaff.24.6.1436.

Chapter 3

The Care Continuum

Kathleen M. Ferket

Contents

The Accountable Care Act is contributing to a disruptive cycle of change within the healthcare system. The current changes impacting the healthcare environment has been described as "changing the battery in your car while driving 80 miles per hour." The move from a volume-based care model to a value-based care model is impacting hospitals, physicians, and patient choice like never before. Consistent reimbursement for high volume, over-utilization of services, readmissions, and hospital-acquired conditions were routinely obtained in the hospital–physician centric model of care. One by one, disorders that could be treated through the judgment and skill of the experienced physician in expensive hospitals are becoming diagnosable and treatable by less expensive caregivers working in more accessible and affordable venues of care.[1]

The Triple Aim is the guiding principle for care in the "new world," rewarding hospitals and physicians for high quality and appropriate utilization at the most competitive cost (Figure 3.1). Excellent patient experience, reduced per capita cost of care, and improvement of the health of populations have historically not been a focus of physicians or hospitals. Effective communication, collaboration, team-based care, and clinically integrated network are essential to achieving the Triple Aim goal. Coordinated care will be required as patients move across the healthcare continuum. The shift from a physician centric model to a consumer driven model has begun and it will impact every aspect of healthcare.

Practitioners within the healthcare continuum previously have not needed to understand the various care venues in the continuum. The following review outlines the various entities and identifies implications for future change.

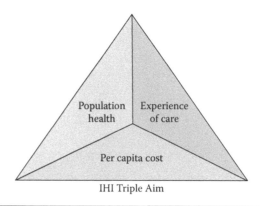

IHI Triple Aim

Figure 3.1 IHI Triple Aim framework was developed by the Institute for Healthcare Improvement in Cambridge, MA. (Available at https://www.ihi.org)

Acute Inpatient Care

The hospital, long viewed as the center of the universe, is reversing directions by 180°. The cycle of disruption is most apparent in the acute care setting.[2] In 2013, the Centers for Medicare and Medicaid Services (CMS) set the stage for change by enacting IPPS 1559, commonly referred to as *the second midnight rule*. This rule has dramatically impacted the number of 1-day inpatient length of stay. This CMS requirement mandated physicians to attest and document specific reasons why the patient may require a minimum 2 days of inpatient care. As a result, observation admissions increased by 10%–20% which subsequently decreased acute inpatient care census. This has particularly impacted Medicare patients, as observation is covered under Medicare part B, resulting in additional out of pocket expense for the patient. Hospitals receive decreased reimbursement for observation stay. For physicians, it has been confusing due to the ever-changing CMS rules but their reimbursement has not yet been affected. Therefore, collaboration between inpatient care managers and physicians is more important than ever before.

Inpatient volumes are decreasing across the country, and hospitals are struggling with a "new normal," adjusting to decreased census due to CMS inpatient criteria and improved readmission management. Hospital census is contracting by 2% annually and many licensed beds go unused. In Illinois, a licensed bed fee of 55.00 per bed has been applied to hospitals to fund the Adverse Events Reporting law. In certificate of need (CON) states, hospitals are reluctant to release any licensed beds due to the arduous process to obtain licensed beds or expand services. State mandated licensed bed reporting monitors hospital occupancy rates. In the future, hospitals not meeting minimum occupancy levels of certain services may be forced to discontinue or repurpose low utilization services.

Intensive care and progressive care units will continue to have adequate volumes. Hospitalized patients will be acutely ill, requiring the highest level of care. The traditional inpatient medical and surgical units will experience a significant census decrease. Observation and critical decision units will expand and may be adjacent to emergency departments for continuity of care. Continued assessment and efficient testing will determine if the patient requires inpatient services or discharge.

As post-acute services enhance their staff competency to care for higher acuity patients, the lower cost skilled facility venue will expand. With technology advances and increased minimally invasive surgical procedures, patients will recover and then be discharged to home. Anterior hip replacements are currently available as an outpatient for selected clients. Orthopedics has set the benchmark for moving procedures to the outpatient setting.

Education and Practice Implications

Hospitals have been the platform for education and training of medical students, nurses, pharmacists, and other multidisciplinary professionals. There will continue to be a need for acute care clinicians to staff/practice in acute care hospitals but the tide is turning. Some medical residency training programs are changing to meet this need. Residency programs now offer a choice, with either a concentration in hospital-based practice or a primary care focus with community integration. Nursing schools are behind the curve and must adopt a similar approach. The majority of nursing clinical rotations are hospital based, with some exposure centered in the community. In the future, nurses may be asked to identify their preferred practice setting concentration. The hospital will remain a practice setting, but ambulatory, post-acute, home care, skilled rehabilitation, and community settings will need to be included. Education and practice must stay current with healthcare changes in order to supply the additional 1.2 million new nurses required by 2020. A strong grasp of accountable care organizations, bundled payment models, outcome-based metrics, health coaching, navigation skills, and the ability to work in a team-based model are requirements to prepare clinicians to practice competently in the future environment.[3]

Acute Care in the Current World

Hospitals are beginning to adopt a team-based care model for patients and integrated care is improving. Specialty units, such as intensive care settings, work collaboratively with nursing, pharmacy, and respiratory care with a lead physician coordinating care. The traditional medical-surgical unit is challenged with a team-based approach due to unit configuration. Primary care physicians and specialty consultants come on their own schedule and may not encounter the nurse caring for their patient. This results in poor communication and fragmented care for the patient.

Hospitalist models have more of a team approach to the patient primarily due to their availability within the hospital. A traditional physician practice model of rounding once a day or after office hours is rapidly fading and may be a thing of the past within the next 3–5 years. Delay in patient care progression due to waiting for physicians to round at the end of the day will no longer be acceptable, as hospitals are pressed to meet CMS standards or risk not being reimbursed for the episode of care. Primary care physicians will be giving office-based care, where they can best focus on the patient-centered medical home and managing rising and high-risk patient population.

The criteria of value-based purchasing (clinical outcomes, quality, cost, and efficiency) continue to act as drivers of change within the hospital. The hospital model will be centered on efficiency, collaboration, patient satisfaction, appropriate utilization, and evidence-based medicine. Hospitalists, with expanded or 24 h per day coverage will help to transform many "5 day per week hospitals" into true 7 day per week hospitals. Procedure-based services will need to expand services to support the 7-day hospital model. Key services unavailable on weekends will be a thing of the past, decreasing avoidable delays for patients. The historic hospital- and physician-centric model is changing to a patient-centric model, largely driven by reimbursement, pay for performance, and consumer healthcare choice.

The Post-Acute Care Continuum

As the *hospital as center of the universe* paradigm shifts, the status of post-acute venue as *second class citizen* is reversing. One consistent issue among hospital-based clinicians is a misunderstanding of the multiple levels of care in the post-acute setting. With the expansion and importance of the post-acute settings it is of primary importance that all healthcare providers understand the various post-acute options. Let's begin with a brief review from the least to most acute settings.

Independent Living Villages

Centered on the older adult, these comprehensive communities offer residents the ability to progress to higher levels of care and support, when and if required. Programs are wellness and fitness focused, offering an array of choices within the compound. The adult only setting allows security and independence. On site fitness, meals, classes, and activities support the resident in all aspects of retirement. Available services may include optometry, podiatry, primary care, and an outpatient pharmacy for convenient care. The homes or apartments are designed to meet the older adult needs for safety and ease of use. When the client requires additional support the next level is assisted living arrangements. This community setting is the model for the senior medical neighborhood with ready access to prevention, wellness, and interpersonal relationships within the community.

Assisted Living

The assisted living setting is often adjacent or connected to a skilled setting. These clients need support with activities of daily living, medication, or meals. This option offers the support needed to maintain the client in as independent a setting, as possible. Scheduled visits by a registered nurse or certified nursing assistants are available, as a part of the contract and may be tailored to client need. Care coordination with clients and consistent communication with family help to support independence for the client. Daily visits are important for social interaction and provide the caregiver an opportunity to assess changes in activity, confusion, or decreases in appetite. Daily visits insure the environment is safe and secure, preventing falls or unintended accidents. Medication adherence is monitored to insure compliance and if chronic disease management is a factor, early recognition of condition changes is noted and acted upon.

Short-Term Skilled Rehabilitative Services

With the focus on length of stay within hospitals, transition from acute care settings to post-acute settings emerged. The rise in orthopedic procedures and subsequent need for therapy is the major driver for skilled facilities rehabilitative transformation. Strict criteria need to be met for hospital-based rehabilitation programs and specific skilled nursing facilities. Short-term patients requiring intensive rehabilitative service now receive this care in a stepped down setting at less cost than an acute care setting. These clients are generally located in a separate area of the campus, away from clients requiring long-term or higher level skilled support. The separate rehab setting has softened the stigma for patients being discharged for "skilled" rehab care. Nurses, physical therapists, occupational therapists, pharmacists, and physiatrists are available to support the client and care coordination with the primary care provider continues. Anticipated length of stay is generally determined by the DRG and the services required. It is expected the patient will discharge to home or home with home care services. The increase in bundled payments for key DRGs will enhance focus on outcomes and LOS in these facilities.

Traditional Long-Term Care Skilled Services

The standard long-term care facility (LTAC) supports clients requiring a higher level of care over an extended or indefinite period of time. The need for mechanical ventilation is the skill differentiator. Clients may require mechanical ventilation or weaning associated with a tracheostomy. This complex acute care precludes the patient from being cared for in a traditional skilled facility. Treatments, feeding tubes, medications, central lines for total parenteral nutrition, and routine care are supported with 24-h nursing care. A long-term placement may be associated with a failed resuscitation event or a traumatic injury in which long-term recovery is required.

Dementia Care Units

These specialized units are designed for clients with memory loss and dementia who are unable to care for themselves and require continuous observation. The secured unit is designed with low stimulation and safety. More and more skilled facilities are adding this service as the need is growing in the population overall.

Palliative Care

The option for a palliative care services is advancing, although slowly in the current fee for the service model. Estimates show that about 27% of Medicare's annual budget of $327 billion goes to care for patients in their final year of life.[4] Advance directives, while somewhat more prevalent continue to be an opportunity especially as families grapple with end of life decision making.

Palliative care options will increase as the "second curve" reimbursement model evolves. As accountable care organization shared savings, bundled payments, and transparent quality/costs become the norm, hospitals and physicians will not be reimbursed for tests, hospitalizations, or procedures deemed as futile care. Significant consumer education and information will need to be applied for adoption and acceptance of this paradigm in the United States.

In 2014, the Institute of Medicine Committee on Approaching Death released its groundbreaking report on Dying in America which address end of life issues. When curative options for a specific disease state are no longer feasible, palliative care is an option for patients to manage symptoms associated with the illness. Palliative care may be provided in a variety of settings, including inpatient, skilled nursing facilities, home care, chronic disease outpatient clinics, and in the home. Palliative care enhances client satisfaction and reduces unnecessary utilization of services. Clients may be under palliative care for symptom management anywhere from several months to several years. It is often confused with hospice but the care modalities are very different.

Hospice Care

Hospice care is rendered when the client and or family recognize that there is no option for further treatment and the patient has a high likelihood of dying. Hospice is most associated with malignant disease states for which no further treatment option exists. Hospice is also associated with end-stage renal, cardiac, and pulmonary disease states. A focus is for pain-free end-of-life care with the opportunity for family presence either at home, in a skilled facility, or dedicated hospice unit as optional settings. In the current state, many patients are transferred to acute care facilities from skilled nursing settings as per family or physician request.

Home Care Services

Home care agencies are pivotal to enhancing care across the continuum. Technology continues to enhance therapeutic modalities which can be safely administered in the home. Nursing assessment, medication review and reconciliation, education, and testing are some of the important interventions performed by home care nurses. Ancillary services by physical and occupational health therapists, as well as unlicensed assistive personnel for routine care, labs, and bathing support the client in a home environment. Physicians who provide home visits are showing an increase across the nation.

Seeing the client in the home setting allows healthcare professionals a glimpse into the client environment. Assessing all domains of health, including adequate heat, nutrition, sanitation as well as falls risks, are key to recognizing if all needs are met. As bundled payment contract increases, a renewed effort to increase the utilization of home health services will be on the rise. From a cost structure, the delivery of home healthcare is less costly and safer then skilled services. In the familiar home environment, there is less of falls and decreased pathogen exposure. Telehealth, electronic scales, home pulse oximetry, and skin sensor glucose monitoring are all available and being used now. Future technology will only enhance the services that will be available in the home. Physicians and nurse practitioners will visit the patient at home, with the goal of client-centered care.

Patient-Centered Medical Home and the Medical Neighborhood

Population health is an approach to care that uses information on a group (population) of patients within a primary care practice or group of practices to improve the care and clinical outcomes of patients within that practice.[5] Core principles of population health management include primary care physician leadership, patient involvement, and responsibility and care coordination programs that range from wellness/prevention to chronic care management.

The patient-centered medical home (PCMH) is the framework for the medical neighborhood. The medical neighborhood model requires relationships and reciprocal communication to integrate the primary and specialty care for the benefit of consistent care coordination. Medical neighborhoods are necessary because care is often fragmented as patients are seen by many different health providers.[6] This is evidenced by frequent acute care readmissions, patient misunderstanding of medications, and follow up. A national survey found that primary care physicians and specialists perceive communication about referrals to be poor and agree this negatively affects quality of care.[7]

Seamless care transition between primary care and specialists as client's transition from hospital discharge to post-acute venues is pivotal. Standardized transfer records, now becoming an expectation, will reduce variation and improve handoff between acute to post-acute care. Medication reconciliation, discharge education, and a post-discharge check by a clinician remain the most important process in preventing unnecessary readmission.

Relationships between hospitals systems and post-acute care venues are more collaborative since the onset of accountable care organizations. The medical neighborhood is now extending from PCMH and hospital to post-acute providers and into the community. Faith-based organizations will play an important role in a medical neighborhood model. Geisinger and Methodist Health Systems are examples of networks which have successfully integrated faith-based congregational model to support both wellness and chronic disease management. This will be explored further in Chapter 5.

Family

The role of family and needs for in-home caregiver support will continue to expand in the future. As more procedures move to the outpatient setting, recovery at home with caregiver support will be necessary. Technology will support E-visits and home monitoring will become routine experiences. Clinician visits to the home offer a unique assessment of the client in their own setting and is helpful in identifying barriers to program compliance.

Federally Qualified Health Clinics

Federally qualified health clinic (FQHC) models are expanding with the increase in coverage for previously uninsured populations. Health system relationships will form with FQHCs through the accountable care entity programs. Cultural competence and access to care will be necessary for the newly insured. Clinically integrated networks with ACE partners will achieve improved care coordination. The role of the community health worker will expand with this population with a focus on education and prevention.

Community Agencies

Community agency growth is determined by community need assessments, demographics, and the tax base of the region. Hospitals have been aware of the agencies in their service area but true relationships have been largely superficial. This is no longer an option in the "second curve" of healthcare. The opportunity to enhance relationships and coordinate services in the community will be a key for healthcare networks. The medical neighborhood will include local community services to support home visits, meals on wheels, education on wellness and prevention, and outpatient behavioral health services, to name just a few. Health systems will need to partner with their community agencies to provide a broad network of resources for their clients. Community agencies will eventually join ACOs or ACEs and will move toward clinically integrated networks to share data, metrics, and outcomes to participate in shared savings. Linking high-risk patients in the community is a successful strategy for decreasing unnecessary hospital utilization.

Employers

Employers who provide health insurance coverage to employees are engaging with payers and health systems to decrease costs and utilization. On site wellness and prevention programs and incentives for participation and achieving wellness goals are on the rise. Bringing clinical experts or community workers on site to support care coordination among employees will decrease costs, improve access, and enhance client satisfaction. Walgreens has moved toward an employee stipend to choose his/her own coverage on the health insurance exchanges. The next five years will show a dramatic shift in employer sponsored health plans as more companies move to this option. Consumers are motivated to get the most for their healthcare dollars, shopping for the best price, quality, and access. The consumer will impact the changes in the continuum of care like never before.

Conclusion

Recognizing the unique contributions of each setting across the care continuum is essential for all healthcare practitioners. The challenge to un-silo the care continuum is daunting and will be a long-term effort. It requires physicians, clinicians, hospital systems, and community agencies to understand the cultural nuances of each particular setting. Clinically integrated networks are the foundation for successful coordination, communication, and collaboration across the continuum and will insure success in an accountable care organization.

Bibliography

1. Foreman M. A medical neighborhood. *Health*, May 2012; 23–25.
2. Christensen CM, Grossman JH, Hwang MD. *The Innovator's Prescription*. New York: McGraw-Hill, 2009.
3. U.S. Census Bureau. *Labor Statistic Projections 2010–2020*. Available at https://www.census.gov.
4. Appleby, J. Debate surrounds end-of-life health care costs. *USA Today*, October 19, 2006. USAtoday.com.
5. Agency for Health Care Research. Available at https://www.ahrc.gov.
6. Greenberg J, Barnett M, Spinks, BA et al. The medical neighborhood: Integrating primary and specialty care for ambulatory patients. *JAMA Internal Medicine*, 2014; 174(3): 454.
7. O'Malley AS, Reschovsky JD. Referral and consultation communication between primary care and specialist physicians: Finding common ground. *Archives Internal Medicine*, 2011; 171(1): 56–65.

Chapter 4

Managing Populations

Bryan N. Becker

Contents

Introduction

Healthcare entities that care for diverse populations have recognized that subsets of patients require more resources than others, have more complications than others, and ultimately cost more than others. High-risk patients are usually a small proportion of the patient population (~5%).[1] They are patients who often have multiple chronic illnesses and comorbid conditions. Patients with minor or no chronic conditions or very well-managed chronic conditions are considered low risk. They represent usually 60%–80% of any population.[2] The remaining 15%–35% of patients are categorized as rising-risk patients. These patients may have two or more chronic conditions and those chronic conditions when out of control can lead to significant complications. It is estimated that one in five rising-risk patients moves to a high-risk category every year due to lack of control of chronic conditions or significant complications. Importantly, the 5% of patients in the United States deemed high risk account for nearly 50% of healthcare spending.[3]

The success of value-based care delivery such as shared savings programs is dependent upon managing the health of populations. With that, risk stratification becomes more important than ever. Healthcare organizations dedicated to succeeding in a "fee-for-value" environment must reduce their cost structure and improve outcomes with a rational approach toward maximizing the effectiveness of the interventions that they deliver. As such, they must be able to target high-risk, high-cost patients who need appropriate management. The fundamental step in targeting these high-risk patients is identifying them. This chapter focuses on three key features around population health: risk stratification, predictive modeling, and key interventions to support population health, such as ambulatory care-sensitive conditions (ACSCs).

Choosing the Population

One of the key features for any successful population health effort is choosing the population. Organizations will often focus on either defined or discrete populations or look at other characteristics such as geography or practice size to focus on community or regional populations. *Defined populations* make sense primarily from business standpoint. Such populations are chosen by the organization around a core feature, for example, group of individuals receiving care within a health system, or a group of individuals covered by the same health plan. *Community or regional populations* are chosen on the basis of either geographic or some other common criteria that align around a set of particular issues, for example, geriatric patients with multiple needs. These individuals may receive care in disparate environments and their information may be more difficult to collect as it may reside in a number of different locations.

The link between value and a selected population is predicated upon understanding as much of the population as possible and identifying where services for that population are optimally delivered. Healthcare organizations that desire to improve outcomes and do so at a lower cost have to know who are the high-cost, high-risk patients who require different forms of management.

Risk Stratification

The process by which patients are categorized into different risk groups such as high-risk, low-risk, and rising risk is called *risk stratification.* Risk stratification tries to accurately capture the risk of future events that would alter healthcare costs and the use of healthcare services based on those events. There are utilization-based systems, for example, the chronic illness and disability payment system (CDPS) index, and diagnosis-based tools, for example, the Charlson comorbidity index, that support risk stratification. While such tools are helpful, it is important to recognize that risk stratification tools often do not incorporate psychosocial information or additional nonclinical information around other social determinants of health that might be useful.[4]

Certain utilization-based risk stratification tools are commonly used (Figure 4.1). These include standard risk adjustments informed by *ambulatory care groups* (ACGs). ACGs use International Classification of Diseases-9 (ICD-9) codes to classify individuals based on clinical judgment and potential resource utilization. The CDPS index uses claims data to predict payment

Utilization based	Predict	Comorbidity based	Predict
Ambulatory care groups	Resource utilization	Hierarchical condition categories	Hospitalization and resource utilization
Chronic illness and disability payment system	Payment costs	Adjusted clinical groups	Predicts morbidity and resource utilization
Probability of repeat admissions	Hospitalization risk	Elder risk assessment	Hospitalization; 2-year mortality and nursing home placement
Assessing care of vulnerable elders survey	Hospitalization risk	Chronic comorbidity count	Sums up chronic conditions to predict healthcare costs
Dorr algorithm	Risk of death or hospitalization	Minnesota tiering	Complexity of illness
DxCG Rx	Resource utilization	Charlson comorbidity index	Predicts utilization and 1-year mortality
Medicaid Rx	Resource utilization		
Impact pro	Care management candidacy		
Ingenix PRG and ERG	Current and future healthcare usage		

Figure 4.1 Additional methods of risk adjustment.

costs.[5] The *probability of repeat admissions* (PRA) examines the risk of repeat hospitalization. This is often combined with data provided from other assessments such as the *assessing care of vulnerable elders survey* (ACOVE) for greater predictive accuracy.[6–8] *Impact Pro* is a proprietary risk stratification tool provided by Ingenix to support care management primarily for commercially insured patients. The *Dorr algorithm* is a tool provided by Care Management Plus that identifies risk of death or hospitalization primarily for older patients and Medicare beneficiaries.[9] *DxCG Rx Groups* and *Medicaid Rx* use drug therapy categories and prescription-related information, respectively, to classify individuals.[10] In DxCG Rx Groups, drug therapy categories can be attributed to more than one category. In Medicaid Rx, prescription drugs are mapped to specific medical conditions and costs are predicted as a result of an algorithm that includes medical conditions, age, and gender. *Ingenix PRG* also creates a set of diagnostic groups based on prescriptions and maps prescription medications to discrete diagnostic categories. *Ingenix ERG* alternatively includes ICD-9 codes and procedure codes in attempting to capture all relevant treatment information related to an episode and adjusts based on that information.

Other methodologies used to stratify patients into various risk categories rely in part on the presence of comorbidities. Diagnostic and demographic data obtained at clinical encounters and through other avenues of information gathering can serve as the basis for determining who might need additional medical services. *Hierarchical condition categories* (HCCs) are disease groups organized by body system or similar disease processes.[11,12] The Centers for Medicare and Medicaid Services (CMS) and HHS-HCC models include both disease and demographic factors, termed coefficients. There are sets of coefficients for new enrollees, members in the community, members in long-term care facilities, and enrollees with end-stage renal disease. The models are cumulative and patients can be assigned to more than one category. Some HCCs take priority over related conditions however. Only one HCC in a category can be assigned to a patient. In total, HCCs contain 70 condition categories selected from diagnostic codes and include expected health expenditures. HCCs are the underpinning of the *DxCG* risk adjustment tool, acknowledging that individuals can have multiple HCCs in this context.

HCCs are part of the Medicare Advantage Program. Interestingly, commercial risk adjustment was one of a small number of new risk stabilization programs that were put into place by the Affordable Care Act. Risk adjustment methods were designed to mitigate the potential impact of adverse selection and help to stabilize premiums. State exchanges or the Department of Health and Human Services (HHS) serve as entities responsible for operating risk adjustment models. The HHS risk adjustment model redirects money from insurers with healthier patient populations to those with sicker patient populations. HCCs used by Medicare and commercial entities are different however.

Adjusted clinical groups (AdCG) use both outpatient and inpatient diagnoses to classify patients into 1 of 93 categories. AdCG often are used to predict hospital utilization. *Elder risk assessments* (ERA) are specifically for individuals more than 60 years of age.[13] ERAs use age, gender, marital status, number of hospital days over the prior 2 years, and selected comorbid medical illness to assign an index score to each patient. The *chronic comorbidity count* (CCC) uses publicly available information from the Agency for Healthcare Research and Quality (AHRQ)'s Clinical Classification Software tools to determine a total number of comorbid conditions grouped into six categories.[14] *Minnesota tiering* (MN) is a risk stratification system based on major extended diagnostic groups.[11] Individuals are tiered into one of five tiers based on the number of major extended diagnostic groups. Finally, the *Charlson comorbidity index* predicts 1-year mortality for patients with a range of comorbid illnesses.[4] The model uses administrative data to assess the presence or absence of 17 comorbidity definitions and assigns patients a score from 1 to 20, with 20 being the more complex patients with multiple comorbid conditions.

There are other risk stratification models of course. Some of these were created to specifically address certain populations, for example, Vulnerable Elders Survey (VES-13)[15,16] and the SCAN Health Plan Method. These tools focus on slightly different variables. The VES-13 addresses functional status and self-reported health, whereas the SCAN Health Plan Method (based on an assessment of its Medicare Advantage population) assessed demographics, medical conditions, use of services, durable medical equipment use, medications, inpatient, pharmacy and other costs, laboratory measures of disease control, health questionnaire responses, other geriatric conditions, and disease interactions not specified in HCCs.[4]

Risk stratification formulae are population tools. Patient health risks are adjusted using the variables based on one of the indices noted above, including age, gender, previous health history, and the presence of chronic conditions. Appropriate, complete, and accurate clinical documentation is

Major conditions that when documented completely and accurately affect contemporary risk stratification methodologies:

    Major depression (rather than depression)
    Old myocardial infarction (old MI)
    Kidney failure
Diabetes with complications
    Angina pectoris
    Breast, prostate, colorectal cancers coded as "history of" rather than active
    Protein calorie malnutrition
    Amputation status
    Drug or alcohol dependency
    Tracheostomy status or respirator dependence

Figure 4.2   Examples of clinical conditions that affect risk stratification.

absolutely necessary for accurate risk stratification. The Centers for Medicare and Medicaid Services (CMS) published information around risk stratification and described conditions that were frequently not documents as adequately as they needed to be to appropriately risk stratify patients[17] (Figure 4.2).

Ultimately, it is important to recognize that risk stratification yields a risk score for a particular individual used in calculating payment to a health plan. For instance, CMS uses risk adjustment factors to pay plans for the risk of the people they enroll, instead of using an average value based on the entire number of beneficiaries. CMS risk adjusts Part C payments to Medicare Advantage (MA) plans and Program for All Inclusive Care for The Elderly (PACE) organizations, and Part D payments.[17]

Health plans must attest to the accuracy of the information though they usually do not review all the coding and/or clinical documentation generated by providers. More precise and appropriate diagnostic code reporting and complete clinical documentation from providers increases the accuracy of risk scores. Each patient's entire risk profile must be reflected in the medical record and coded in claims and encounter data. This promotes better documentation, better risk attribution, and, in certain instances, more consistent provider revenue and competitive premiums for members.

Diagnosis coding however can be counter-intuitive to clinical practice. The mnemonic "MEAT" is often used in risk adjustment coding to represent criteria for capturing a diagnosis code on a specific date of service. The documentation must clearly state that the specific diagnosis was monitored or evaluated or assessed or treated during the face-to-face encounter. Risk adjustment diagnose scan can only be captured from documentation from an approved provider—MD, DO, PA, ARNP, clinical psychologist, PT, OT, audiologist, DPM, etc. Clinical documentation from inpatient hospital, out-patient, hospital, and face-to-face office visits are acceptable for coding and therefore for also calculating risk adjustment.

All relevant diagnostic codes should be reported at least once per year for each patient. They can be reported more frequently too. On January 1 of each year, the patient's diagnosis information is reset in preparation for a new year of diagnosis encounter data. Patients can have up to a maximum of 12 diagnosis codes on an outpatient claim.

Risk Stratification Performance

It is interesting to note that risk stratification models have varying degrees of performance. Retrospective models utilizing prescription drug informa-tion compare favorably in terms of risk prediction to diagnoses obtained from encounter data. These can be measured using a correlation coefficient or R^2 or a mean absolute prediction error (MAPE). While obtaining other variables such as additional chronic condition information can improve the overall predictive value slightly, the impact of including patient-level labora-tory and other clinical data has some of the greatest potential to improve the predictive power of many of the risk stratification tools. The incorpo-ration of prior healthcare expenditures is also an effective way to predict future healthcare costs.

There are challenges with present risk stratification schema focused on only claims data, medical conditions, and prescription medication to encompass the totality of the patient. Several healthcare systems have started to examine how to incorporate other features of the patient to bet-ter stratify and segment risk. Lack of access to care is important in select-ing patients who might fail to control their chronic conditions and need additional support. Social support represents another variable not normally accounted for in traditional risk stratification schema. Lack of social support and social isolation may identify high-risk individuals. Add both of these variables to medical complexity and there is a higher likelihood of a patient using excess healthcare resources and having difficulty in managing his or her chronic conditions well. Finally, there are some patients who have behavioral and mental health conditions or simply have no desire to engage in their own healthcare. These individuals also represent significantly at-risk patients, if not high-risk patients.

Predictive Analytics

Risk stratification and other clinical data provide a new platform for decision making for healthcare organizations.[18] Increasingly, availability of these data along with more accurate patient- or service-specific cost data allows healthcare organizations to venture into analytics around their populations.[19] Predictive analytics, the use of computing to mine and assess data and predict performance, are relatively new to healthcare overall. They have been used most recently and frequently to manage healthcare capacity utilization. Analytics platforms are adjuncts to electronic health records, claims databases, and other data sources, such as billing, driving population, and patient-specific analytics. They are useful as health system tools for identifying areas of quality performance or quality improvement depending on the quality metrics being assessed. In addition, such platforms today help identify gaps in care for patients.

Data inputs for analytics include clinical and utilization variables as well as financial information (Figure 4.3). Historically these data were somewhat limited. They were focused on claims data and inpatient data primarily. Data quality was less than optimal and unstructured data, such as information embedded in clinic notes in the electronic health record was inaccessible. What is transpiring in the quest to access more data is an understanding of how to unlock many of these data sources and incorporate them. Increasingly, there are expanding data sets for health systems in a variety of digital formats. These include data embedded in the electronic health record as well as financial data, claims data, socioeconomic and demographic data, and care coordination and care management data. Moreover, data clarity and

Clinical	Utilization	Financial
Major medical conditions	Provider visits	Prescription claims
Other chronic conditions	Hospitalizations	Historical medical expenditures
Preventive health screening results	Emergency department visits	
	12-month prescription activity	
	Primary treating physician	

Figure 4.3   General data categories for population health analytics.

accuracy continue to improve and tools such as natural language processing can access unstructured data.

A primary objective in compiling this information into an analytics format is to help the healthcare organization predict potential clinical utilization and financial impact over a period of time. The healthcare organization then can identify patients most likely to benefit from specific programs designed to improve health, control chronic conditions, and reduce unnecessary care, such as preventable readmissions. Case studies continue to suggest that predictive analytics can shift management from reactive to proactive and thus stem excess use of the emergency department visits and hospital admissions for specific conditions.

There is great belief in predictive analytics of having a positive impact on healthcare. Simple tools can predict hospital readmissions with up to 80% accuracy.[20–23] Clinical prediction models have even identified how to incorporate subjective data to some extent. The Rothman index was created as a single score compiling 26 common observations and results already embedded in standard electronic health records. The index graphically displays a picture of the patient's condition and critical to it is the incorporation of nursing notes. Theoretically, algorithmic modeling, scenario modeling, pattern identification, and even simulation are all possible and potentially helpful in determining the optimal approach for a patient, his or her conditions, and the best access to the right types of services. That noted, the evidence that predictive analytics can improve overall patient outcomes, reduce waste, and more appropriately align care with need is not overwhelming.[24] The challenge in this regard may not be simply improving the precision and accuracy of the algorithms using the data available. There are obvious questions as to the best timing of when to use analytics for populations, how to manage the iterative changes in the analytics introduced by new variables, and new members of the population, be the patients or clinicians. Finally, it may be that the corresponding care interventions and programs to improve health are still in the development phase of their impact capabilities.

Care Models That Account for Risk

There are several fundamental categories of care models addressing differential risk among patients. There are patients who have well-controlled chronic conditions. Many of these individuals are adequately engaged in self-care and do not experience significant complications. There are also individuals with chronic conditions who may benefit from additional management support. Both groups of patients are candidates for traditional disease management. These programs developed in the latter part of the last century focused most commonly on specific diseases. The payer sector adopted chronic disease management programs along with larger healthcare companies as a means of addressing quality-of-care parameters and as a way to identify opportunities to reduce per patient expenditures. Disease management programs have been tremendously successful in certain conditions. However, their adoption by the primary care community was challenging at times due to payer or healthcare organization communications, the lack of uniformity in certain disease management programs, and often the small sample size of patients covered by a specific payer or healthcare organization. The advancement of value-based purchasing and the measures for meaningful use and the Physicians Quality Reporting System have harmonized some of the disease management metrics together in a slightly more comprehensive way (Figure 4.4).

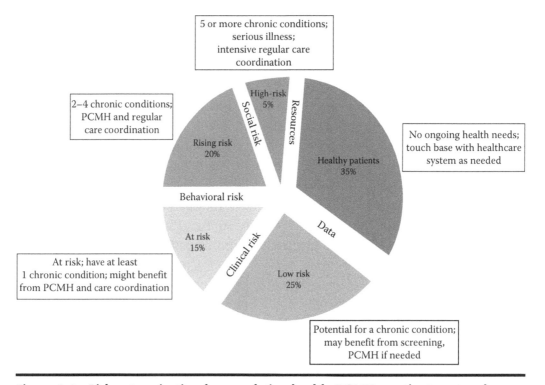

Figure 4.4   Risk categorization for population health. PCMH—patient-centered medical home.

Care Management Programs and the Patient-Centered Medical Home

Many organizations have examined their traditional disease management programs and enhanced them with personnel and/or information features to create a portfolio of care management programs. These programs may not be disease-specific and in fact, can be population-specific, for example, patients with multiple chronic care needs, geriatric patients, etc.

Care management programs have some specific features at their core. They must provide specific services to individuals. The services must be delivered to that individual at a certain start point in their care or health process. There is often an automated referral process or a referral by a member of a care team based on objective criteria. The care management services also have a point of termination. This could be when the individual has "graduated" or reached a different level of self-efficacy or condition control.

Care management programs also have to have one or more objective outcomes to be achieved through the interventions or actions of the program. Finally, successful care management programs should include one or more of the following: self-management, care coordination, or care team care planning. Examples of care management programs include wellness programs and high-risk clinics (Figure 4.5).

	Type of program	Specific example
Care management protocols	Wellness	Combined fitness and nutrition program for health plan members
	Disease management focused on patient management, self-efficacy, and education	Chronic kidney disease education programs
	Care coordination for certain conditions	Diabetes management programs or cancer patient navigation programs
	Care transitions—moving from acute care setting to home	Complex patient discharge program using home care
	Medication therapy management	Pharmacist-led program supporting medication adherence for patients with congestive heart failure and other chronic conditions
Interdisciplinary clinical settings	High-risk clinics	Geriatric patients with multiple chronic conditions or children with disabilities
	Clinical centers	Clinical support teams for patients with neurologic conditions such as Parkinson's

Figure 4.5 Examples of care management programs.

Some patients might be more suitable for a different approach, the patient-centered medical home (PCMH). PCMHs have been a vehicle to care for rising-risk patients.[25] Originally constructed for pediatric patients, the PCMH model identifies a personal physician to provide continuity of care, a physician-led interdisciplinary team that works to support the patient, efforts to integrate care across delivery environments (ambulatory, acute care, and specialty care), effective use of information technology, and open access along with enhanced patient-focused communication. The PCMH actually is derived from the term "medical home," derived by the American Academy of Pediatrics in 1967. While its initial connotation was a single source of information about a patient, it grew to encompass a "partnership approach with families to provide primary healthcare that would be accessible, family-centered, coordinated, comprehensive, continuous, compassionate, and culturally effective."[26] To formalize this, the American Academy of Pediatrics developed an operational definition of the medical home with 37 specific activities embedded in the model.[27] The World Health Organization adopted principles related to the medical home as early as 1978[28] and as primary care evolved in the United States in the 1990s, the concept of the medical home gained more traction. In 2004, the American Academy of Family Physicians merged concepts from the Wagner Chronic Care Model and primary care to prompt new modes of thinking around medical homes. Ultimately, they defined seven core features of a PCMH that have been agreed upon by the American Academy of Pediatrics, the American Academy of Family Physicians, The American College of Physicians, and the American Osteopathic Association. The core features are: personal physician, physician-directed medical practice, whole person orientation, care is coordinated and integrated, quality and safety, and enhanced access and payment reform.

The National Committee for Quality Assurance (NCQA) has been a supporter of PCMH models for some time and serves as the largest PCMH recognition program in the United States.[29] It has envisioned several key facets to a successful medical home, including enhanced after hours and online access, long-term patient and provider relationships, shared decision making, patient engagement on healthcare matters and on health in general, team-based care, better quality and experience of care, and lower costs due to decreased emergency department and hospital utilization.

Given its promise as an entity that could revitalize primary care, the PCMH has been studied for its efficacy. The PCMH model also decreases income-based disparities in care and clinician burnout in some contexts.[25,30,31] However, an aggregate assessment of the PCMH model the AHRQ published a summary paper in 2012 examining available information around PCMH models and their effectiveness in achieving the Triple Aim: better quality, lower costs, and improved experience of care.[32] It reviewed 498 published studies from 2000 to 2010 and determined that more evaluations of the medical home were needed to refine and improve the model. There was some favorable benefit to the model though no significant improvement in costs, and the results of the studies were for the most part inconclusive.

The enthusiasm around PCMH models has prompted exploring other ways in which they might be able to care for higher risk patients. Patient-centered specialty practices, medical homes led by specialists, are one such tactic to support patient care and information flow for certain patients with chronic conditions. This model has been advanced in particular in oncology.[33–36]

PCMH models are challenged as they mature to continue to incorporate key resources for patients (whole person orientation) and how to fund these models given the resources needed to truly address the health of a population with ongoing chronic care needs. Notably however, the PCMH and specialty PCMH are appropriate ways at present to address patient care for populations of rising-risk patients. However, incrementally increasing risk can strain resources and such higher risk patients may need even more intensive care and use of resources. Probably one of the most extreme but necessary developments to address high-risk patients was the creation and subsequent evaluation of ambulatory intensive care units (A-ICUs).[37] Initially it was crafted by Dr. Arnold Milstein to care for patients with multiple complex chronic conditions who would be deemed high-risk. The initial assessment of A-ICUs was published in a white paper, "Redesigning Primary Care for Breakthroughs in Health Insurance Affordability" in 2005.[37] The cost models initially developed were predicted to deliver 37%–40% reduction in healthcare spending with approximately half of this savings offset by the increased expense of the A-ICU versus traditional primary care models. Initial estimated A-ICU start-up costs to serve 18,000–20,000 high-risk adults were $10.8 million. Practical implementation of similar models actually led to 15%–20% less total healthcare spending (risk-adjusted) per year versus peer organizations.[38] Some of the conditions addressed in A-ICUs include diabetes, kidney failure, and hypertension.

Ambulatory Care-Sensitive Conditions

ACSCs are ones for which appropriate ambulatory care could prevent hospitalization. The term was first used in 1993 by Billings et al.[39] Examples of ACSCs include conditions in which acute management could prevent admissions to the hospital, for example, dehydration and gastroenteritis. In addition, chronic conditions in which preventive care could delay or prevent admission, for example, management of diabetic complications, are ambulatory-sensitive conditions. ACSCs are often used as a marker for health system quality. Traditionally, it is believed that hospitalization rates for ambulatory-sensitive conditions are potential surrogates for decreased quality of care and less than optimal access. However, there may be geographic conditions. Moreover, difference in rates of ACSC hospitalization may suggest disparities in access to care.

In the United States, ACSCs are used as a measure of primary care effectiveness. These are measures defined by the Agency for Healthcare Quality and Research such as the age-standardized acute care hospitalization rate for conditions where appropriate ambulatory care would prevent or reduce the need for admission to the hospital per 100,000 individuals in the population less than 75 years of age. The traditional list of ACSCs includes a number of clinical problems (Figure 4.6).

There are several important observations around ACSCs in the United States. Data suggest that African-American patients, Hispanic patients, those insured by Medicaid, or those without insurance tend to comprise a larger proportion of individuals with common ACSCs who presented to emergency departments for evaluation[40] or were hospitalized.[41] Many of the same trends were evident when examining ACSCs among children.[42] Furthermore, ACSCs may be heightened among individuals with behavioral health as an ongoing concern.[43,44] In a 24-month longitudinal analysis of a large cohort of individuals seen in five Department of Veterans Affairs primary care sites, rates of ACSC admissions were found to be significantly greater among patients with mental illness compared to those without it.

Medicaid managed care programs do seem to be associated with decreased hospitalizations attributable to ACSCs.[45] Access to primary care seems to be important in limiting hospitalizations and the use of acute care resources for patients with ACSCs. Basu et al. examined hospital discharge records in New York state and found a negative association between primary care physicians per capita and ACSC admission.[46] The same observation was made on a larger scale examining county ACSC hospitalizations compiled

Congenital syphilis	Secondary diagnosis for newborns only
Failure to thrive	Age <12 months
Dental conditions	
Vaccine preventable conditions	Haemophilus meningitis for ages 1–5 only
Iron deficiency anemia	Primary and secondary diagnoses
Nutritional deficiencies	Primary and secondary diagnoses
Acute Conditions	
Bacterial pneumonia	Excludes cases with secondary diagnosis of sickle cell anemia and patients <2 months
Cervical cancer	
Cellulitis	Excludes cases with a surgical procedure, except when incision of skin and subcutaneous tissue is the only listed surgical procedure
Convulsions	
Dehydration–volume depletion	Principal/secondary diagnoses examined separately
Gastroenteritis	
Hypoglycemia	
Kidney/urinary infection	
Pelvic inflammatory disease	
Severe ear, nose, and throat infections	Excludes otitis media cases with myringotomy tube insertion
Skin grafts with cellulitis	Excludes admissions from skilled or intermediate care nursing facilities
Chronic Conditions	
Angina	Excludes cases with surgical procedures
Asthma	
Chronic obstructive pulmonary disease	Includes acute bronchitis only with certain secondary diagnoses
Congestive heart failure	Excludes cases with certain surgical procedures
Diabetes	Excludes diabetes with renal manifestations, diabetes with ophthalmic manifestations, diabetes with neurological manifestations, and diabetes with peripheral circulatory disorders
Grand mal and other epileptic conditions	
Hypertension	Excludes cases with certain procedures
Tuberculosis (non-pulmonary)	
Pulmonary tuberculosis	

Figure 4.6   Ambulatory care sensitive conditions and ICD-9CM code. (From AHRQ. With permission.)

by the Safety Net Monitoring initiative of the Agency for Healthcare Quality and Research (AHRQ)[41,47] as well as a larger federally qualified health center (FQHC) population.[48] Notably, patient education seems to be a critical feature in influencing potential reductions in ACSC-related hospitalization. Survey data suggested that parent and children education about conditions, medications, and disease triggers could be simple strategies with beneficial effects on health and reduction in need for acute care.[49]

The problem of ambulatory-sensitive conditions is not unique to U.S. healthcare. The Longitudinal Health and Administrative Data (LHAD) initiative recently published the first national-level population-based study of patient factors (e.g., socioeconomic status) and other factors that can be affected by PHC (e.g., comorbidities) associated with ACSC-related hospitalizations in Canada. The LHAD report estimated that 4.2 million persons aged between 12 and 74 have been diagnosed with one or more ACSCs, with approximately 46% suffering from hypertension, 43% heart disease, 36% diabetes, 30% asthma, and 16% chronic obstructive pulmonary disease. Among these, 161,000 (3.8%) reported one or more hospitalization over a 4-year period.[50]

The prevention of complications, unnecessary hospitalizations, and use of acute care resources such as emergency department visits attributable to ACSCs have several critical implications for primary care teams.[51] First, there is a need to identify patients on an ongoing basis who are at a high risk for hospitalization for ACSCs, especially with broadened consideration not just of the medical condition but also social circumstances, medication adherence, and self-management capacity. Second, there is a need to consider how to incorporate regular review of medications and enhanced understanding of the patient and caregivers of medical therapy, medication dosages, and a better overall understanding of the treatment plan, reinforced by shared decision making. Notably, there also has to be a system in place for regular monitoring of symptoms and treatment adherence using in-person, telephonic, or other messaging technology. Furthermore, to take advantage of patient engagement, it is important to identify how to expand self-management training for patients and their caregivers, affording them the ability to address acute changes in clinical condition prior to or in conjunction with seeking additional primary care resources.

There are also additional features that are integral to successfully limiting ACSC-related hospitalizations at least. They include identification of existing social support systems and community resources for patients to access; use of health technology to facilitate access to resources; and increased communication between physicians. Specific tactical approaches that at least address care delivery include after-hours care, optimal use of ambulatory services, intensive monitoring of high-risk patients be it in the home or in an A-ICU environment, and education around how individuals can access clinical care in a timely and effective manner.

Summary

The shift in mindset underway in U.S. healthcare today is increasingly directed toward how to manage populations of patients. The importance of the individual encounter as it has traditionally been considered as an end to itself is now understood to be a part of care continuum. Yet, the underlying way that information around that care continuum and that encounter come together is still evolving. The use of risk stratification and predictive analytics in clinical practice is new, yet evolving rapidly and for a good reason. Understanding how to care for higher risk patients without increasing their cost of care yet increasing the effectiveness of the care that they receive is important as is the understanding how to anticipate patient needs in such a way that optimal services are delivered in advance to prevent or markedly reduce the likelihood of potential complications or problems. Finally, finding the right care model for the patient is now more possible than ever.

Bibliography

1. Cohen CJ, Flaks-Manov N, Low M, Balicer RD, Shadmi E. High-risk case identification for use in comprehensive complex care management. *Population Health Management*, 2015; 18: 15–22.
2. Struijs JN, Drewes HW, Heijink R, Baan CA. How to evaluate population management? Transforming the Care Continuum Alliance population health guide toward a broadly applicable analytical framework. *Health Policy*, 2015; 119: 522–9.
3. Cohen SB, Uberoi N. *Differentials in the Concentration in the Level of Health Expenditures across Population Subgroups in the U.S., 2010.* Statistical Brief #421. Rockville, MD: Agency for Healthcare Research and Quality, 2013.
4. Levine SH, Adams J, Attaway K, Dorr DA, Leung M, Popescu B, Rich J. Predicting the financial risks of seriously ill patients. California Healthcare Foundation, December 2011, pp. 1–33.
5. Kronick R, Gilmer T, Dreyfus T, Lee L. Improving health-based payment for Medicaid beneficiaries: CDPS. *Health Care Financing Review*, 2000; 21(3): 29–64.
6. Shekelle PG, MacLean CH, Morton SC, Wenger NS. Acove quality indicators. *Annals of Internal Medicine*, 2001; 135(8 Pt 2): 653–667.
7. Wenger NS, Shekelle PG. Assessing care of vulnerable elders: ACOVE project overview. *Annals of Internal Medicine,* 2001; 135(8 Pt 2): 642–646.
8. Westropp JC. ACOVE. New tools address unmet need in quality assessment for older patients. *Geriatrics,* 2002; 57(2): 44, 7–8, 51.

9. Dorr DA, Wilcox AB, Brunker CP, Burdon RE, Donnelly SM. The effect of technology-supported, multidisease care management on the mortality and hospitalization of seniors. *Journal of the American Geriatrics Society,* 2008; 56(12): 2195–2202.
10. Gilmer T, Kronick R, Fishman P, Ganiats TG. The Medicaid Rx model: Pharmacy-based risk adjustment for public programs. *Medical Care,* 2001; 39(11): 1188–1202.
11. Haas LR, Takahashi PY, Shah ND et al. Risk-stratification methods for identifying patients for care coordination. *American Journal of Managed Care,* 2013; 19(9): 725–732.
12. Pope GC, Kautter J, Ellis RP, Ash AS, Ayanian JZ, Iezzoni LI, Ingber MJ, Levy JM, Robst J. Risk adjustment of Medicare capitation payments using the CMS-HCC model. *Healthcare Financing Review: CMS,* 2004; 25: 119–141.
13. Takahashi PY, Chandra A, Cha S, Borrud A. The relationship between elder risk assessment index score and 30-day readmission from the nursing home. *Hospital Practice (1995),* 2011; 39(1): 91–96.
14. Naessens JM, Stroebel RJ, Finnie DM et al. Effect of multiple chronic conditions among working-age adults. *American Journal of Managed Care,* 2011; 17(2): 118–122.
15. McGee HM, O'Hanlon A, Barker M et al. Vulnerable older people in the community: Relationship between the Vulnerable Elders Survey and health service use. *Journal of the American Geriatrics Society,* 2008; 56(1): 8–15.
16. Min L, Yoon W, Mariano J et al. The vulnerable elders-13 survey predicts 5-year functional decline and mortality outcomes in older ambulatory care patients. *Journal of the American Geriatrics Society,* 2009; 57(11): 2070–2076.
17. Risk adjustment. In *Medicare Managed Care Manual.* Chapter 7, 2014; pp. 5–56.
18. Bates DW, Saria S, Ohno-Machado L, Shah A, Escobar G. Big data in health care: Using analytics to identify and manage high-risk and high-cost patients. *Health Affairs (Millwood),* 2014; 33(7): 1123–1131.
19. Liyanage H, de Lusignan S, Liaw ST et al. Big data usage patterns in the health care domain: A use case driven approach applied to the assessment of vaccination benefits and risks. Contribution of the IMIA Primary Healthcare Working Group. *Yearbook of Medical Informatics,* 2014; 9(1): 27–35.
20. Ben-Chetrit E, Chen-Shuali C, Zimran E, Munter G, Nesher G. A simplified scoring tool for prediction of readmission in elderly patients hospitalized in internal medicine departments. *Israel Medical Association Journal,* 2012; 14(12): 752–756.
21. Bradley EH, Yakusheva O, Horwitz LI, Sipsma H, Fletcher J. Identifying patients at increased risk for unplanned readmission. *Medical Care,* 2013; 51(9): 761–766.
22. Burke RE, Whitfield E, Prochazka AV. Effect of a hospitalist-run postdischarge clinic on outcomes. *Journal of Hospital Medicine,* 2014; 9(1): 7–12.
23. Hasan O, Meltzer DO, Shaykevich SA et al. Hospital readmission in general medicine patients: A prediction model. *Journal of General Internal Medicine,* 2010; 25(3): 211–219.

24. Wharam JF, Weiner JP. The promise and peril of healthcare forecasting. *American Journal of Managed Care,* 2012; 18(3): e82–e85.
25. Aysola J, Bitton A, Zaslavsky AM, Ayanian JZ. Quality and equity of primary care with patient-centered medical homes: Results from a national survey. *Medical Care,* 2013; 51(1): 68–77.
26. Center RG. *The Patient Centered Medical Home: History, Seven Core Features, Evidence and Transformational Change.* Washington, DC: The Robert Graham Center, 2007.
27. Medical Home Initiatives for Children with Special Needs Project Advisory Committee. American Academy of Pediatrics. The medical home. *Pediatrics,* 2002; 110(1 Pt 1): 184–186.
28. International Conference on Primary Health Care. *Declaration of Alma Ata.* World Health Organization Chronicles; 1978; pp. 428–430.
29. Assurance NCfQ. The Future of Patient-Centered Medical Homes Foundation for a Better Healthcare System. In: Assurance NCfQ, editor. Washington, DC, 2014.
30. Helfrich CD, Dolan ED, Simonetti J et al. Elements of team-based care in a patient-centered medical home are associated with lower burnout among VA primary care employees. *Journal of General Internal Medicine,* 2014; 29(Suppl 2): S659–S666.
31. Nocon RS, Gao Y, Gunter KE et al. Associations between medical home characteristics and support for patient activation in the safety net: Understanding differences by race, ethnicity, and health status. *Medical Care,* 2014; 52(11 Suppl 4): S48–S55.
32. Peikes D, Zutshi A, Genevro J, Smith K, Parchman M, Meyers D. Early Evidence on the Patient-Centered Medical Home. Final Report. (Prepared by Mathematica Policy Research, under Contract Nos. HHSA290200900019I/HHSA29032002T and HHSA290200900019I/HHSA29032005T). Rockville, MD: AHRQ Publication No. 12-0020-EF; 2012.
33. Butcher L. Specialty medical homes taking root. *Physician Executive,* 2013; 39(3): 6–8, 10, 2–3.
34. Kuntz G, Tozer JM, Snegosky J, Fox J, Neumann K. Michigan oncology medical home demonstration project: First-year results. *Journal of Oncology Practice,* 2014; 10(5): 294–297.
35. Reinke T. Oncology medical home study examines physician payment models. *Managed Care,* 2014; 23(6): 9–10.
36. Sprandio JD, Flounders BP, Lowry M, Tofani S. Data-driven transformation to an oncology patient-centered medical home. *Journal of Oncology Practice,* 2013; 9(3): 130–132.
37. Milstein A. Redesigning primary care for breakthrough in health insurance affordability. In: Mercer Human Resource Consulting, editor. *Model 1: the Ambulatory Intensive Caring Unit.* California Healthcare Foundation; 2005, pp. 1–79.
38. Milstein A, Gilbertson E. American medical home runs. *Health Affairs (Millwood),* 2009; 28(5): 1317–1326.

39. Billings J, Zeitel L, Lukomnik J, Carey TS, Blank AE, Newman L. Impact of socioeconomic status on hospital use in New York City. *Health Affairs (Millwood),* 1993; 12(1): 162–173.
40. Oster A, Bindman AB. Emergency department visits for ambulatory care-sensitive conditions: Insights into preventable hospitalizations. *Medical Care,* 2003; 41(2): 198–207.
41. Laditka JN, Laditka SB. Race, ethnicity and hospitalization for six chronic ambulatory care-sensitive conditions in the USA. *Ethnicity & Health,* 2006; 11(3): 247–263.
42. Parker JD, Schoendorf KC. Variation in hospital discharges for ambulatory care-sensitive conditions among children. *Pediatrics,* 2000; 106(4 Suppl): 942–948.
43. Yoon J, Yano EM, Altman L et al. Reducing costs of acute care for ambulatory care-sensitive medical conditions: The central roles of comorbid mental illness. *Medical Care,* 2012; 50(8): 705–713.
44. Yoon J, Bernell SL. The role of adverse physical health events on the utilization of mental health services. *Health Service Research,* 2013; 48(1): 175–194.
45. Bindman AB, Chattopadhyay A, Osmond DH, Huen W, Bacchetti P. The impact of Medicaid managed care on hospitalizations for ambulatory care-sensitive conditions. *Health Service Research,* 2005; 40(1): 19–38.
46. Basu J, Friedman B, Burstin H. Primary care, HMO enrollment, and hospitalization for ambulatory care-sensitive conditions: A new approach. *Medical Care,* 2002; 40(12): 1260–1269.
47. Laditka SB, Laditka JN, Fisher Drake B. Home- and community-based service use by older African American, Hispanic, and non-Hispanic white women and men. *Home Health Care Services Quarterly,* 2006; 25(3–4): 129–153.
48. Falik M, Needleman J, Wells BL, Korb J. Ambulatory care-sensitive hospitalizations and emergency visits: Experiences of Medicaid patients using federally qualified health centers. *Medical Care,* 2001; 39(6): 551–561.
49. Flores G, Abreu M, Chaisson CE, Sun D. Keeping children out of hospitals: Parents' and physicians' perspectives on how pediatric hospitalizations for ambulatory care-sensitive conditions can be avoided. *Pediatrics,* 2003; 112(5): 1021–1030.
50. Sanmartin C, Khanand S, and the LHAD Research Team. *Hospitalizations for Ambulatory Care-Sensitive Conditions (ACSC): The Factors That Matter.* Ottawa, Canada: Statistics Canada, 2011, pp. 1–16.
51. Freund T, Campbell SM, Geissler S et al. Strategies for reducing potentially avoidable hospitalizations for ambulatory care-sensitive conditions. *Annals of Family Medicine,* 2013; 11(4): 363–370.

Chapter 5

Patient-Centered Medical Home and Its Brethren: New Care Delivery Models

Kathleen M. Ferket and Kevin S. Attride

Contents

Traditional Primary Care

The traditional primary care practice is a physician-centric business model with the MD/DO as quarterback of the team. Goals of the traditional model included adequate volume growth, retaining volumes, and revenue generation for the practice to support physician partner financial success. The office staffing model is largely nonprofessional, using nonlicensed medical assistants and front end staff for appointments and insurance verification. Offices employing registered nurses are the exception rather than the rule. Billing and payment cycle may be internal or outsourced. The provider may belong to a Physician Hospital Organization (PHO) for managed care contracting and discounted practice supplies. In the current system, patients and their families frequently serve as their own navigators, often communicating, to the extent they are willing or able, information among primary care providers and specialists. This approach is ineffective for a variety of reasons, including a lack of patient understanding of the clinical care details and a limited ability of patients to advocate for themselves.[1]

Patient education and teaching resources in the office are limited, if available at all. Immediate need appointments are restricted or unavailable. Office hours do not support working families or urgent care needs. Weekend hours, if available, are generally half days on Saturdays. An office visit around holidays is often unavailable and could necessitate an emergency department (ED) referral, even for minor illness. Medication renewals are a part of an annual visit but do not include full medication reconciliation or teaching. The primary care physician (PCP) may receive information regarding a patient ED encounter but timeliness regarding the information varies. In other words, a traditional primary care practice delivers highly fragmented care, which contributes to decreased quality and increased costs.

In some settings, the PCP may choose to manage their patients in the acute care setting but this model is becoming less common each day. The traditional PCP discharge follow-up appointment occurs 10 days to two weeks and contributes to medication noncompliance, often resulting in an avoidable hospital readmission. With ever-increasing Centers for Medicare & Medicaid Services (CMS) demands in hospitals for efficiency, expectations on PCPs as inpatient attending is becoming prohibitive.

The "fee for service" payment model does not reimburse PCP's for office care coordination, education, wellness, or prevention services. These factors, as a key to optimal patient care, went unaddressed, contributing to a fragmented system of care.

Patient-Centered Medical Home

One approach to decreasing fragmentation, improving coordination, and placing greater emphasis on the needs of patients is the patient-centered medical home (PCMH).[2] Care coordination has been defined as "the deliberate integration of patient care activities between two or more participants involved in a patient's care to facilitate the appropriate delivery of healthcare services."[3] The American Academy of Pediatrics coined the idea of a medical home in 1967 with the aim of improving the health of chronically ill children with special needs.[4]

In 2007, seven joint principles for the PCMH were drafted by four physician organizations. The seven principles include

■ Personal physician—each patient has a relationship with a personal physician.
■ Physician directed medical practice (modified in 2011 to team-based approach).
■ Whole person orientation.
■ Care is coordinated and integrated across the healthcare system.
■ Quality and safety are hallmarks of the medical home.
■ Enhanced access to care is available.
■ Payment recognizes the added value provided to patients in a medical home.[4]

The National Committee for Quality Assurance (NCQA) Patient-Centered Medical Home (PCMH) is a recognition program for improving primary care. In a set of standards that describe clear and specific criteria, the program gives practices information about organizing care around patients, working in teams, and coordinating and tracking care over time. There have been several important changes to the content of the PCMH 2014 from PCMH 2011 including the following:

■ *Integration of behavioral health*—Expectations rise, as they did in previous NCQA standards, that a practice support patients' behavioral health. Practices are expected to collaborate with behavioral healthcare providers and to communicate behavioral healthcare capabilities to patients.
■ *Care management focus on high-need populations*—Practices are expected to address socioeconomic drivers of health and poorly controlled or complex conditions. Practices should also focus on the special needs of patients referred from the "medical neighborhood" of practices that surround and inform the medical home.
■ *Enhanced emphasis on team-based care*—Revised standards emphasize collaboration with patients as part of the care team and establish team-based care as a "must-pass" criterion for NCQA recognition.
■ *Alignment of improvement efforts with the Triple Aim*—Practices must show that they are working to improve across all three domains of the Triple Aim: patient experience, cost, and clinical quality.
■ *Sustained transformation*—In keeping with the goal of continuous improvement, practices show that they comply with NCQA standards over long periods.[5]

With the passage of the Affordable Care Act in 2010, the payment model has shifted and created an incentive for treating illness and disease early, providing more primary care, managing chronic diseases well, avoiding redundant and expensive tests, and reducing hospital readmissions. The goals of the PCMH are closely aligned with those of Accountable Care Organizations (ACOs), to increase quality and reduce cost. Though an ACO is a group of provider entities organized in a legal structure to achieve these specified objectives, the PCMH is foundational for accountable care.[6]

Strong care coordination within the PCMH results in improved outcomes and decreased utilization of acute care services. ACOs that incorporate a care continuum focus will be successful in population health strategies and shared savings. The PCMH within the ACO can be viewed as interlocking components in support of systemic healthcare reform.[4] Within the ACO model, patients will often be assessed and stratified into three categories as highlighted earlier based on actuarial review of past claims utilization. However, a somewhat different approach segments the population into multiple categories depending on utilization risk (high, rising, at-risk, or healthy) as well as environmental risk (clinical, social, and behavioral) to indicate how to approach patient intervention (Figure 5.1).

No matter what the model, effective population management will be centralized in the primary care practice; however, evidence-based decision support to treat them appropriately using the latest data to identify the targeted patients is essential. The PCMH must ensure they are capturing all necessary data to identify and support care coordination activities. Patients must have updated problem lists, allergies, vitals, and risk assessment to be appropriately

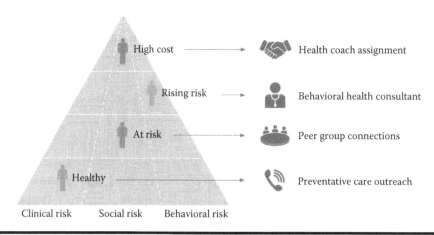

Figure 5.1   Take Action Pyramid. (The Advisory Board Company. © 2014. All rights reserved. With permission.)

segmented for intervention. This is especially necessary for the population of 65 years and older and the reason they should receive preventive visits annually, a comprehensive assessment of their clinical, social, and behavioral status.

A care coordination focus will be based on patient stratification and the care model will shift from physician centric to consumer centric. The lowest risk patients will have a wellness and prevention focus. Annual prevention and wellness visits are becoming the expectation with required documentation criteria and processes to review a host of health maintenance and environmental factors from BMI to depression screening.

In addition to wellness visits, the at-risk population must be screened more routinely to prevent the acceleration of their chronic diseases. More frequent reminders and points of contact will keep these patients more aware of their risks, especially digital contact through secure messaging or automated calls. Telehealth technology can also play a valuable function in mitigating risk escalation.

The rising risk population will be monitored closely, including medication review, education, monitoring, and compliance with treatment and care goals. This group of patients will require regular care coordination by phone consultation. The role of disease-specific nurse navigators or nurse practitioners will focus on this population in the ambulatory setting, supporting them with goals to improved care, including self-management.

A strong care coordination focus will be on the approximate 5% of the patients with high risk factors, working with the patient and physician to reach mutually agreed-upon goals of care as well as remove barriers preventing improvement. Education, medication reconciliation, social services assessment, and support will be provided within the office or through the care management network. The physician and nurse practitioner will focus the majority of their time on the rising and high-risk patients. It is critical for care coordinators to collaborate with the patient and family as well as any community services in which the patient is involved. Extended visits and access to immediate appointments for these patients will be the norm, which will positively impact patient satisfaction.

Successful primary care practices will decrease overutilization of high-risk patients by working to avoid hospitalization, improving rising risk population compliance to regimens, and supporting overall wellness activities of the low-risk population within the practice. The breakpoint for a successful PCMH is a 17% reduction in ED utilization.

Ensuring continuity of care is also a function of the care coordination focus. The PCMH has the responsibility to assist patients with their care beyond the clinical walls and follow-up appropriately. Tracking testing, especially for abnormal labs and imaging studies, and physician referrals is paramount for ensuring successful continuity of care. Managing transitions from specialty clinics, acute settings, postacute settings, and community organizations is critical for effective care and meeting the objectives of the PCMH.

The PCMH emphasizes that all clinicians work as a team at the top of their licenses. The physician will function as a part of a team with the focus on communication, collaboration, and care coordination. Mid-level providers may see low-risk patients, with a focus on prevention and healthy life style practices. The model of care will expand to include RNs, social workers, care coordinators, nutritionists, and patient resource centers for education and training. This will contribute to additional office overhead but will enhance efficiency, quality, and satisfaction. Shared savings or healthcare system subsidy for the participating PCP may offset the additional costs.

The PCMH is also a practice that focuses on clinical and operational improvement quantitatively. The team uses current data to identify areas of opportunity to improve care and prevention. In addition to identifying vulnerable populations to measure quality performance, all patients are checked to ensure routine screenings and other preventive services. Chronic disease performance metrics also help the practice determine its effectiveness to improve outcomes. Practices also measure areas of utilization to determine efficiency and lower costs. Measuring and improving communication and patient experience are priorities to ensure patients understand their care. Measuring and understanding patient engagement is critical. Not only do these practices set improvement targets, but high performing PCMHs are demonstrating continuous improvement over time, exhibiting high clinical quality and safety. Robust and specific documentation, as well as the latest EHR, adhering to the most current meaningful use standards, is always essential to achieve these goals and the ability to measure them.

A founding principle central to the PCMH is improved patient access. The team of clinicians is dedicated to ensuring patients can be seen when necessary by reserving additional slots, even having access to same-day appointments, whether routine or urgent. Practicing hours are also extended beyond the normal 9 a.m. to 5 p.m. to improve continuity of care to reduce urgent care or emergency department visits when possible. Alternative clinical encounters, such as group visits, and electronic communication through patient portals are additional avenues to connect with patients and care for their needs. More advanced EHRs allow patients to setup future appointments, refill medications, review clinical documentation, track test results and specialty care referrals, review educational material about their diseases, as well as securely message clinic team members. The practice also provides off-hours access to provide clinical advice whether by telephone or secure messaging.

Patient-centeredness is at the heart of the PCMH. Each process builds upon the foundation of effective primary care delivery to ensure each team member supports the practice's goals and is culturally aligned. In fact, the most challenging obstacle in the PCMH model is one of culture. Cultural transformation from the traditional primary care model, focused on making activities easier for the physician or just maximizing profitability, to that of the true PCMH, dedicated to building processes around the patient and delivering effective care, are challenging many practices today. Clinics will also continue to shift to larger, team-oriented, multi-disciplinary practices involving many more clinicians than just physicians and medical assistants. Clinical excellence and improvement become the goals in the ever-changing healthcare environment and age of consumerism. As consumers develop expertise in managing their healthcare dollars, a continued focus on consumer satisfaction will ensue. Patient engagement and accountability are keys to the success of the patient-centered medical home.

The Medical Neighborhood

The medical neighborhood is a set of principles and expectations, supported by the requisite systems and processes, to ensure efficient and coordinated care for all patients. The foundation of the medical neighborhood is the collaborative care agreement, which outlines mutual expectations for PCPs and the specialists as they care for patients together.[7]

The PCMH is the framework for the medical neighborhood (Figure 5.2). The medical neighborhood model requires relationships and reciprocal communication to integrate the primary and specialty care for the benefit of consistent care coordination. Medical neighborhoods are necessary because care is often fragmented as patients are seen by many different health providers.[2] This is evidenced by frequent acute care readmissions, patient misunderstanding of medications, and poor follow up. A national survey found that PCPs and specialists perceive communication about referrals to be poor and agree this negatively affects quality of care.[2]

Seamless care transition between primary care and specialists as consumer's transition from hospital discharge to post-acute venues is pivotal. Standardized transfer records, now a CMS expectation, will reduce variation

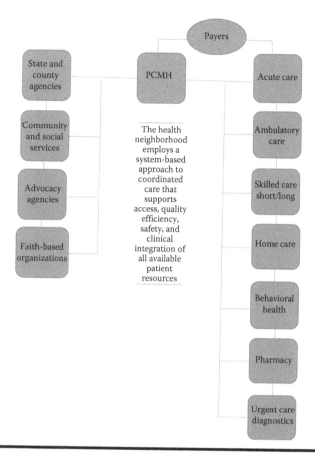

Figure 5.2   Health neighborhood key stakeholders and information flow. (Adapted from Agency for Healthcare Research and Quality. Coordinating Care in the Medical Neighborhood: Critical Components and Available Mechanisms; White Paper, No. 11-0064, 2011; available at https://www.ahrq.gov [accessed in 2014].)

and improve handoff between acute and post-acute care settings. Medication reconciliation, discharge education, and a postdischarge check by a clinician remains the most important process in preventing unnecessary readmission.

Researchers estimate that inadequate management of care transitions was responsible for $25–45 billion in wasteful spending in 2011 through avoidable complications and unnecessary hospital readmissions. Relationships between hospitals systems and post-acute venues are more collaborative since the onset of ACOs and the bundling of payments for certain episodes of care.

The medical neighborhood extends from the PCMH, hospital, post-acute setting, and into the community. Faith-based organizations will play an important role in a medical neighborhood model. Geisinger Health System and Advocate Health Care, innovative healthcare networks, have integrated a faith-based congregational model to support both wellness and chronic disease management.

Care coordination is the focal point of population health management. There are many different models for care coordination. Activities of care coordination include support for self-management, education for patient and family, cross setting communication, coaching, teamwork and collaboration, understanding of information systems, data and advocacy.[6]

Chronic disease management will focus on the rising- and high-risk population. Disease management programs for chronic obstructive pulmonary disease (COPD), heart failure, and diabetes have proven to be successful in the moderate- and high-risk category of patients. Working with the PCMH, the nurse practitioner manages the specific disease modality but works with care coordinators to ensure client compliance, understanding and follow up. The care coordinator role ensures engagement and satisfaction with processes around the chronic disease. Measures of a successful care coordination model include decreased acute care hospitalizations, decreased emergency visits, and adoption of preventative health practices.

Ensuring clinical integration and interoperability with post-acute providers is the next crucial step in the process. Health information exchanges may provide the link to address the fragmentation of data within multiple EMRs across the health system. In the future, an advanced medical neighborhood model may provide interoperability between the PCMH and community agencies providing services to the client.

An important supporting role for the medical neighborhood is the community health worker. Community health workers are being deployed into specific communities to assist the newly enrolled participants from the health exchange navigate the complexities of the healthcare system. The community health worker in the United States dates back to the 1960s with efforts to reach people in underserved communities for health promotion and disease screening programs.[7]

The Center for Public Awareness describes several global functions of community health workers, including decreasing healthcare costs, increasing healthcare access, strengthening the family, community, and the local economy. Community health workers will need a full understanding of access points of care. Successful community workers are home grown from the "neighborhood" and are generally trusted and more impactful. Training programs for this new role are supported through grants allocated by the ACA. Collaborative relationships between community health workers and hospitals, clinics, physicians, social agencies, and faith-based organizations will be pivotal to their success in an effective medical neighborhood. It will be important for physicians and hospitals to partner with programs deploying new community health workers and incorporate them into a medical neighborhood team.

Conclusion

The world outside the traditional hospital is rapidly transforming. Collaborative relationships across settings, clinical integration, and a focus on value for the consumer will be the ingredients for success in the future of population health management.

To provide the full spectrum of services and ensure care is delivered in the most cost efficient and clinical appropriate setting, population health management programs must maintain a network of community-based acute-care and post-acute care resources.

This will require strong leadership and a commitment to a high-functioning system of care, which seamlessly coordinates information flow, clinical decisions, and operations across a variety of care settings and providers.[9]

Bibliography

1. Agency for Healthcare Research and Quality. Coordinating Care in the Medical Neighborhood: Critical Components and Available Mechanisms; White Paper, No. 11-0064, 2011; available at https://www.ahrq.gov [accessed on 2014].
2. Greenberg J, Barnett M, Spinks BA et al. The "Medical neighborhood" integrating primary and specialty care for ambulatory patients. *JAMA Internal Medicine* 2014; 174(3): 454–457.
3. Foreman M. A medical neighborhood. *Health*, 2012; May: 23–25.
4. Sanford ST. Designing model homes for the changing medical neighborhood: A multi-payer pilot offers lessons for ACO and PCMH construction. *Seton Hall Law Review* 2012; 42: 1519–1547.
5. The National Committee for Quality Assurance; Available at https://www.ncqa.org, accessed on 2014.
6. Haas S, Swan BA, Haynes T. Developing ambulatory care registered nurse competencies for care coordination and transition management. *Nursing Economics* 2013; 31(1): 44–49.
7. Bodenheimer T. Coordinating care—a perilous journey through the health care system. *The New England Journal of Medicine, Health Policy Report* 2008; March: 1064–1071.
8. Swider S. Outcome effectiveness of community health workers: An integrative literature review. *Public Health Nursing* 2002; 19(1): 11–20.
9. SG2. Population Health Management, 2013. Available at https://www.sg2.com, accessed on 2014.

Chapter 6

The Value Proposition for Prevention and Screening

David J. Ballard, Briget da Graca,
Neil S. Fleming, and Cliff T. Fullerton

Contents

Greater prioritization of prevention is frequently touted as the solution
to the United States' dual problems of poor health outcomes and disproportionate healthcare spending relative to other developed countries.[1-3]
Certainly, few would argue with the general premise that preventing disease
is beneficial, but considerable uncertainty exists as to whether prevention—
particularly with its contemporary emphasis on *clinical* preventive services
and screening tests—can deliver the expected improvement in population
health and reduction in healthcare costs. Challenges in determining what
might be realistic expectations include inconsistency between studies in
how "prevention" was defined, which "population" was considered when

examining the impacts of prevention, and the methods by which those impacts were quantified.

What Constitutes "Prevention"?

The scope of prevention has broadened over time, to the point where its meaning has become ambiguous. Key resources, such as the *Guide to Clinical Preventive Services* produced by the Agency for Healthcare Research and Quality (AHRQ) and the United States Preventive Services Task Force (USPSTF), do not include a definition.[4,5]

A 1967 textbook titled *Preventive Medicine* defined prevention, in a narrow sense, as "averting the development of a pathological state" (i.e., primary prevention), and, in a broader sense, as including "all measures—definitive therapy among them—that limit the progression of disease at any stage of its course" (i.e., secondary prevention).[4,6] It took a little over a decade for the detection of disease in early/asymptomatic stages to be added to secondary prevention, shifting actions to reverse, arrest or delay progression of disease into tertiary prevention.[4,7] In 1998, the World Health Organization phrased primary prevention in terms of "risk factor reduction", and, not long thereafter, the Australian National Health Partnership added "primordial" prevention (preventing the emergence of predisposing social and environmental conditions that can lead to causation of disease) to the terminological soup.[4,8] "Quaternary prevention" may, however, be the most baffling, having been variously defined as: (1) actions to protect patients from over-medicalization;[9] (2) quality assurance and improvement processes within a healthcare system;[10] or (3) rehabilitation or restoration of function.[11]

One factor contributing to the inconsistencies in how prevention is defined is the separation that has occurred between the domains of clinical care and public health. Medical education has focused on hospital-based care and clinical research since the nineteenth century, isolating the previously integrated public health in a separate discipline.[12] Lacking in-depth knowledge of each other's fields, the resulting two disciplines tasked with health promotion and disease prevention are frequently unable to coordinate and integrate their efforts as needed.[12–14] Thus, while urban planning, design, and transportation decisions are known to have tremendous impacts on health through air and water quality, traffic safety, and other social and environmental determinants of health, the medical community is unlikely to be involved in making them—and, conversely, generally overlooks these arenas in its own efforts related to prevention.[12]

This status quo is both reflected and maintained in the ways in which the public health and clinical disciplines define the population in which they are seeking to prevent disease (or worsening of disease): in public health, a "population" refers to all residents of a particular geographic area (possibly stratified by race/ethnicity, gender, age, disease status, disability, or language spoken), while clinicians frequently define populations by aggregating the individuals to whom they have delivered care during a particular period of time.[12,15–18] This latter definition is the one applied to the Medicare Shared Savings accountable care organizations (ACOs) in the Patient Protection and Affordable Care Act,[19] and being used by at least some private ACOs,[20] which may further entrench the divide between clinical and public health prevention efforts—especially in urban areas where multiple providers (and potentially ACOs) serve a single neighborhood.[15]

The problem with the clinical population definition is that it may reinforce the tendency of clinicians to view prevention primarily from the perspective of the clinical services they deliver,[14] blurring the lines between "risk for disease" and disease itself,[21,22] and between prevention and treatment.[23] For example, classifications like "pre-diabetes" and "pre-hypertension" were introduced to help identify high-risk individuals in whom lifestyle modification was urgently needed to stop or slow their progression into disease, but studies show there is heavy reliance on medications to prevent these individuals from crossing the relevant blood sugar and blood pressure thresholds into diagnosed disease—despite a lack of evidence showing that the benefits of these treatments outweigh the risks below these levels.[23] Given that individuals have to take these medications long term to sustain their below-threshold measures, just as they would for treatment of the actual disease, such approaches have a dubious place in the "prevention" category, and really represent a shift in the treatment threshold to a lower value that needs to be validated by research.[23,24] Analogously, at the other end of the clinical spectrum, should an intervention for patients who survived a myocardial infarction that involves four drugs, lifestyle advice, and cardiac rehabilitation be considered "prevention" as it is named in the National Institute for Health and Clinical Excellence (NICE) guidelines?[24,25] Or would "treatment" or "disease management" be more accurate terms?

Who Is Responsible for Prevention?

As the definition of prevention has expanded, so has the list of key players, although not all are involved in all levels of prevention. "Primordial prevention" (preventing the emergence of predisposing social and environmental conditions that can lead to causation of disease) falls within the domain of local, state/provincial, and national governments, which enact and enforce zoning laws, and health and safety regulations, and provide urban planning, and funding for education. But while governments are the primary actors in primordial prevention, they cannot be effective alone. Success requires cooperation from industry, advice and educational resources from professional associations and community organizations to prioritize and implement initiatives, and the support of the healthcare community in communicating and reinforcing the health benefits of the program. A successful example of such cooperation is the set of actions taken to reduce tobacco use over the past half century: During the 1960s, public health service announcements regarding the dangers of smoking were so effective that the tobacco industry agreed to stop advertising on television, and public opinion was swayed to support limitations on smoking in public and higher tobacco taxes. This led to a steady decline in per capita cigarette consumption from 1965 to 2000.[26–28]

Given the large portions of time most adults spend in the workplace, employers also have a role to play in primordial prevention, ensuring workplaces that are safe and enable employee access to key determinants of health such as affordable healthy food and locations where they can be physically active, and offering wellness programs and health insurance incentives that encourage employees to incorporate healthy living into their workday and lifestyle.[29]

Primary prevention (reduction of risk factors and health promotion) is where individual responsibility comes into play, particularly for chronic diseases that are strongly associated with lifestyle choices such as diet and exercise. The preferred method of reducing cardiovascular risk is lifestyle based—not smoking; eating a diet that emphasizes fruits, vegetables, and whole grains, and limits intake of sodium, sugar, and saturated fats; and exercising for at least 30 minutes five times a week. Such a lifestyle is far from the norm, however, with fewer than 15% of adults and children in the United States exercising sufficiently, and <10% meeting the dietary recommendations for the consumption of fruits, vegetables, and whole grains.[30,31] Part of this poor compliance is due to the lack of primordial prevention, the point of which is to make healthy choices easy—or even automatic—for the individual. The powerful combination of primordial and primary prevention is demonstrated by the public health messaging on the dangers of saturated fat and cholesterol in the 1960s, which led to a greater than 50% reduction in the intake of saturated fat and a 10 mg/dL decrease in mean population cholesterol level. These lifestyle changes accounted for half of the >30% decrease in incidence of coronary heart disease seen in the United States from 1965 to 1978.[26–28] Unfortunately, public health agencies in the United States have largely abandoned such strategies,[26] leaving healthcare providers and nonprofit organizations to try to fill the gap in providing patients and members of the general public with the necessary information to encourage and support healthy choices.

A second arm of primary prevention is vaccination against infectious diseases. This still requires individual responsibility to seek out vaccination, but falls among the range of preventive services for which healthcare providers can be held accountable for delivery—for example, by including quality metrics for influenza and pneumonia vaccination among those to which a provider's income is tied in a pay-for-performance program.[32] Childhood vaccinations are a second example of the successful combination of primordial and primary prevention. Primordial prevention has ensured the necessary support for the healthy choice of vaccinating is in place: in all 50 states, vaccination against specific diseases is required to enroll children in public schools, although medical and religious exemptions are available,[33] and programs such as the Centers for Disease Control and Prevention's "Vaccine for Children" ensure that inability to pay is not a barrier to any child receiving the necessary vaccinations.[34] By 1999, 99% of children enrolled in public school in most states had received their recommended vaccinations,[35] and 9 of the 11 diseases for which vaccination was universally recommended for children before 1990 had been eradicated or showed dramatic reductions in incidence.[36] In contrast, the delivery rate of the pneumococcal vaccination recommended for individuals older than 65 years, which, although covered by Medicare,[37] is not supported by any primordial structure analogous to the school enrollment requirement for childhood vaccinations, had reached only 60% in 2008.[38]

Screening for early detection of disease, depending on the definition of prevention being used, may fall either within primary prevention or make up its own category of secondary prevention. Depending on the classification, this is an area where responsibility is shared between the individual and the healthcare provider. The formal mechanisms for accountability, such as public reporting tend to fall on the provider rather than the patient.

Insurance premium incentive/penalty programs for at least basic screening such as body mass index, blood pressure, and fasting blood glucose and lipids are increasingly being used to encourage engagement from the patient's side as well.[39] The underlying primordial prevention supporting such clinical service components of prevention lie largely in ensuring patients have access to the appropriate screening, including removing or reducing financial barriers. The Patient Protection and Affordable Care Act took steps in this direction through its attempts to increase the proportion of the United States population with healthcare coverage, and the requirement that insurers cover preventive care without cost-sharing for the patient.[19]

By the time prevention is focused on reversing, arresting, or delaying disease progression (either secondary or tertiary prevention), it has moved firmly into the clinical realm. While healthy lifestyle choices remain important in preventing exacerbation of disease, and may be sufficient to control the disease in some cases, at this point in the continuum of care, the patient has substantially more contact with the healthcare system, and, most likely, providers in multiple roles. Responsibility expands beyond the patient and primary care provider to the broader healthcare delivery system. It is at this stage that new structures, encouraging coordination across healthcare components come into play. These structures are intended to ensure that responsibility and accountability are shared and that incentives and rewards are allocated appropriately.

Determining the Costs and Benefits of Prevention

The approaches typically used to combine the monetary and nonmonetary costs and benefits associated with an intervention are *cost–effectiveness, cost–utility, cost–benefit*, and *cost–minimization* analyses.

Cost–effectiveness analysis looks at the effects of interventions in terms of naturally occurring units (e.g., deaths) or intermediate outcomes (e.g., changes in blood glucose levels), and the monetary costs of the interventions.[40,41] The aim is to provide information about the relative efficiency of alternative interventions that serve the same goal.[40,41]

Cost–utility analysis is a type of cost–effectiveness analysis that employs quality-adjusted life years (QALYs) as its outcome measure, and applies to budget allocation problems requiring maximization of health under fixed budget constraints. It can be used to decide the best way of spending a given treatment budget or the healthcare budget as a whole.[40–42]

Cost–benefit analysis, with the outcome reported as net monetary gain or loss, enables consideration of broader perspectives—for example, showing where higher costs of a healthcare service may be tolerable based on benefits gained in some other segment, such as work productivity. This may be controversial because it requires assigning monetary values to the benefits, and to death and disease.[40,41]

Cost–minimization analysis applies when the health effects (including quality of life) of two or more interventions are known to be equal, so that the decision between them revolves purely around cost. Its use is limited since it can only compare alternatives with the same outcomes, and in the rare case these alternatives have already been demonstrated to be equally effective.[40,41] Figure 6.1 summarizes the main differences between these methods in terms of how they measure effects, and the type of evaluation to which they apply.

Economic evaluations of preventive measures offer particular challenges because of the typically wide separation in time between costs and benefits, and because benefits being sought do not accrue solely to the individual. Thus, the typical means of economic evaluation run risks of understating (or overstating) the cost–effectiveness of prevention, and these risks need to be taken into account when interpreting the result of such evaluations.[43] The three areas where under- or overestimation may creep in are (1) estimating the costs and benefits over time; (2) estimating the costs and benefits to others; and (3) estimating the costs and benefits to the individual.

Economic evaluations that need to account for costs and benefits over time typically discount future costs and benefits to a present value, based on the assumption that people prefer to have a benefit now and a cost later.

Method	Costs	Effects	Evaluation question
Cost–effectiveness analysis	Monetary units	Natural units (life-years gained, burns prevented, etc.)	Comparisons of interventions with same objective
Cost–utility analysis	Monetary units	Utility and quality-adjusted life years (QALYs) or disability-adjusted life years (DALYs)	Comparison of interventions with different objectives
Cost–benefit analysis	Monetary units	Monetary units	Are the benefits worth the costs?
Cost–minimization analysis	Monetary units	The effects are not measured, since they are considered to be equal	Least-cost comparisons of programs with the same outcome

Figure 6.1 Characteristics of different types of economic evaluation. (From WHO report, http://www.euro.who.int/data/assets/pdf_file/0007/144196/e95096.pdf.)

While there is some disagreement in general about the appropriateness of discounting nonmonetary future benefits, the issue is magnified in the case of prevention because of the extended period across which the discounts are applied—particularly if a high discount rate is chosen (e.g., 7%–10%).[43] A frequently used illustration is the cost–benefit analysis of treatment and prevention of myocardial infarction in a cohort of 10-year-old boys: the cost per added year of life of treatment (special coronary care units) ranged from $1782 with 0% discounting to $5037 with 10% discounting over the lifetime of the cohort, but the cost per added year of life of prevention (cholesterol screening and change in diet initiated at age 10 years) went from $2855 with 0% discounting to $94,460 with 10% discounting.[44] Moreover, while economic evaluations typically apply a discount rate of either 3% or 5%, studies show that, with respect to health states, there is wider variation between individuals regarding to what extent the assumption of preferring immediate to future benefits (and future to immediate costs) holds true.[43] Particularly for prevention, since individuals vary in their preferences for risks (uncertainty increases over time), preferences likely range from willingness to pay upfront costs for prevention to reduce that uncertainty, to choosing to ignore the long-term risks and forgo prevention—or, at least, postpone it until the uncertainty of obtaining individual benefit decreases.[45] While it may not be possible to determine what discount rate reflects the prevention preferences of the population, applying discount rates ranging from 0% to high values (7%–10%), can provide decision makers with a clearer picture of the extent to which discounting may be driving the result. This will also provide insight into how sensitive the result is to variation in preferences either within or between populations.

Unlike curative treatment, which typically benefits only the individual patient and a relatively small group of close associates (e.g., dependent family members), prevention can involve costs and benefits to others ("externalities"), both in and outside of the healthcare system, immediately and in the future. Examples include the herd immunity from vaccination programs that protects individuals who, for one reason or another, cannot be vaccinated, as well as the health benefits from reduced exposure to second-hand smoke that follow from smoking cessation.[43] Prevention needs to be examined from the societal perspective to ensure all these ramifications are considered. Since total benefits may be substantial but diffuse (meaning no one set of stakeholders has sufficient incentive to invest in prevention), decisions regarding what services should be offered and who should pay for them need to be made at the societal level rather than being left to market forces.[43] Economic evaluations will under-state the value of prevention if the benefits to people other than the individual receiving the preventive measure are not considered, but will overstate it if downstream and external costs—for example, off-setting effects, such as an increase in average driving speed, leading to increased fatalities, after seat-belt use is made mandatory—are also not included. Including these downstream and external effects is challenging in terms of establishing the link to the preventive measure, which may occur through a chain of uncertain events.[43]

A major debate in cost–utility analyses of prevention strategies is whether unrelated medical care during the life years gained should be included in the calculation of cost.[42] Inclusion or exclusion can make a substantial difference to the outcome of the evaluation—particularly for primary prevention, where the costs of unrelated medical care may be substantially greater than those of related medical care.[42] The argument for inclusion is based on internal consistency: since the outcome of interest (quality-adjusted life years [QALYs]) captures the benefits not only of the preventive measure but also of subsequent care to treat conditions that developed during the life years gained, all the costs contributing health-related benefits need to be included. Inclusion also provides consistency across cost–utility analyses where limiting included costs to related medical care leads to seemingly arbitrary inclusions/exclusions that hamper comparisons across interventions. For example, consider an individual who is both obese and a smoker. Under two different scenarios, prevention averts a fatal myocardial infarction, leading to the same number of life years gained in both cases. During those years, the individual develops arthritis, and the quality of life gains from normal treatment of that arthritis are included in the QALYs attributed to the prevention strategy. If the prevention strategy that averted the myocardial infarction was a smoking cessation program, then the treatment costs for the arthritis are considered unrelated and would be excluded from the cost–utility analysis. However, if the prevention strategy was weight loss, they are considered related and would be included. A comparison of these costs–utilities would therefore make the smoking cessation program appear to provide better value for money than the weight loss program.[42]

The third aspect of economic evaluations of prevention that run the risk of over- or understatement of value is the treatment of intangible costs and benefits—such as increased or decreased pain and suffering.[43]

Intangibles often have substantial impact on the relative cost effectiveness of prevention programs. Unlike treatment, in which key benefits are typically the tangible reductions in morbidity and mortality, benefits an individual gains from prevention are in the form of reduced uncertainty or anxiety about something that might otherwise happen in the future. Likewise, the individual costs include the anxiety induced by false-positive results on screening tests, and, for lifestyle-based prevention strategies, the loss of pleasure through having to devote leisure time to exercise activities they do not enjoy, or forgoing favorite foods.[43,46–50] Cost–utility analysis captures individuals' preferences (utilities) of this sort for health/healthcare through use of outcome measures like QALYs, but the accuracy of the utility data is unknown. For example, do the utilities chosen for measurement include the relevant range of utilities for the measure being evaluated?[43] Cost–benefit analysis also captures preferences/utilities, although indirectly, through contingent valuation surveys of people's willingness-to-pay (i.e., the maximum amount of income an individual is willing to forego to ensure a particular service or good is available), which captures the total value the individual assigns to it.[43]

Prioritizing Prevention Activities: Getting the "Biggest Bang for the Healthcare Buck"

Because there are so many areas of health that need to be improved across broad segments of the United States' population, health resources need to be allocated wisely. Essentially, every choice to devote resources to a specific prevention effort—whether it targets a particular disease, behavior, geographic area, or demographic subgroup—comes at the cost of improvements that could have been achieved in some other area. To make informed decisions that, over time, will provide the incremental gains needed to establish a healthy population, decision makers at all levels of the healthcare system need guidance regarding the effectiveness of different preventive strategies, the short- and long-term costs and benefits the strategies each involve and provide, and the number of people affected in their population. Priorities may differ between populations or between subgroups in a population because of differences in prevalence even when the relative risk based on the exposure is the same, and preventive strategies that work in one setting or population may not work in another.[4] The United States Preventative Services Task Force (USPSTF) is tasked with evaluating and synthesizing the evidence into guidelines that support informed decision making in these regards—at least with respect to preventive strategies that fall within the scope of clinical preventive services such as screenings, counseling services, and preventive medications.[51]

The USPSTF was created in 1984 as an independent, volunteer panel of experts in the fields of preventive medicine and primary care, including internal medicine, family medicine, pediatrics, behavioral health, obstetrics and gynecology, and nursing. Based on review of the existing peer-reviewed evidence, the USPSTF devises recommendations for preventive services and assigns each a grade that reflects the strength of the evidence supporting it. The grades range from A (a recommendation with high certainty that the net benefit is substantial) to D (a recommendation against the service based on moderate to high certainty of no net benefit), or an I report (indicating insufficient evidence to assess the benefits and harms).[51] The USPSTF also makes an annual report to Congress, identifying critical gaps in the evidence base for preventive services and recommending priority areas for research.[51]

The USPSTF's scope of activity is specific: "Its recommendations address primary or secondary preventive services targeting conditions of substantial burden in the United States and are provided in primary care settings."[52] It does not consider either costs or coverage of services in making recommendations.[52] Its recommendations therefore represent only a starting point for decisions regarding the efficient allocation of healthcare resources in pursuit of population health. Other groups, such as the National Commission on Prevention Priorities, convened by the Partnership for Prevention (a nonprofit organization comprised of leaders from the business community, the health sector, health voluntaries, and government[53]) have analyzed the economic and societal benefits of clinical preventive services to develop targeted recommendations for expanded access to services that would improve health outcomes for large segments of the population at reasonable cost.[54,55] Their review of the evidence identified three clinical preventive services that, based on the published literature, appear to be cost saving, as well as several that are highly cost effective (Figure 6.2).

Cost-saving clinical preventive services
• Discussing aspirin use with high-risk adults • Childhood immunizations • Tobacco-use screening and brief intervention
Highly cost-effective clinical preventive services
• Influenza and pneumococcal vaccinations • Cervical and colorectal cancer screening • Vision screening for adults age ≥65 years • Hypertension screening • Cholesterol screening • Alcohol abuse screening

Figure 6.2   Clinical preventive services identified as cost-saving are highly cost-effective. (Adapted from Maciosek MV et al., *American Journal of Preventive Medicine* 2006; 31(1): 52–61.)

Many factors can influence a preventive strategy's cost effectiveness. These include[57,58]

1. The definition of the target population (i.e., should the preventive service be applied to all individuals, or just to a particular demographic, or just to individuals already identified as high risk for developing disease?)
2. Frequency
3. The technology used for delivery (e.g., the cost–effectiveness of colorectal cancer screening depends greatly on whether it is done via colonoscopy, sigmoidoscopy, or fecal occult blood test)
4. Whether prevention is compared to doing nothing or to effective treatment after disease develops
5. The proportion of the population already receiving the service

A prevention strategy's initial failure to demonstrate cost–effectiveness should, therefore, not necessarily be taken as evidence that it is not worth pursuing, but rather that its method of delivery should be reviewed or restructured to align the costs with the health benefits.

Delivery rates for many of the cost-effective services are low, often ≤50% of the target population. Thus, there is significant opportunity to improve the delivery of care in these areas and in the related health outcomes (assuming compliance with treatment where disease is diagnosed). However, delivery rates of other services, such as cholesterol and hypertension screening, are estimated to approach 90%, although compliance with treatment among those who screen positive is far lower.[56] In such cases, greater health gains are likely to be achieved by focusing on increasing treatment compliance than by attempting to reach a 100% screening rate.

Most reviews attempting to rank the cost–effectiveness of prevention strategies have focused on clinical preventive services; however, if prevention strategies were truly to be prioritized according to the greatest health benefits per dollar spent, the list would be topped by primordial prevention—such as mandated limits on the salt content of bread, margarine, and cereal to reduce cardiovascular disease,[59] and coordinated national campaigns similar to those against tobacco and consumption of saturated fats in the 1960s that placed pressure on industry to comply with marketing restrictions and changed public opinion as to what constituted acceptable and healthy behavior.[26] These strategies "win" in terms of value because they reach whole populations simultaneously, and require little conscious effort at the individual level. The importance of this approach to prevention is recognized in the National Prevention Strategy that was established under the Patient Protection and Affordable Care Act. The first of its four strategic directions is *Healthy and Safe Community Environments*, followed by *Clinical and Community Preventive Services, Empowered People, and Elimination of Health Disparities*.[60] Moreover, several priorities addressed within each of these four domains relate to lifestyle and environment, including tobacco-free living, preventing drug and alcohol abuse, healthy eating, active living, injury and violence prevention, sexual and reproductive health, and mental and emotional well-being.[60]

Some primordial prevention efforts are underway in the United States. For example, at the federal level, H.R. 5729 "Sugar-Sweetened Beverages Tax Act of 2014" (or "SWEET Act"), introduced in the House of Representatives on July 30, 2014, proposed a national tax of one penny per teaspoon of sugar, high-fructose corn syrup and other sweeteners in beverages, to be paid by the manufacturer or importer. The resulting revenue would be channeled into the Prevention and Public Health Fund.[61] Illinois has a similar state tax on sweetened beverages under consideration,[62] and on November 4, 2014, Berkley, CA, enacted the first soda tax in the United States.[63] Based on evidence of the effects of tobacco taxes (which shows that every 10% increase in cigarette price was associated with a 6.5% decrease in youth smoking, and 2% decrease in adult smoking[64]) and preliminary results of Mexico's taxes on sugar-sweetened beverages and calorie-dense food (with PepsiCo and Coca-Cola reporting volume declines of up to 3% in sugary beverage sales since the tax took effect in the first half of 2014),[65] SWEET Act–type measures may lead to substantial health gains—particularly if expanded to other calorie-dense, nutrient-poor foods.

Will Increased Focus on Prevention Decrease Healthcare Costs? Does It Matter?

One of the principal promises made for health reform under the Patient Protection and Affordable Care Act was that "devoting more of our healthcare funds to prevention will save tens of millions of dollars and improve millions of lives" (p. 1928).[66] Unfortunately, this is unlikely to be the case.

A greater focus on prevention can achieve better health in populations. Increasing delivery of USPSTF-recommended adult preventive services from 70% to 86% over a period of six years in a physician network caring for ~245,000 patients was estimated to have prevented 36 deaths and 97 incident cases of cancer; 420 coronary heart disease events (including 66 sudden deaths) and 118 strokes; 816 cases of influenza and pneumonia (including 24 hospital admissions); and 87 osteoporosis-related fractures.[67,68] However, there is little evidence that increased use of preventive services (other than lifestyle modifications related to diet, exercise and tobacco use, and child-hood immunizations[56,69]) lead to reduced expenditures.[57,70] In fact, greater use of preventive care can increase total lifetime healthcare costs. These costs come from two directions: first, the costs associated with delivering the preventive services themselves (which may require significant amounts of clinician time and/or expensive technology), plus the costs of investigating false positives in the screening tests, and the costs of treating disease found through screening;[57,70] second, successful prevention of disease increases lifespan, creating additional opportunity to develop other health conditions that then require treatment, increasing total lifetime costs of care.[57,70]

Furthermore, while the Patient Protection and Affordable Care Act requires coverage of preventive services graded A or B by the USPSTF with-out cost-sharing (such as co-pays) from the patient, the same is not true for the ancillary tests and follow-up visits or treatment that might follow from a positive screening test.[71] This raises questions about the extent to which increased screening will actually lead to more definitive early diagnoses and early treatment. There is also doubt that earlier treatment leads to decreases in overall treatment costs as is typically assumed,[75] and concerns that increased screening will exacerbate the problem of over-diagnosis (already estimated to account for 10%–30% of localized breast cancers and 40%–60% of prostate cancers[72,73]), resulting in delivery of "early treatment" that is unnecessary and carries risks of sequelae that require further intervention.

Some argue that cost savings are the wrong goal for prevention, and what should be considered is what value the preventive measure achieves.[54] From that perspective, health promotion and disease prevention can provide high value to society by improving lives at relatively low cost and, when pitted against treatment, have a better chance of providing a good return on investment. One example of this is workplace health promotion/disease prevention sponsored by an employer. If employee participation leads to greater lifetime healthcare costs through lifespan extension, these costs may be outweighed by what the employer gains through increased productivity, and decreased absenteeism and staff turnover, in a healthier workforce.[54] Employers need to be included in the debates regarding the economic benefits of prevention because they have the ability to influence the envi-ronments in which most adults spend large portions of their time. They also have incentives to keep their workers healthy—both to keep productivity high and to reduce the utilization of employer-provided health insurance—and can create incentives for employees to participate in wellness programs or to achieve specific health indicators by tying these to reductions in the employee's health insurance premium costs. In 2012, 63% of companies with three or more employees that offered health benefits also offered at least one wellness program.[74] Unfortunately, despite this widespread popularity, there is limited evidence regarding the effectiveness of these workplace-based wellness interventions, and the existing evidence suggests only modest benefit.[29] Part of the problem with evaluating these programs is the heterogeneity across employers, making it impossible to aggregate results; other problems relate to the poor quality of the research designs that sought to evaluate the effects.[29] More rigorous evaluations are needed, not only of the health effects, but also of how they translates through increased productivity and less frequent healthcare utilization into a return on investment for employers.

Conclusion

Greater focus on health promotion and use of preventive services may not produce the reductions in healthcare costs anticipated by the framers of the Patient Protection and Affordable Care Act. Nonetheless, many such measures offer considerable value in terms of the improvements in health and quality of life at reasonable costs. Primordial prevention, which creates a healthy environment and culture that encourages individual lifestyle choices that promote health and reduce risks for disease, offers the best value for money spent in terms of improving health outcomes. Further research is needed to determine how the costs of these measures can be best aligned with benefits to ensure these accrue to the same stakeholders—as is the case with most quality-related interventions.[75] A critical aspect of that alignment is determining how the population being targeted for health improvement should be defined, and what perspective should be considered. If benefits are experienced within a community—as, for example, with childhood immunizations—the relevant definition might be the geographic population, with the costs covered by that community through public mechanisms such as taxes. In contrast, if the benefits accrue to the healthcare system—for example, when prevention of progression of chronic illnesses such as diabetes and heart failure leads to reduced need for hospitalization—a more relevant population definition might be based on patient panels or enrollees in a health plan. Meanwhile, in wellness programs, where at least some benefits accrue outside the realm of health and healthcare, the population may be best defined according to the employer. This adds complexity to an already complicated situation, since all aspects of health and prevention are to some extent, interrelated. Structures that make some populations identical, such as employer-based ACOs, offer opportunities for coordination that provide incentives for more of the stakeholders whose engagement is needed to maximize the value that health promotion and prevention can offer.

Bibliography

1. Lorenzoni L, Belloni A, Sassi F. Health-care expenditure and health policy in the USA versus other high-spending OECD countries. *Lancet* 2014; 384(9937): 83–92.
2. Squires DA. *Explaining High Health Care Spending in the United States: An International Comparison of Supply, Utilization, Prices, and Quality.* New York: The Commonwealth Fund; 2012.
3. *U.S. Health in International Perspective: Shorter Lives, Poorer Health.* Washington, DC: The National Academies Press; 2013.
4. Starfield B, Hyde J, Gervas J, Heath I. The concept of prevention: A good idea gone astray? *Journal of Epidemiology and Community Health* 2008; 62(7): 580–583.
5. Guide to Clinical Preventive Services, 2014: Recommendations of the U.S. Preventive Services Task Force. June 2014. Agency for Healthcare Research and Quality, Rockville, MD. http://www.ahrq.gov/professionals/clinicians-providers/guidelines-recommendations/guide/index.html. Accessed November 17, 2014.
6. Clark DW, MacMahon B. *Preventive Medicine.* Boston, MA: Little, Brown & Co; 1967.
7. Nightengale EO, Cureton M, Kalmar V, Trudeau MB. *Perspectives on Health Promotion and Disease Prevention in the United States.* Washington, DC: Institute of Medicine; 1978.
8. National Public Health Partnership. *Preventing Chronic Disease: A Strategic Framework. Background Paper.* Melbourne, Australia: National Public Health Partnership; 2001.
9. Bentzen N. *WONCA Dictionary of General/Family Practice.* Copenhagen, Denmark: Laegeforeningens Forlag; 2003.
10. Gofrit ON, Shemer J, Leibovici D, Modan B, Shapira SC. Quaternary prevention: A new look at an old challenge. *Israel Medical Association Journal* 2000; 2(7): 498–500.

11. Mensah GA, Dietz WH, Harris VB, Henson R, Labarthe DR, Vinicor F, Wechsler H, Centers for Disease C, Prevention. Prevention and control of coronary heart disease and stroke—nomenclature for prevention approaches in public health: A statement for public health practice from the Centers for Disease Control and Prevention. *American Journal of Preventive Medicine* 2005; 29(5 Suppl 1): 152–157.

12. Zusman EE, Carr SJ, Robinson J, Kasirye O, Zell B, Miller WJ, Duarte T, Engel AB, Hernandez M, Horton MB, Williams F. Moving toward implementation: The potential for accountable care organizations and private-public partnerships to advance active neighborhood design. *Preventive Medicine* 2014; 69(Suppl 1): S98–101.

13. Caron RM. Population health management: An approach to improve the integration of the health care and public health systems. *Academic Medicine* 2014; 89(5): 698.

14. Ferguson JH. Curative and population medicine: Bridging the great divide. *Neuroepidemiology* 1999; 18(3): 111–119.

15. Gourevitch MN, Cannell T, Boufford JI, Summers C. The challenge of attribution: Responsibility for population health in the context of accountable care. *American Journal of Preventive Medicine* 2012; 42(6 Suppl 2): S180–183.

16. Kindig D, Stoddart G. What is population health? *American Journal of Public Health* 2003; 93(3): 380–383.

17. Hacker K, Walker DK. Achieving population health in accountable care organizations. *American Journal of Public Health* 2013; 103(7): 1163–1167.

18. White KL. *Healing the Schism: Epidemiology, Medicine, and the Public's Health.* New York, NY: Springer-Verlag; 1991.

19. Patient Protection and Affordable Care Act, 124 Stat. 119, §3022 (2010).

20. Couch CE, Winter FD, Jr., Roberts WL. Engaging STEEEP care through an accountable care organization. In: Ballard DJ, Fleming NS, Allison JT, Convery PB, Luquire R, eds. *Achieving STEEEP Health Care.* Boca Raton, FL: CRC Press; 2013: 217–226.

21. Greene JA. *Prescribing by Numbers: Drugs and Definition of Disease.* Baltimore, MD: Johns Hopkins University Press; 2007.

22. Rosenberg C. Managed fear. *Lancet* 2009; 373(9666): 802–803.

23. Kreiner MJ, Hunt LM. The pursuit of preventive care for chronic illness: Turning healthy people into chronic patients. *Sociology of Health and Illness* 2013; 36(6): 870–884.

24. McInnes G. Pre-hypertension: How low to go and do drugs have a role? *British Journal of Clinical Pharmacology* 2012; 73(2): 187–193.

25. Skinner JS, Cooper A, Feder GS. Secondary prevention for patients after a myocardial infarction: Summary of NICE guidance. *British Medical Journal* 2007; 334(7603): 1112–1113.

26. Egan BM, Lackland DT, Jones DW. Prehypertension: An opportunity for a new public health paradigm. *Cardiology Clinics* 2010; 28(4): 561–569.

27. Goldman L, Cook EF. The decline in ischemic heart disease mortality rates. An analysis of the comparative effects of medical interventions and changes in lifestyle. *Annals of Internal Medicine* 1984; 101(6): 825–836.

28. Moser M. A decade of progress in the management of hypertension. *Hypertension* 1983; 5(6): 808–813.

29. Cahalin LP, Myers J, Kaminsky L, Briggs P, Forman DE, Patel MJ, Pinkstaff SO, Arena R. Current trends in reducing cardiovascular risk factors in the United States: Focus on worksite health and wellness. *Progress in Cardiovascular Diseases* 2014; 56(5): 476–483.

30. Rodrigo R, Korantzopoulos P, Cereceda M, Asenjo R, Zamorano J, Villalabeitia E, Baeza C, Aguayo R, Castillo R, Carrasco R, Gormaz JG. A randomized controlled trial to prevent postoperative atrial fibrillation by antioxidant reinforcement. *Journal of American College of Cardiology* 2013.

31. Kones R. Primary prevention of coronary heart disease: Integration of new data, evolving views, revised goals, and role of rosuvastatin in management. A comprehensive survey. *Drug Design Development and Therapy* 2011; 5: 325–380.

32. Scott A, Sivey P, Ait Ouakrim D, Willenberg L, Naccarella L, Furler J, Young D. The effect of financial incentives on the quality of health care provided by primary care physicians. *Cochrane Database of Systemic Reviews* 2011; Issue 9: Art no. CD008451.

33. Constable C, Blank NR, Caplan AL. Rising rates of vaccine exemptions: Problems with current policy and more promising remedies. *Vaccine* 2014; 32(16): 1793–1797.

34. Centers for Disease Control and Prevention. Vaccines for Children Program (VFC). http://www.cdc.gov/vaccines/programs/vfc/index.html. Accessed November 17, 2014.

35. Orenstein WA, Hinman AR. The immunization system in the United States— the role of school immunization laws. *Vaccine* 1999; 17 Suppl 3: S19–24.

36. Centers for Disease C, Prevention. Impact of vaccines universally recommended for children—United States, 1990–1998. *MMWR Morbidity and Mortality Weekly Report* 1999; 48(12): 243–248.

37. Centers for Medicare and Medicais Services. Immunizations. http://www.cms.gov/Medicare/Prevention/Immunizations/index.html?redirect=/immunizations/. Accessed November 19, 2014.

38. Lu PJ, Nuorti JP. Pneumococcal polysaccharide vaccination among adults aged 65 years and older, U.S., 1989–2008. *American Journal of Preventive Medicine* 2010; 39(4): 287–295.

39. Wong V. A Choice for Employees: Get a Health Screening or Pay an Extra $600. 2013; http://www.businessweek.com/articles/2013-03-22/a-choice-for-employees-get-a-health-screening-or-pay-an-extra-600. Accessed November 17, 2014.

40. Polinder S, Toet H, Panneman M, van Beeck E, (eds.). Methodological approaches for cost-effectiveness and cost-utility analysis of injury prevention measures. http://www.euro.who.int/__data/assets/pdf_file/0007/144196/e95096.pdf. Accessed 18 November, 2014.

41. Torrance GW, Siegel JE, Luce BR. Framing and designing the cost-effectiveness analysis. In Gold MR, Siegel JE, Russell LB, Weinstein MC, eds. *Cost-Effectiveness in Health and Medicine.* New York: Oxford University Press; 1996: 54–81.

42. van Baal PH, Feenstra TL, Hoogenveen RT, de Wit GA, Brouwer WB. Unrelated medical care in life years gained and the cost utility of primary prevention: In search of a "perfect" cost-utility ratio. *Health Economics* 2007; 16(4): 421–433.

43. Phillips KA, Hotlgrave DR. Using cost-effectiveness/cost-benefit analysis to allocate health resources: A level playing field for prevention? *American Journal of Preventive Medicine* 1997; 13(1): 18–25.

44. Cretin S. Cost/benefit analysis of treatment and prevention of myocardial infarction. *Health Services Research* Summer 1977; 12(2): 174–189.

45. Rogers EM. *Diffusion of Innovations.* 4th edn. New York: Free Press; 1995.

46. Cohen D. *Health, Prevention and Economics.* New York: Oxford University Press; 1988.

47. Berwick DM, Weinstein MC. What do patients value? Willingness to pay for ultrasound in normal pregnancy. *Medical Care* 1985; 23(7): 881–893.

48. Viscusi W, Magat W, Huber J. An investigation of the rationality of consumer valuations of multiple health risks. *RAND Journal of Economics* 1987; 18(4): 465–473.

49. Weinstein MC. The costs of prevention. *Journal of General Internal Medicine* 1990; 5(5 Suppl): S89–S92.

50. Hatziandreu EI, Koplan JP, Weinstein MC, Caspersen CJ, Warner KE. A cost-effectiveness analysis of exercise as a health promotion activity. *American Journal of Public Health* 1988; 78(11): 1417–1421.

51. US Preventive Services Task Force. About the USPSTF. http://www.uspreventiveservicestaskforce.org/about.htm. Accessed November 17, 2014.

52. Guirguis-Blake J, Calonge N, Miller T, Siu A, Teutsch S, Whitlock E, Force USPST. Current processes of the U.S. Preventive Services Task Force: Refining evidence-based recommendation development. *Annals of Internal Medicine* 2007; 147(2): 117–122.

53. Prevention. Pf. About Us. http://www.prevent.org/About-Us.aspx. Accessed November 17, 2014.

54. Goetzel RZ. Do prevention or treatment services save money? The wrong debate. *Health Affairs (Millwood)* 2009; 28(1): 37–41.

55. Partnership for Prevention. National Commission on Prevention Priorities. http://www.prevent.org/Initiatives/National-Commission-on-Prevention-Priorities.aspx. Accessed November 17, 2014.

56. Maciosek MV, Coffield AB, Edwards NM, Flottemesch TJ, Goodman MJ, Solberg LI. Priorities among effective clinical preventive services: Results of a systematic review and analysis. *American Journal of Preventive Medicine* 2006; 31(1): 52–61.

57. Neumann PJ, Cohen JT. Cost savings and cost-effectiveness of clinical preventive care. The Synthesis Project. Research Synthesis Report No. 18. Princeton, NJ: The Robert Wood Johnson Foundation; 2009.

58. Cosgrove J. *Health Prevention: Cost-effective Services in Recent Peer-Reviewed Health Care Literature.* Washington, DC: U.S. Government Accountability Office; 2014. GAO-14-789R.

59. Cobiac LJ, Magnus A, Lim S, Barendregt JJ, Carter R, Vos T. Which interventions offer best value for money in primary prevention of cardiovascular disease? *PLoS One* 2012; 7(7): e41842.

60. National Prevention Council. National Prevention Strategy. In: Services USDoHaH, ed. Washington, D.: Office of the Surgeon General; 2011.

61. Sugar-Sweetened Beverages Tax Act of 2014, H.R. 5279, 113th Cong. (2014).

62. Schmidt J. New Soda Tax Proposed in Illinois. 2014; http://taxfoundation.org/blog/new-soda-tax-proposed-illinois. Accessed November 17, 2014.

63. Waters R. Soda Tax Votes In Berkeley And San Francisco Energize Health Advocates, Who Call It A 'Breakthrough Moment'. 2014; http://www.forbes.com/sites/robwaters/2014/11/17/soda-tax-votes-in-berkeley-and-san-francisco-energize-health-advocates-who-call-it-a-breakthrough-moment/. Accessed November 17, 2014.

64. Winterfeld A. Chronic costs: Making healthy choices easier for Americans can prevent deadly diseases and save money. *State Legislatures* 2009; 35(10): 30–32.

65. Choi C. Mexico's junk food tax squeezes Pepsi, Coke. 2014; http://www.shreveporttimes.com/story/money/business/2014/10/09/mexicos-junk-food-tax-squeezes-pepsi-coke/17014887/. Accessed November 17, 2014.

66. Obama B. Affordable health care for all Americans: The Obama-Biden plan. *JAMA* 2008; 300(16): 1927–1928.

67. Ballard DJ, Nicewander DA, Qin H, Fullerton C, Winter FD, Jr., Couch CE. Improving delivery of clinical preventive services: A multi-year journey. *American Journal of Preventive Medicine* 2007; 33(6): 492–497.

68. Silverstein MD, Ogola G, Mercer Q, Fong J, Devol E, Couch CE, Ballard DJ. Impact of clinical preventive services in the ambulatory setting. *Proceedings (Baylor University Medical Center)* 2008; 21(3): 227–235.

69. Molinari C. Prevention under the Affordable Care Act (ACA): Has the ACA overpromised and under delivered?: Comment on "Interrelation of preventive care benefits and shared costs under the Affordable Care Act (ACA)". *International Journal of Health Policy and Management* 2014; 3(3): 155–156.

70. Rappange DR, Brouwer WB, Rutten FF, van Baal PH. Lifestyle intervention: From cost savings to value for money. *Journal of Public Health (Oxf)* 2010; 32(3): 440–447.

71. Dixon RB, Hertelendy AJ. Interrelation of preventive care benefits and shared costs under the Affordable Care Act (ACA). *International Journal of Health Policy and Management* 2014; 3(3): 145–148.

72. Brawley O, Rice S. Redefining cancer to reduce unnecessary treatment. *Modern Healthcare* 2014; 44(10): 28–29.

73. Beck M. Some Cancer Experts See "Overdiagnosis," Question Emphasis on Early Detection. 2014; http://online.wsj.com/articles/some-cancer-experts-see-overdiagnosis-and-question-emphasis-on-early-detection-1410724838. Accessed November 18, 2014.

74. James J. Workplace Wellness Programs (Updated). *Health Affairs Health Policy Briefs* 2013; http://www.healthaffairs.org/healthpolicybriefs/brief.php?brief_id=93. Accessed November 17, 2014.
75. Corrigan JM, Donaldson MS, Kohn LT, Maguire SK, Pike KC. *Crossing the Quality Chasm. A New Health System for the 21st Century.* Washington DC: Institute of Medicine, National Academy of Sciences. National Academy Press; 2001.

Chapter 7

Big Data Enables Population Health

Kevin S. Attride

Contents

What Is So Great about Big Data?

If you listen to the news, then you're hearing about "big data." This week it is education, next week it will be retail. So it begs the question: is big data just hype or the most useful innovation of the twenty-first century? The answer lies somewhere in the middle. Will it be as impactful for healthcare as it is for other industries? What are the implications for providers, payers, and other healthcare organizations?

Big data can often be described in a number of ways, though the overarching characteristics are always the same: our world is complex and technology has advanced enough to be able to capture much of the complexities digitally. Big data aims to turn complex data into actionable information.

The U.S. government has defined big data as "large volumes of high velocity, complex, and variable data that require advanced techniques and technologies to enable the capture, storage, distribution, management, and analysis of the information."[*]

It identifies healthcare data fairly well considering the complexities of the human body and the potential for numerous data points to be collected each second from each individual. The organization of this data is a daunting effort in itself, and there lies the objective of big data: making sense from senseless data. When working with data for any length of time, one understands the difference between data and information. Healthcare providers are inundated with reports covering a range of topics and opportunities, but what can actually be accomplished with this data? Information is actionable and leads one to an understanding or decision. Big data attempts to turn nonactionable data into end-user actions. It is quite a big task, especially for an industry that has embraced paper since its inception.

---

[*] IHTT: Transforming healthcare through big data strategies for leveraging big data in the healthcare industry.

Four Vs of Big Data

Big data in healthcare is best described by four variables (Figure 7.1):

Volume: It is called big data for a reason. The amount of information being captured digitally is enormous. Healthcare generates large data-sets for each patient, especially for technologically advanced organizations who capture live metrics.

Variety: Modern technology now allows organizations to capture a whole range of details. The types of data and numerous sources instantly create a complexity that feeds the big data principle. Whether the data is collected automatically or inputted manually, organizations, physicians, and patients generate a diversity of information.

Velocity: In today's environment, information moves quickly and big data is no exception. Not only is the speed of data generation accelerating, but also the necessity to process the data quickly is becoming more critical. Whether the data is necessary in real time for critical care or an organization's entire decision support, healthcare demands fast processing.

Veracity: "Dirty data in, dirty data out" is a phrase often repeated, and veracity speaks to the difficulty in effectively managing abnormalities and variability in data. Humans are often to blame in creating inconsistent data, though there are multiple reasons healthcare data can be so variable.

Data Sources

While these four components explain the structure, data sources and the information within provide the raw material for big data analytics.

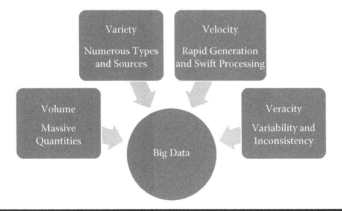

Figure 7.1   Major components of big data.

	Biometrics	Human-Generated	Transactional	Machine-to-Machine	Internet-Centric
Complexity	High	High	Moderate	Moderate	High
Format	Range of Unstructured to Structured	Majority Unstructured with Minority of Structured	Primarily Structured	Primarily Structured	Primarily Unstructured
Examples	Images, Vitals, Retinal Scans, Fingerprints, Genomic Mapping	Electronic Health Records, Physician Notes, Emails, Faxes	Billing Records, Adjudicated Claims, Financial Cost Data Operational Details	Remote Scales, Telehealth Monitors, FitBits, GPS Trackers, Health Watches	Social Media, Internet Searches, Blogs, Smartphone Apps, Website Data

Figure 7.2 There is an abundance of big data sources for healthcare.

Healthcare data is broadly segmented into the following sources (Figure 7.2):

Biometrics: Potentially the most obvious data in healthcare, biometrics consist of common data types, such as radiology images, vital signs, and genetic markers. It is foundational to clinical operations and was one of the first types of data collected beyond patient charts, though the industry has advanced tremendously since storing the first x-ray.

Human-Generated: Most elements from electronic health record (EHR) fields like diagnosis codes or patient information to physician notes are generated by humans. Although EHR data took over from paper charting, much of it remains unstructured and more difficult to process.

Transactional: Though often behind the scenes, transactional data provides valuable insight. Billing records and claims are common, but any operational or financial data that can be captured could be used to build a more complete picture of patient care.

Machine-to-Machine: Device and sensor data is becoming more prolific, from telehealth devices to digital pedometers. The onerous is on healthcare organizations to turn the data into actionable information, especially when much of the data lies in the hands of the patient.

Internet-Centric: The next frontier of valuable data lies in patient information created on the Internet. Whether the information is housed in social media networks or search engine interactions, information can be collected to provide a better understanding of population trends or diagnosing patients.

The Gigabyte

- 1 gigabyte = 7 min of high-definition (HD) video
- 1 gigabyte = 10 yards of books stacked on one another

The Petabyte

- 1 petabyte = 13.3 years of high-definition (HD) video
- 1 petabyte = 20 million four-drawer filing cabinets completely filled
- 20 petabytes = Total hard drive space manufactured in 1995
- 140 million petabytes = 1 human genome stored digitally

Figure 7.3   Most people are familiar with the gigabyte, but this storage size is far too small in the new reality of big data. 1 petabyte = 1,000,000 gigabytes.

When thoroughly scrubbed and integrated, data from multiple sources becomes a powerful tool, one that will change healthcare like never before. The consulting firm McKinsey & Company estimates that if leveraged appropriated, healthcare could achieve $300–450 billion in savings annually using the power of big data. Many organizations have already launched their big data strategy or attempted to utilize a number of data sources. One system has connected multiple sources to collect over five million patient records generating 5.4 petabytes of information. At the rate of data connections, that is expected to double every 18 months.

As is quite evident, a petabyte is quite large (Figure 7.3). Challenges begin to emerge just storing all the information being captured at a dizzying rate, but that is actually the "easy" part. Far greater challenges face the efficacy of big data.

Why Big Data Is Hard to Achieve

Big data offers tremendous possibilities, but there are major challenges turning large datasets into actionable information. Healthcare especially brings a number of barriers due to the intimate details of patients (Figure 7.4).

Industry Preparedness

While many industries depend on elaborate data systems, healthcare has been protected from intense competition and scrutiny, thwarting its ability to provide real-time analytics and measure improvement. Neither Google nor Apple would be capable of delivering results if they could not report the outcomes of their core services. Yet healthcare providers often lack similar

Figure 7.4   Plethora of challenges prevent big data actualization.

capabilities having underinvested in information systems for years. If it was not for Meaningful Use, the governmental program to improve and extend digital capabilities for patient care, many physician practices would still be using paper charting. Most organizations are incapable of determining the cost of services either. There are large informational gaps, whether asking a physician about his rates of adherence to evidence-based metrics or the expense to a patient for a surgical procedure.

Much of the responsibility lies in the perverse incentives of the industry. When a physician or hospital gets paid to perform activity, the volume approach, instead of being paid to provide outcomes, the value approach, innovation and process improvement wither. While incentives have begun to shift over the last decade, misaligned incentives are still the rule rather than the exception. Physicians, hospitals, and payers are often pitted against each other.

Data Reliability

If it were not hard enough that the whole industry is underprepared to tackle the growing complexities of reform and population management, one of the biggest obstacles in attaining actionable information is data reliability. Due to underinvestment in information technology, many systems lack the ability to provide standardize data. The lack of industry standards is often to blame, but many systems were not designed to create the necessary reporting and information bridges. For example, most EHRs were built to capture data in a digitized medical record. Without conceptualizing future functionalities, many EHR solutions were built on a framework with little thought to robust reporting mechanisms.

Gaining insight into data origination and data context remains difficult. While this may seem hard to believe upon first glance, understanding why a patient's screening returned abnormal and the rationale for the result requires investigation. The answer could be the difference between life and death. This also states the complexities of data timeliness. Some data points can be measured monthly or annually, while others must be captured in real time.

Data accuracy has become a tremendous issue because humans are often central to data collection. Was the right metric recorded? Was it placed in the right field? Beyond human errors, the data must be mapped from one system to another. Additional challenges emerge as to whether the data is placed in fields that can be processed. Many big data solutions have not yet begun to process unstructured data, so patient notes become problematic. These complexities compound to create dirty and multifaceted data that must be cleaned and processed more thoroughly.

After algorithms have thoroughly cleansed and normalized the dataset, reaching actionable information is still another hurdle. While numerous correlations can be found, issues arise as to which ones are meaningful and which are causal. Just because acute readmissions increase as office hours are extended does not mean that have a meaningful relationship. Outliers must also be validated and processed in a manner to provide explanation.

Environmental Concerns

Architectural and infrastructural complexities lead to further big data "environmental" concerns. The central issue is the lack of talent. While there are plenty of talented people in healthcare information technology (HIT), the demand for those with expertise in specialized analytics, often called data scientists, far exceeds the supply. Provider organizations, payers, and innovators in HIT will continue to be hampered until the market reaches human resource equilibrium with those having capabilities to solve the current and future challenges.

Gathering the right data through interconnectivity continues to plague the industry. Most systems, especially EHRs, were not built to produce reports or transmit data to other systems. A physician colleague recently asked, "Were office-based EHRs not built with the ability to provide communication and data transfer?" Unfortunately, those capabilities were not in the original blueprints. If primary care physician A on system Y wants to securely communicate patient information to specialist B on system Z, currently, it can only be accomplished using a software bridge, usually by a third party, which is different from their primary systems. While new Meaningful Use rules propose to fix this challenge, actual implementation is still many years away. This is just one of the many HIT issues preventing well-coordinated care.

This simple example shows just one aspect of the difficulties HIT professionals have working with systems being stretched to functions beyond their original design. Most often, systems were built to support a fee-for-service, volume-based environment of care, which lacks the value-emphasis targeting coordinated care and performance outcomes. Gathering data from these systems also remains a challenge. Most systems are not built with interconnectivity standards, so connecting two systems takes dozens to hundreds of hours to accurately map elements, with the number of data points multiplying the resources necessary to validate the proper mapping. Often, this is due to incentives. As EHR companies look for additional revenue, the low hanging fruit has become data interconnectivity. Professionals must be cautious of the sales pitch promising interconnectivity. Past experiences have shown this to be both challenging and time intensive, no matter the system. These obstacles prevent data analysis and are a real concern for healthcare innovation.

Much more foundational than technical is the topic of privacy. While other industries require tight measures to ensure data security, healthcare organizations have additional regulations through federal law in the Health Insurance Portability and Accountability Act (HIPAA) which mandates strict privacy compliance. Returning to the example of the two physicians attempting to share patient information, primary care physician A must only share the specific patient's details with specialist B. Once the bridge is built, what sounds simplistic becomes complex, especially due to lack of patient identification standards. Even if the systems match the same name and birthday, a different patient could be called into question. EHRs across the United States do not have a unified medical record identifier to match patients. Even with the unique identifier in a social security number, which is highly protected, the privacy that accompanies the number due to financial considerations makes it a poor identifier. Without an identifier, the process is complex.

The topics of who owns the data and who is available to use the data also highlight unspoken concerns. When a provider captures the details of the patient, does the provider own the data, the patient, or both? Providers from different organizations often own only slices of the data and lack the complete picture of a patient's health history or know who else is providing treatment. Worse still, in some cases, the patient can actually withhold information from the provider. For example, the Medicare Shared Savings

Program (MSSP) allows patient beneficiaries to opt out of data sharing with the Accountable Care Organization (ACO) caring from them. In effect, the patient can choose to withhold information from the care providers. This calls into question that who can use data to treat patients. The value-based model of healthcare requires data to be much more transparent to allow coordinated care.

Cultural Impediments

Privacy bleeds into the concept of cultural impediments. Siloed information is the cultural norm for healthcare with different organizations "owning" their own data when patients are shared between providers. A physician group in Florida told a newly forming clinically integrated network (CIN), which joins physicians, hospitals, and other entities for the expressed purposes of enhancing the quality of care delivery, that it was interested in joining, so long as the CIN would pay them for their data. In essence, the data was not a transparent, transferrable tool in the process of enhancing patient care, but more like intellectual property that must be purchased. While this ideology is fading, it still hinders coordinated efforts to enhance care. Larger organizations experience challenges appropriately sharing data intraorganizationally. Often, they lack processes to share data between systems or integrate it into different functions. Healthcare must learn how to share data to meet the demands of population health.

Medicine has a long history of limited data, so the healthcare culture comes from the baseline of intuition and expertise. Until digital records became popularized toward the end of the twentieth century, decisions were driven by opinions through experience and the art of medicine. Much of healthcare has embraced the new reality of data transparency and availability, but the old guard bristles when their knowledge is challenged, even when the data is accurate and valid. This challenge stems from resistance to change. The new challenge will be presenting new data that supports improved decision making. While new analytics are demonstrating protocols and decision support relying on rich data to provide far superior results, change management will become the critical catalyst.

Though big data challenges in healthcare are numerous, it only indicates growing opportunity. Healthcare cannot afford to concede defeat, for the future is far brighter with the rich analytics of big data. Knowing the momentous efforts to achieve this new innovation, what improvement does big data bring to healthcare, especially for population health?

Big Data Impact on Population Health

Healthcare sits at the crossroads of volume and value, which raises the question as to why results have not received greater emphasis in the past. While some well-known organizations have worked to achieve world-class performance for a few decades, most of the industry has lagged. There are a number of reasons, but lacking actionable information has been the missing pillar. As a result, readmissions, adverse events, complications, severely uncoordinated care, and skyrocketing costs have crescendoed to the point when the nation cries out for change. Population health can now answer that cry using timely, actionable information from big data. The steps to gathering the right data and preparing it for population health management can be complex and involve sophisticated software, but the steps are fairly straightforward (Figure 7.5).

Source Determination

While an organization must determine the desired objectives to achieve population health, available information becomes a major determinant of what is achievable. Retrievable data becomes the first important step to achieving big data for population health. Some sources become fairly obvious: EHRs, claims, and lab data. For CINs and integrated delivery networks (IDNs), the challenges become more complex when attempting to select multiple data sources. A fairly robust data warehouse can combine data from EHRs that span inpatient facilities, ambulatory services, and physician offices; adjudicated claims data from the Center for Medicare and Medicaid Services (CMS, but also simplified to Medicare) and a majority of health plan payer claims data; patient experience surveys; post-acute data, whether from EHRs or self-reported data; patient-submitted information, such as health-risk assessments

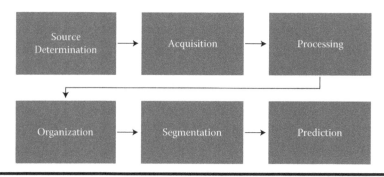

Figure 7.5 Process of capturing and evaluating big data.

(HRA); remote monitoring data from equipment like telehealth scales or patient monitors. Each source is unique and brings a number of complexities when retrieving its data.

Acquisition

After the sources have been identified and prioritized, the most difficult task begins: gathering valid and accurate data from each source. Gleaning EHR data from inpatient facilities and office-based physicians is often the first step for many provider organizations, but even if they are advanced enough to have all their employed physicians on the same system, for creating a transparent ecosystem, like that of the Epic EHR, most are not closed networks that force every physician to use their software. Therefore, a percentage of care remains outside the captured network. Many physician hospital organizations (PHOs) have numerous EHRs, creating barriers to capturing the data. Standardization has been and continues to be a key obstacle. EHR vendors have traditionally lacked the capability to deliver a complete patient chart in a feed easily readable by another system. While that is changing, it still presents a key hurdle. Payers have traditionally refused to provide claims data unless the provider organization participates in value-based contracting. The sources can be placed on a continuum from easily attainable such as lab results, to nearly impossible, such as data residing outside of the network. Each dataset must be weighed for its return on investment and time intensity to retrieve.

Processing

Though each has varying levels of expertise in data acquisition, IBM, Oracle, Qlik, SAP, and Microsoft, as well as healthcare-oriented solutions like Epic, Cerner, Health Catalyst, Premier, Optum, and Advisory Board are the well-recognized data analytic solutions. Their greatest expertise centers on the ability to process and analyze numerous disparate data sources. While large organizations may have the capital and resources to build their own data warehouses, the fierce market competition keeps these companies innovating far faster than most provider organizations. Advanced techniques to clean, curate, normalize, and standardize are important factors to prepare data before it can be integrated. With the current state of nonstandardized data outputs and dirty data inputs, data scientists must build advanced algorithms to ensure that the processing generates highly reliable and cleansed data. Once the variety of data sources is standardized, then they can begin the process to convert raw data into actionable information.

Organization

The newly integrated information is ready to be organized into useful data for population health management. Visualization tools are capable of generating scorecards to measure outcomes, provide patient lists for targeted populations, and provide point-of-care actions. The information enables a variety of powerful decision-making opportunities with the necessary sources. The challenge for the tools is to organize the data to prioritize the most pertinent details. For example, if a patient has 15 gaps in evidence-based care, certain screenings or tests become much more important and others lose pertinence if the patient is 90 and highly acute. Data organization and visualization become essential. Critical lab values, the most pertinent diagnoses, the complete medication list and when it was last reconciled, environmental hazards, and a variety of other details must be brought to the forefront for clinicians to take the most appropriate actions.

Segmentation

After risk scores are ascribed to patients, they can be grouped into different risk categories, each for specificity of disease, severity, and costs. The Advisory Board Company breaks down patient populations into four categories: high-cost, rising-risk, at-risk, and healthy (Figure 7.6). High-cost patients will typically represent approximately 5% of the dataset unless the organization has a preponderance of healthy or sick patients. The data will indicate high-risk scores for this segment because they typically have multiple comorbidities with highly acute disease states, such as heart failure or chronic obstructive pulmonary disease. Rising-risk represents a variety of chronic diseases and psychosocial concerns. At-risk represents those developing chronic disease, participating in a risky lifestyle, or already having one chronic disease. Advanced analytics provide the framework through a variety of indicators, whether an elevated HgA1c indicating prediabetes, an HRA pointing to poor nutrition, or highly infrequent or missed checkups. Healthy patients comprise the rest of the population. Various outreach and supportive tools can help keep them in this designation or determine when their risks have elevated. While this segmentation is more common, analytics allow for other uses that involve quality metrics or patients connected to certain care environments.

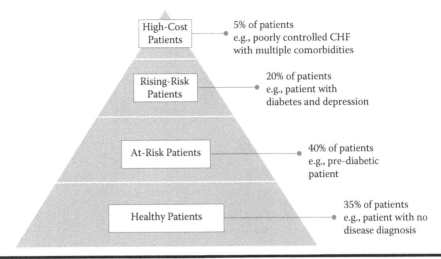

Figure 7.6 Patients can be placed in different risk categories as commonly seen in this pyramid. (From The Advisory Board Company. *Managing Multiple Patient Groups.* **© 2013. All rights reserved. With permission.)**

Prediction

While understanding near current or past patient information via segmentation is important, predictive modeling is foundational to any successful population health management program. Risk management takes different forms with innovators providing advanced predictive analytics. Tools are quickly moving from retrospective insight into direct intervention to risk forecasting. The market has a range of different analytical risk engines, some of which are simplistic and others advanced. CMS' hierarchical condition categories (HCCs) risk model is fairly basic, focusing primarily on patients' documented diagnoses with demographic information contributing a small impact. Other commercial models such as the Johns Hopkins ACG or VeriskDxCG can use additional data points to predict mortality or future costs. Advanced models are able to predict a number of indicators from readmissions to utilization of emergency services to broken appointments. Advanced models are recommended for targeting patient subsegments to prevent cost and improve outcomes. For example, not all high-cost patients from the current year will be high-cost patients next year. The rising-risk population tends to rise, so it becomes critical that predictive modeling forecasts future risk to ensure that these patients receive treatment before escalation.

The importance of big data shines when grouping populations because the organization can understand not only the severity of their illness and predicted risks, but also the cost they generate. High-risk patients generally

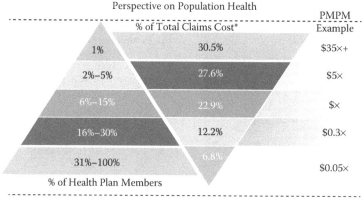

Figure 7.7 shows that the top 5% of health plan members drive a majority of healthcare expenditures. (For licensed content titled *Perspective on Population Health*. Lew Altman Consulting. © 2013. All rights reserved. With permission.)

account for a large portion of a population's healthcare costs, but as a sampling of Verisk data shows (Figure 7.7), the top 1% combined with the top 2% to 5% account for 58% of total cost with an astonishing range of 5 to 35 times the average cost. This data also shows that the healthy population account for less than 7% of the costs at one-twentieth the average cost. Integrating rich biometric data with claims and other data sources provides a wealth of information that can be used to leverage predictive modeling and patient engagement.

Application to the Triple Aim

The steps to activate big data in a provider organization clearly demonstrate the usefulness in a population health approach, but how are organizations using big data? The Triple Aim, developed by the Institute for Healthcare Improvement (IHI), focuses on three integral aspects of care delivery: improving population health, enhancing experience of care, and reducing per capita cost. Since its inception, healthcare organizations across the country have adopted its model with fury. Since big data is central to population health's effectiveness and population health is central to the effectiveness of the Triple Aim, let us look at big data uses in elements of the Triple Aim (Figure 7.8).

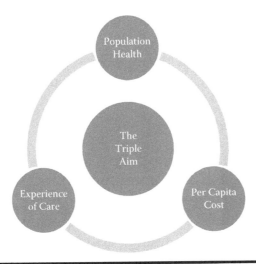

Figure 7.8   Big data support the elements of the Triple Aim.

Improving Population Health

Improving population health is the banner over healthcare's ability to deliver quality outcomes for more than just individual patients. Readmission reduction is easily identified but much more difficult to correct without analytics. Health Management Associates Inc., which operates nearly 70 hospitals across the nation, is tackling this problem using big data and prediction analytics. Using patterns in their clinical and operational data, they are able to predict patient behaviors. Depending on the factors involved, they are able to rank the likelihood of a patient's return in the inpatient setting.

Coordinating care across the continuum is critical for Texas-based Methodist Health System's ACO. They've combined claims and other data sources to manage their own employees and Medicare population to improve outcomes. Predictive analytics allow their nurse navigators to achieve better outcomes by coordinating care, providing education, and overcoming barriers to care. Their tools and tactics allow them to enhance communication and achieve quality goals.

Notoriously difficult to diagnose, heart failure affects more than five million adults in the United States each year. The Centers for Disease Control (CDC) reports that more than half of affected patients will not survive more than 5 years after diagnosis. Virginia-based Carilion Clinic is tackling the issue with the help of IBM. Using natural language processing and predictive modeling, they have developed a pilot that first identifies individuals at risk for heart disease. Using both structured data and unstructured physicians' notes, which are much more difficult to translate into actionable information, Carilion Clinic is able to correctly diagnose heart failure 85% of the time, allowing them to deliver superior quality and improve the health outcomes for this patient population.

Enhancing Experience of Care

Enhancing experience of care draws from healthcare's ability to produce results in a way that satisfies the patient. This can be achieved in a number of ways but is often complex when attempting to measure a patient's opinion of care. Dignity Health, a health system spanning 20 states, plans to do just that. One of their priorities is to use advanced analytics to monitor and enhance patient experience within its care settings. They have implemented SAS' cloud-based analytics platform to create tools for analyzing, optimizing, and customizing individual treatment to improve the care experience of each patient.

California-based Health Fidelity believes that HIT is the cornerstone of their care delivery, including big data's ability to deliver a superior care experience. They use actionable information to ensure that patients receive proactive care, especially during routine appointments. Elements are easily added to patient care to safeguard the visit experience, such as nutrition consultations and advice about exercise.

For Massachusetts-based Eliza Corporation, a health engagement management solution, the Triple Aim is foundational, especially in their efforts to enhance experience by empowering patients to make better decisions about their health. One of the ways they use big data to affect patient care is through support with what they term "unmentionables," of which stress is a major factor. Their research suggests that 40% of people were experiencing four to six "unmentionables" at any moment, from workplace strain to financial concerns to relationship anxiety to the pressures of caring for a sick family member. They attempt to enhance the experience of care by directing patients to support resources.

Reducing Per Capita Cost

Reducing per capita cost is foundational for value-based care through efficiency and waste reduction. Numerous organizations are attempting to break the cost curve in the hope to deliver care more efficiently, and big data is a key enabler. Massachusetts-based Brigham and Women's Hospital (B&W) recently produced a study demonstrating how big data can lower healthcare costs across a number of activities, including treatment optimization. Since chronic disease affects multiple organ systems, correctly managing treatment necessitates minimizing treatment costs. Big data is enabling their clinicians to deliver more targeted treatment to autoimmune disorders like rheumatoid arthritis. B&W is able to provide care for these patients at lower cost by predicting the trajectory of the patient's disease process and customizing treatment therapies in a more targeted way.

Carolinas Healthcare System is leveraging big data in its quest to cut cost under the weight of falling reimbursement after their first forecasted loss in 30 years. New software allows them to track patients with chronic conditions, such as chronic obstructive pulmonary disease (COPD), to predict health crises and stratify patient risk factors. Specific patients are assigned to care teams who remotely support them in managing their conditions. They are even cutting costs by preventing hospitalizations by connecting with patients by phone or text messages. Patients are also encouraged to leverage the online medical records portal to better understand their health.

The University of Pittsburgh Medical Center (UPMC), one of the largest health systems in the country, is attempting to leverage analytics to reduce expenditures as well, especially since they own a health plan for over two million individuals. Being in the position of both provider and payer, UPMC not only focuses on outcome performance, but also monitors financial and operational efficiency from a critical perspective. They combine claims data with biometric data from 48 major clinical systems to better identify care deficiencies. Harmonizing the data on each patient determines the ideal course of care with evidence-based guidelines. Their analysis has enabled earlier interventions with preemptive diagnoses. The new process has supported cost reductions and operational waste elimination by closing gaps in research outcomes and physician performance.

Where Will Big Data Take Us?

Big Data Leverages New Technology

Where will big data take healthcare in the next 10 years, and more specifically, how will it be able to leverage new technology to accomplish population health in the future? With the rapid growth of consumer devices, research, and computing power, the metaphorical sky becomes the limit. While the horizon provides numerous innovations such as processing unstructured data to measuring body functions outside of traditional care settings, four areas are blazing the trail to enhance big data delivery in the population health: wearable technology, social media, stretchable electronics, and genomics.

While telehealth technology is currently being used in the healthcare space, it is often limited to stationary devices such as remote scales. The future is in technology worn with everyday use. Most people are familiar with wearable technology currently on the market by Nike or FitBit, but wearables with advanced sensor technology will innovate the space far beyond counting steps. Wrist-worn devices are capable of tracking more body signals in real time. The Apple Watch will be a game changer because more advanced sensors provide health indicators during every moment of the day, from heart rate activity to movement measured by accelerometers. While some wearables offer more health-tracking features, Apple's ability to penetrate the market and accelerate innovation bodes well for wearable technology. ABI Research even estimates that $52 million will be invested in this space over the next 5 years. It is healthcare's opportunity to leverage this enormously valuable content to promote wellness, manage chronic disease, and avoid acute events. Ochsner Health System, a healthcare provider based in southeast Louisiana and industry leader in digital technology, has begun piloting the use of the Apple Watch with patients who struggle with high blood pressure to remind them about medication and exercise. The possibilities for engagement and intervention through wearable technology are endless and far more efficient when patient data can be tracked in real time.

Social media is ubiquitous in the twenty-first century, so it is only natural to utilize this dataset. While much of the data is currently unstructured, Facebook, Twitter, and a host of other networks offer intimate details about the health of individuals. Growing research indicates that patients share more medical information with their friends through public avenues than with their own physicians. The fact is social media activity is built around behaviors, so there is a smaller chance that patients obfuscate the truth when interacting online. This carries an important implication beyond the opportunity for clinicians to enhance motivational interviewing: social media is the new gold mine for the indicators of a person's health. Whether through Twitter analysis or Facebook "likes," healthcare organizations will soon have the ability to tap into better indicators for wellness, prevention, and chronic disease, not to mention patient engagement or medical adherence.

Science fiction is now upon us. Capsules detecting vitals and health monitoring chips are no longer a dream. These new technologies, termed stretchable electronics, will provide healthcare with even greater insight into real time functions of the human body. These sensors are measuring heart rate, hydration, temperature, and even brain activity. As these sensors get more advanced and less expensive, they'll become common in the population health environment as care coordinators and physicians recommend stretchable electronics for patients diagnosed with chronic diseases like diabetes. They are capable of improving wellness by providing both the individual and the clinician new metrics to improve health, such as rest, nutrition, and hydration. This technology will also heavily impact severely sick patients with heart failure to ensure that they are monitored and alerted to changes in the status of their disease. The difficult-to-diagnose, like chronic fatigue, will also have breakthroughs to provide more impactful treatment to better understanding when they received pain, what they ate, or how well they slept.

Genomics, the study of an organism's entire genetic makeup, called a genome, provides an understanding of how a person's genome is affected and interacts with the environment and lifestyle behaviors. While genetics has led to the ability to screen certain diseases affected by certain genes, genomics provides the ability to better understand complex diseases like heart disease and diabetes. It also demonstrates how to improve treatment for those diseases. Since the mapping of the human genome in 2003, the cost to map and analyze one's genome has been falling, spurring the growth of consumerization in genomic data. While physicians have been using genetic data to understand disposition to certain diseases, genomics will provide far more rich information about populations to treat and prevent advanced diseases. Due to the large 140 million petabytes of information for each person, there are still large challenges to store and process the data, but the future brings great possibilities of enhancing care for an entire population.

Healthcare big data 1.0 is here and impacting care every day, but innovating organizations will quickly move past EHR data for readmissions and chronic disease. Healthcare big data 2.0 will soon be upon us using real-time data to monitor patient health or prevent acute episodes. Even unstructured data from the Internet will provide physicians the tools to enhance care in the modern age of medicine.

What Are the Implications?

Big data presents a bright future with these new technologies, especially as the data feeds move to real time. The details will provide physicians and care coordinators a more advanced position for clinical decision support to enhance patient care. Improved data availability and transparency will lead to improved outcomes with the right infrastructure. But transparency of data will involve the alignment of multiple stakeholders united for the cause of improving population health, enhancing experience of care, and reducing cost. Patients, by necessity, must extend private data to their care providers even though many are providing relevant information via the Internet anyway. Though society is choosing with their mouse clicks, many will defy data transparency in the name of their privacy, even when it hampers health innovation. Full transparency or not, incentives will begin to play a role in collecting data. The environment of explosive healthcare expenditures is a harbinger for change, and rich analytics will be a critical tool to get us there.

Bibliography

1. Big Data. *Wikipedia*. Wikimedia Foundation, 2015. Available at http://en.wikipedia.org/wiki/Big_data. Accessed on July 20, 2014.
2. Bustos L. The big 9 big data sources [Infographic]. *Get Elastic Ecommerce Blog*, 2014. Available at http://www.getelastic.com/big-data-infographic/. Accessed on October 8, 2014.
3. Cottle M, Kanwal S, Kohn M, Strome T, Treister N. eds. Transforming health care through big data: Strategies for leveraging big data in the health care industry. *New York: Institute for Health Technology Transformation*, 2013. Available at http://ihealthtran.com/big-data-in-healthcare. Accessed on July 20, 2014.
4. Diana A. Healthcare dives into big data. *Information Week*, 2014. Available at http://www.informationweek.com/healthcare/analytics/healthcare-dives-into-big-data/d/d-id/1251138. Accessed on July 20, 2014.
5. Diamond D. A hospital is already giving Apple Watch to its patients. *Forbes*. Forbes Magazine, April 24, 2015. Available at http://www.forbes.com/sites/dandiamond/2015/04/24/can-apple-watch-make-patients-healthier-how-one-hospital-is-trying-to-find-out. Accessed on July 13, 2015.
6. Diaz J. How large is a petabyte? *Gizmodo*. Gawker Media, 2009. Available at http://gizmodo.com/5309889/how-large-is-a-petabyte. Accessed on October 21, 2014.
7. Farr C. Health developers, doctors want to see more from Apple's watch. *Thomson Reuters*, 2014. Available at http://www.reuters.com/article/2014/09/11/us-apple-launch-health-idUSKBN0H62IA20140911. Accessed on October 21, 2014.
8. *Genomics versus Genetics: What's The Difference?* University of Washington, n.d. Available at http://depts.washington.edu/cgph/GenomicsGenetics.htm. Accessed on October 22, 2014.

9. *Healthcare Is BIG DATA.* Explorys, n.d. Available at https://www.explorys.com/ solutions/big-data-in-healthcare. Accessed on July 20, 2014.

10. Hoffman R. Big love for big data? The remedy for healthcare quality improvements. *Information Week*, 2013. Available at http://reports.informationweek. com/abstract/105/11840/Healthcare/Big-Love-for-Big-Data-The-Remedy-for-Healthcare-Quality-Improvements.html. Accessed on July 20, 2014.

11. Hwang K. Sources of big data in health care. *About Health*, 2015. Available at http://healthtech.about.com/od/Population-Health/fl/Sources-of-Big-Data-in-Health-Care.htm. Accessed on October 8, 2014.

12. Jacob S. Health systems use 'big data' to cut costs, improve quality. *Healthcare Daily*, 2013. Available at http://healthcare.dmagazine.com/2013/06/13/health-systems-use-big-data-to-cut-costs-improve-quality/. Accessed on October 20, 2014.

13. Kayyali B, Knott D, Kuiken SV. The big-data revolution in US health care: Accelerating value and innovation. *Insights & Publications*. McKinsey & Company, 2014. Available at http://www.mckinsey.com/insights/health_ systems_and_services/the_big-data_revolution_in_us_health_care. Accessed on July 20, 2014.

14. Kerschberg B. Big data and health care get engaged. *Forbes*, 2012. Available at http://www.forbes.com/sites/benkerschberg/2012/06/12/big-data-and-health-care-get-engaged. Accessed on July 21, 2014.

15. Marcus G, Davis E. Eight (No, Nine!) problems with big data. *The New York Times*, 2014. Available at http://www.nytimes.com/2014/04/07/opinion/eight-no-nine-problems-with-big-data.html. Accessed on October 8, 2014.

16. Milliard M. 6 Ways big data can lower costs. *Healthcare IT News*. HIMSS Media, 2014. Available at http://www.healthcareitnews.com/news/6-ways-big-data-can-lower-costs. Accessed on July 21, 2014.

17. Monegain B. Dignity health goes big for data. *Healthcare IT News*. HIMSS Media, 2014. Available at http://www.healthcareitnews.com/news/dignity-health-goes-big-data. Accessed on October 20, 2014.

18. Olavsrud, T. 4 barriers stand between you and big data insight. *CIO*. CXO Media Inc., 2013. Available at http://www.cio.com/article/2386908/enterprise-software/4-barriers-stand-between-you-and-big-data-insight.html. Accessed on October 8, 2014.

19. Portillo E. Carolinas healthcare seeks to cut costs through prevention, technology. *The Charlotte Observer*, 2014. Available at http://www.charlotteobserver. com/news/business/banking/article9103286.html. Accessed on October 21, 2014.

20. Raghupathi W, Raghupathi V. Big data analytics in healthcare: Promise and potential. *Health Information Science and Systems*, 2014. Available at http:// www.hissjournal.com/content/2/1/3. Accessed on October 8, 2014.

21. Rowe J. Top 3 paths big data will blaze. *Healthcare IT News*. HIMSS Media, 2013. Available at http://www.healthcareitnews.com/news/top-3-paths-big-data-will-blaze. Accessed on October 20, 2014.

22. SAS. *Five Big Data Challenges*. Cary, NC: SAS Institute Inc., SAS Campus Drive, n.d. Available at http://www.sas.com/resources/asset/five-big-data-challenges-article.pdf. Accessed on October 8, 2014.

23. Shinal J. If 'clean', big data can improve U.S. health care. *USA Today*, 2014. Available at http://www.usatoday.com/story/tech/columnist/shinal/2014/05/14/medical-privacy-health/9087873/. Accessed on October 22, 2014.
24. Tibken S. Numbers, numbers and more numbers. *The Wall Street Journal*, 2013. Available at http://www.wsj.com/news/articles/SB10001424052702304692 80457728582112934 1442. Accessed on July 21, 2014.

Chapter 8

Managed Care and Payer Models

George Mayzell

Contents

Managed care organizations (MCOs), like all aspects of the healthcare delivery puzzle, are trying to decide to identify their strategy for the New World of options for healthcare delivery system options. This includes both population health and the engine behind this which is the shift from "volume to value."

Currently, MCOs provide several key services and these include the following:

1. Benefit structure
2. Marketing
3. Actuarial evaluation
4. Network contracting and assessment
5. Claims adjudication and processing
6. Medical management
7. Care management

As there are major shifts in the delivery system, many of the big managed care companies are evaluating various ways to provide value that will depend on the core functions listed above. As a healthcare delivery system, account-ability for cost, quality, and outcomes are being forced down to the provider level, in some cases through an accountable care organization (ACO) model (or some alternative mechanism). Many of these functions are now considered unnecessary at the payer level and in particular, medical management and networking contracting are shifting down to MCOs (Figures 8.1 and 8.2).

Current MCOs have a quality function, which historically focused on the healthcare effectiveness data and information set (HEDIS) measures. Evaluation of results of both quality and outcomes is based on historical claims data. The focus is on quality often under the guise of utilization review and customer service. There's no question that much time and effort are expended on quality with selection of network providers and sharing of profiling data. What is missing is real-time analytic level electronic medical record (EMR) data and the critical connectivity at the patient–physician level. Payers have done a lot to improve quality from an administrative data and marketing perspective, but it is difficult for them to take quality to the next level which is a key component of population health.

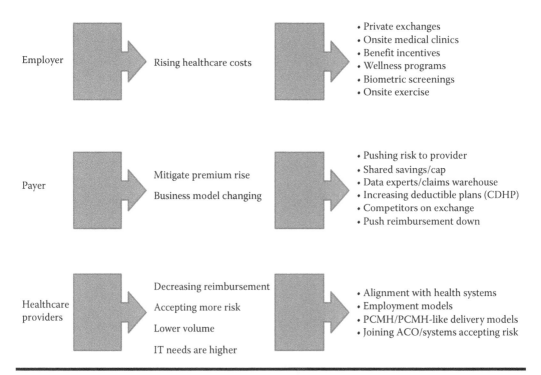

Figure 8.1   Market segment strategies.

Who	Motivation	Examples
Physician groups	They have the patient relationship	Many
Pharmacies	They are looking for a feeder to their retail and Rx business and expansion in the healthcare space	Walgreens Medicare ACOs
Disease management companies	Current DM is in decline and this is a new revenue opportunity	Texas Health Resources ACO with Healthways
Management services organizations	Extension of services already offered to physicians; new revenue opportunity	Imperium
Insurance companies	Would like to be able to offer cheaper products in the market to increase market share	Aenta ACS, United Optum, Cigna, BCBS
Insurance brokers	Concerned that fewer people will be insured through employers and this will impact their revenue model	A private exchange that will offer population health management
Medicare advantage insurers	Partnering with physician groups to start ACOs as a market expansion strategy	American Health Network; Collaborative Health Systems
Dialysis companies	Would like to expand services to other populations	Davita purchase of Healthcare Partners
Group purchasing organizations	Expand services to be more value-added than just purchasing	Premier ACO Collaborative
Associations	Additional benefit to members	MGMA Ancetta tool
Revenue cycle companies	With less FFS revenue, less need for revenue cycle management; need to branch out into population health management	Accretive Health; MedSynergies

Figure 8.2   Getting into the population health revenue stream. (From Silverstein BJ, *Moving Forward,* **Executive Summary, Winter 2013, http://governanceinstitute.com. With permission.)**

Additional limitations of payers are that many of them are for profit and have Wall Street and shareholders to answer to. Historically, the time frame in which the MCOs think is often short term. Because most of the contracts to provide care through the employer model are generally on a year-to-year basis it may be longer but is rare to have a multi-year contract. This makes it particularly challenging to focus on "rising-risk" patients and preventive care both critical to population health models. An additional challenge is the fact that many of these payers function as an ASO or "administrative services only plans." In this case, the actual medical costs are paid directly by the employer from the employer's own bank account. The MCO handles everything else, but does not actually take financial risk for the cost of these patients since these are paid by the employer. The plan simply gets a fixed monthly payment to manage the other duties. In this model, the financial risk of managing medical cost is really at the employer level, even though the health plan has indirect responsibilities. As healthcare becomes more of a significant line on the balance sheet, employers are taking more of an interest in healthcare costs. This includes things such as an emphasis on worksite wellness programs, incentive packages to encourage healthy behaviors, and on-site clinics. The critical pieces here are not just rising healthcare costs, but an effective, healthy workforce that feels better. There is also a corresponding impact on productivity.

As the future unfolds, there is no question that we will be moving to a value-based reimbursement model. This means that physicians and other providers will be paid based on outcomes and improved processes of care and not just based on the number of visits. Currently, our fee-for-service system reimburses on a "per click basis"; therefore, each visit is paid whether it has the right outcome or the right care. In this model, price drives volume and volume drives price, so the more patients that are admitted to a hospital or more patients that a physician sees, the more revenue that is generated. In this model, items such as telephone time and charting time are considered "non-value-added" from a reimbursement point of view, therefore have not been reimbursed by payers (Figure 8.3).

In Figure 8.3, we can see the potential trends of Medicare reimbursement over a period of time. The current margin in this example is positive; however, given the current price and utilization trends you can see that it quickly goes very negative. Even after making multiple adjustments to optimize the care delivery model it still has a negative impact. It takes significant care transformation, including coordination of care and diligent avoidance of excess utilization to impact the revenue in a positive manner. Therefore, in this example, with current reimbursement trends and the same delivery model, the result will be an unsustainable negative cash flow (Figure 8.4).

Payment Models

You can see by the prior charts that doing nothing or simply keeping the business the same as usual may be easy on the surface, but is not sustainable. Moving to some moderate strategies, as depicted above are only interim strategies for a short-term positive impact. Healthcare delivery must move to a more complex model of care management and integration to truly stay profitable and remain viable. The challenge is not to move faster in the care delivery model than the payment model financially supports. As the

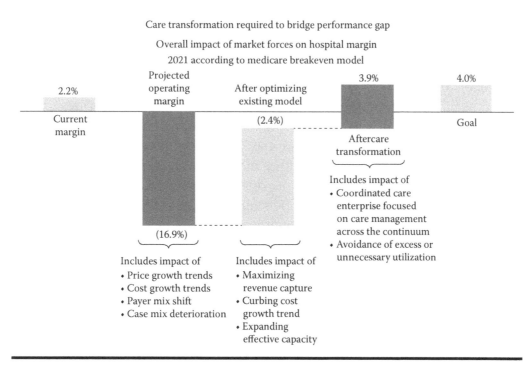

Care transformation required to bridge performance gap

Overall impact of market forces on hospital margin
2021 according to medicare breakeven model

Figure 8.3 Hospital margins with care transformation. (Adapted from Healthcare Advisory Board Interviews and Analysis; The Sustainable Acute Care Enterprise. Copyright 2013, The Advisory Board Company. All rights reserved. With permission.)

current fee-for-service model declines at the unit cost level and the utilization level changes to a new care coordination model, the cost of this transition will also be challenging to the revenue stream. It is in this transition from volume-based reimbursement to value-based reimbursement that will be a challenge over the next several years?

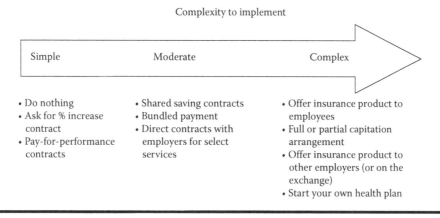

Figure 8.4 Tying payment models to population health. (From Silverstein BJ, *Moving Forward,* Executive Summary, Winter 2013, http://governanceinstitute.com. With permission.)

We are moving from a fee-for-service environment to a "shared savings" or a "pay-for-performance" environment. In these scenarios, reimbursement is primarily based on a fee-for-service basis, but there's an additional incentive that is based on either achieving certain quality metrics and cost savings (it is usually a combination of both). More efficient care provides some financial incentive back to the provider. This is clearly an interim model since in many cases the cost savings may get diluted quickly. The simplest type of cost sharing is "pay-for-performance." In this situation, additional payment is simply allocated to the provider group based on achieving defined quality metrics. These can be simple things, such as percent of generic use of pharmaceuticals, or more complex measures, such as ensuring A1C levels are measured appropriately for the diabetic population. This is often the first step in creating a shared payment model.

An obvious example is a shared savings model where many of these cost savings come directly out of the hospital in the way of decreased admissions and decreased length of stay. The savings then gets shared in some fashion with the providers and the hospital. Often more money is taken out of the hospital than they will ever get back in the shared savings model. The data have shown that 80% of the savings in these models actually come out of the hospital side. These models place a lot of demand on physicians in terms of time and effort and it is difficult to determine a methodology to share the savings in a fair and equitable manner that will be agreed upon by both parties (Figure 8.5).

In Figure 8.5, one can see that by decreasing admissions from 2000 to 1400 there's a significant drop in hospital revenue. As the revenue shifts to the ACO, the savings are shared 50-50, very little of this lost revenue actually comes back to the hospital. Therefore, these models are actually a form of revenue shifting from the hospital back to the physicians or ACO. Even if the hospitals are an active player in this model, there is still inadequate compensation for lost revenue. Hospitals must develop new models of care and reimbursement to survive and thrive in this new reimbursement arena.

One of the more common types of shared savings model is to compare trend over trend. Since healthcare costs continue to increase faster than inflation, it is unfair to ask a provider organization to reverse that trend. In most models, the trend of the patient population is compared against a similar market of patients and the difference or delta is then shared back with the plan providers or employers in an equitable fashion (Figure 8.6).

The next iteration of movement along the continuum of payment reform will be toward either partial risk or full risk reimbursement. In this model,

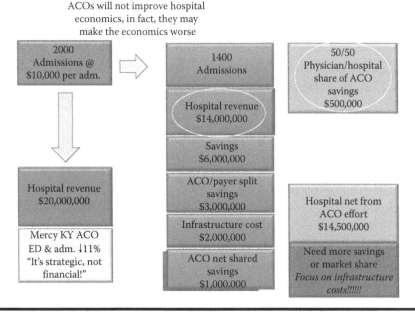

Figure 8.5   Shared savings: A transitional model. (Kaufman Hall Research 2007-B. Research study by Kaufman, Hall, & Associates, LLC, Skokie, IL, 2013.)

the financial risk of healthcare delivery is now at the delivery system level. An example would be a fixed monthly payment, usually on a per member per month (PMPM) basis, is given to the organization and the entire cost of care must come out of this revenue stream. If the care is efficient and there's overall savings left over, this can be shared back with the participants; however, if the care is inefficient and has costly outliers, then the providers will be at risk and might potentially have to pay this back, depending on the

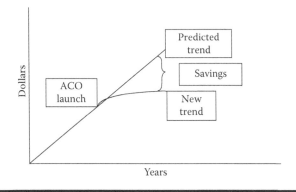

Figure 8.6   Shared savings: Healthcare costs.

structure of the program. Often there is stop-loss insurance built into these programs to help mitigate this downside risk.

There are many ways to migrate to full financial risk. Often groups start with a full professional risk arrangement. In this situation the provider, ACO, or other party are taking risks only for the physician or professional services. Because the amount of reimbursement for each visit is relatively small and the number of visits somewhat predictable, this mitigates the variability and potential for outliers. From here providers often move to pharmacy risk and Medicare Part D risk. Eventually groups must tackle the high-risk part of the equation which is the hospital risk and Medicare Part A risk. Sick patients and expensive outliers can affect this number dramatically; therefore, it makes sense to have a large population in order to spread the risk. Stop-loss insurance may also help protect the group against large outlier claims. It is often possible to also set up risk corridors which might mitigate the risk at the high and low-end to help protect provider groups. This can be done on a cost or utilization basis or by "carving out" certain high-end services, such as transplants or claims in excess of a defined threshold. This can become very complex.

As payers and MCOs face these new realities, there are various strategies to compete in this new environment. Many MCOs have started collaborative models where they are working directly with providers and healthcare delivery systems to provide care under a shared savings model. Often the shared savings models are set up so that certain defined quality metrics must be met, and then there would be shared savings after that. The shared savings are based on comparing last year's trend to this year's trend or measuring a comparative market trend year over year.

Payers are often providing the support for these projects including claims processing, marketing, and connecting with employers to provide actionable data and information. One of the models that some of the MCOs and payers are focusing on is becoming an information broker. They are positioning themselves as data and analytic information experts focusing on claims data, health-risk assessments, and other data streams. As the financial risk shifts further down the healthcare delivery system, this is a reasonable strategic focus for many MCOs/payers.

Other MCOs are actually buying providers including physician groups and hospitals to vertically integrate the entire structure. In this scenario, there is only one organization delivering care and handling the insurance and financial risk part of the equation. This is becoming an important strategy for both the payers and healthcare delivery systems. Much of the future revenue stream is predicted to be on the insurance or risk side, so it is important to align strategies to take advantage of this. This can be done either by MCOs buying the healthcare delivery system or by the healthcare delivery system either buying insurance companies or by taking on full risk on agreements and partnering with third-party administrators that process/adjudicate claims. The ability to get closer to the financial risk is an important strategy for future success.

One of the greatest challenges in this model, as stated earlier, is the time frame in which the payers are working. To truly mitigate the risk and costs of members/patients, it should be a multi-year process. This is why it makes sense to shift some of this responsibility to the employer, especially since often the employers typically take a longer view than a payer. While it is not unusual for an employer to market their health plans every year or every couple of years, employees stay at a particular company much longer. It makes sense for the employer to understand and drive population health-based payment models whether through a payer or healthcare delivery system. Most large employers contract with payers for administrative services only. In this scenario, the employer is 100% responsible for the cost of healthcare for its own employees. As employers become more sophisticated and knowledgeable about healthcare delivery, wellness prevention, presenteeism, and absenteeism, they are demanding more from there managed care partners.

The Financial Drivers

While it may seem a bit cynical, one adage of managed care and healthcare delivery is to always "follow the money." As we look at managed care we can see that it was arguably successful initially. The focus at this point was on being prescriptive on benefits design, limiting network option, and contracting with aggressive pricing.

As we move along the continuum, the focus shifted to the care management process, typically focused on utilization review. This includes activities such as precertification or preauthorization, as well as an evaluation of medical appropriateness. This is where payment denials became such a panacea. Historically, a focus on utilization review and much of managed care in general was focusing on limiting hospital stays, moving patients into observation status rather than inpatient, and trying to eliminate hospitalization when appropriate. In addition, there was also a focus on complex care coordination, that is, case management and controlling medical costs by better transitions of care and coordination of that care. For many years there was also a focus on disease management. This included care coordination specifically for asthma, depression, congestive heart failure, and diabetes among others. This provided challenges as many of these patients had multiple comorbidities and it was difficult to engage in disease-specific initiatives.

Another strategy for managing cost was transferring some of the responsibility to the providers. This was often done in the form of capitation payments both at the primary care and specialist level. For some time, there was a big focus on doing specialty capitation to limit some of the specialist' volume and using primary care fee-for-service to augment the care. This was a way of predicting spending and limiting financial risk at the health plan level. This was effective to a point.

Technology and demographics will continue to drive medical costs. Care management initiatives at the payer level are becoming increasingly challenging.

Population Health

What is prompting the move to population health is the criticality of controlling the ever-increasing medical cost. Care management must be expanded and refocused. Health plans must now collaborate with the healthcare delivery systems and the payer, either the patient or the employer, to focus on more long-range preventions. The future will be dealing with behavioral and other determinants of healthcare, rather than the disease management models of the past. For employers this is an imperative. As they try to come complete in an international and global environment, they must have comparable medical costs to their competitors in other countries. Employers should and will be driving much of this change.

As we take a look at Figure 8.6, we can see at the top of the pyramid are the high-risk groups. These patients were the focus of the MCOs and other healthcare delivery systems because of their high utilization and high cost. These tend to have a short-term return on investment (ROI), making them a good target. The next level of the triangle is the "rising-risk" patients whose risk has the potential to escalate into the high-risk area. These include patients with multiple disease state and comorbidities. These patients require disease management approaches and a more holistic care management approach, since most of them have multiple comorbidities. As we look

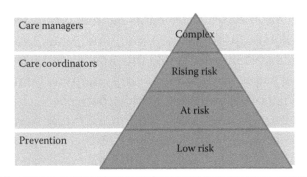

Figure 8.7   Care and risk pyramid.

at the bottom of the pyramid, we see the lowest risk patients. These are patients with risk factors for disease, but at this point have a low healthcare cost. There is where focusing on the mitigation of potential disease and prevention can be very effective (Figure 8.7).

One of the biggest challenges in managed care and population health management is the fact that is very difficult to predict which patients in these groups are going to move into the next level of risk and will be likely increasing the healthcare cost. There have been many predictive models to help with this; however, we have learned over the years that patients with those high expenditures in 1 year are not consistent with the ones that incur high health expenditures in the following year.

The next group is the prevention group, which traditionally had a limited focus. Some of the reasons for this are the inability to get data on this population, the difficulty of engaging this population which is relatively healthy, and the long-term return on investment that would be required. In this group, the most effective way to engage them is through their employer (and/or payer). This group requires a different type of engagement, since they have few healthcare needs on a chronic basis. They are often younger and more tech literate and have a need for health education and acute episodic needs.

One of the great challenges in engaging this group is the fact that they are hard to identify. Since these patients often have few or no medical claims, they cannot easily be identified through analysis of claims data because of their sporadic use of the healthcare system. One-way employers have engaged this population is by requiring them fill out a health-risk assessment and incentivizing a lower premium contribution. This is an excellent way of identifying patients that have high-risk behavior, such as smoking, obesity, etc., and that have not yet had many encounters with the healthcare system. Another way of identifying this group is mining social networking data. Much can be gleaned from understanding one's shopping habits and social network habits. While this may sound very controversial, it is already starting to occur. Much time and energy is being spent on engaging this population of relatively healthy patients.

In summary, patient engagement is critical for future healthcare efficiency for both cost and outcomes. In our current third-party payer system, and our great inequity of healthcare literacy and insurance coverage, this has been a major challenge. In the future, we must engage the patient in their own healthcare and outcomes. This engagement may also extend to their family and friends and even their community's healthcare needs.

Bibliography

1. Illinois Hospital Association, Commitment to Transformation. Navigating the Journey to the "New H," IHA Transforming Illinois Health Care Task Force, 2014.
2. The Advisory Board Company, The Scalable Population Health Enterprise. Generating Clinical and Financial Returns from Cost-Effective Care Management, Study, April 9, 2014.
3. Kirkner RM. Urgent care finds its place in the age of ACOs. *Managed Care Magazine*, November 2014.
4. The Big Idea. The strategy that will fix health care. *Harvard Business Review*, October 2013.
5. Bodenheimer T. Coordinating care—A perilous journey through the health care system. *The New England Journal of Medicine*. Health Policy Report. 2008; 358: 1064–1071. DOI: 10.1056/NEJMhpr0706165. Available at www.nejm.org (Accessed on March 6, 2008).
6. Improving Care Transitions. *Health Affairs Health Policy Brief,* 2012.
7. Bush H. *Caring for the costliest.* Hospitals and Health Networks, 2012. Available at www.hhnmag.com.
8. Larkin H. How Will You Adapt to Population Health? October 14, 2014, H&HN.
9. Boyarsky V, Parke R. *The Medicare Shared Savings Program and the Pioneer Accountable Care Organization.* Milliman Healthcare Reform Briefing Paper, May 2012. (peer reviewed by Bill O'Brien).
10. Smithback EL, Spector JM, Dieguez G, Mirkin DP. Milliman White Paper. Accountable care organizations: Financial, clinical and implementation considerations for academic medical centers, 2012.
11. Silverstein BJ, *Moving Forward*, Executive Summary, Winter 2013, http://governanceinstitute.com.

12. Management Healthcare Executive.com. December 2014. Specialty ACOs: A promising option.

13. Edmondson WR. The per capita payment model. *Journal of Healthcare Management.* January/February 2015; 60(1): 14+. © 1998 American College of Healthcare Executives.

14. Doerr TD, Olson HB, Zimmerman DC. The accountable primary care model: Beyond medical home 2.0. *The American Journal of Managed Care, December* 2014; 1–3.

Chapter 9

Physician Compensation Models

Pam Williams

Contents

Traditional Physician Compensation Models

Physicians traditionally worked as solo practitioners. Their income was
what was left after collecting from their patients and insurance partners for
services rendered and paying their practice expenses. As physicians began
to practice in groups of two or more physicians, models were developed to
allow for allocation of expenses between physicians. Models evolved over
time based upon partnership with senior (or founding) physicians funding the initial practice start-up. This involved purchasing assets and funding initial cash flow and losses incurred as new physicians were hired.
The partners' net income was distributed based on individual or "equal
shares" distribution or based on their group's productivity. They initially
invested and later received the benefit of having employed physicians who
worked at a fixed rate of pay initially before being invited to participate as
a partner.

Employed physicians within a practice were eventually offered the opportunity to "buy in" to the medical partnership. This "buy in" was variable
from practice to practice and between various specialties, and was historically based on the assets and size of the practice in addition to the retirement agreements of the senior partners.

As financial pressures increased and profit margins decreased, nonpart-
ner physicians increasingly found that working on a fixed salary with excess
earnings inuring to the benefit of the partners unacceptable. The amount
expected to "buy in" to a practice could no longer be justified in terms of
future return on investment. A large portion of the value of the practice was
considered the "ownership" of its patients. Physicians who would "buy in"
to a practice would effectively be buying access to those patients or patient's
medical records. Beginning in the late 1980s and 1990s, the concept of

patient panels was developed by managed care organizations and in many cases the control and ownership of these patients shifted from the practice to the payer. As a result, buying into the practice did not necessarily mean direct access to patients, since patients often shifted at the payer's direction or through plan and/or insurer changes. Instead, many physicians left without becoming partners and the partners in established practices had difficulty continuing to fund the model that was intended to provide for their practice growth and ultimate retirement.

As hospitals and health systems began employing physicians in increasing numbers in the 1980s and 1990s, many based compensation on a fixed salary, which did not naturally promote productivity. As a result, physician productivity frequently declined. This lower level of productivity, combined with many hospital's difficulty in managing physician practices, resulted in significant and unsustainable losses. During these early periods, hospitals were notoriously bad at running small "mom-and-pop" type practices. Hospital's overhead structures, wage scales, and benefits packages led to much higher overhead.

Over the past two decades, health system and large multispecialty group compensation models have become increasingly sophisticated in an attempt to create incentives for desired behaviors. A variety of compensation models have since been developed for employed physicians.

Guaranteed Salary

In this model, a guaranteed salary was established in an employment contract. Advantages of guaranteed salary included the ability to establish the market rate for a given physician and specialty in advance, the ability to budget for that cost and the simplicity of administration. Disadvantages included the lack of connection to actual productivity levels, reimbursement and/or expenses in a practice. Physicians had no incentive to increase their level of activity or assist management in containing expenses. Hospitals found that when physicians were put on a guaranteed salary structure they often scaled back their activity level and/or motivation, making profitability even more difficult. Many physicians shifted to "bankers hours" and easier lifestyles given the protection of a guaranteed salary. Additionally, payer mix did not affect their compensation and as previously addressed, a combination of low-paying insurance plans and self-pay patients could dramatically skew a practice's (but not the physician's) income.

Basic component	Basis
Base salary	Based on local or regional market
Base salary plus annual or periodic bonus for volume above predetermined level	Predetermined based on visit volume, gross charges, or net patient revenue
Base salary plus annual bonus shared equally among all physicians in a practice	Profits above guaranteed salary after expenses

Figure 9.1   Productivity models.

Productivity Models

Ultimately, productivity-based models evolved in an attempt to incentivize physician behavior to increase patient volume (Figure 9.1). Various models were developed including base salaries with added incentives for productivity delivered above predetermined benchmarks, equal share models that split total revenue within the practice, the addition of incentive distributions based on individual productivity, and in some cases there were models that included accountability for individual and practice expenses. Compensation models evolved based on work RVUs, actual billings, or on actual collections (Figure 9.2).

Productivity Measures

As productivity models became more sophisticated, a number of productivity measures and other benchmarks were utilized. These included gross

Measure	Pros	Cons
Gross charges	Measure of activity and complexity	Unrelated to net revenue received for patient care
Net collections	Measure of activity, complexity, and payer reimbursement	Dependent upon good revenue cycle management. Became unrelated to productivity as capitation emerged
Patient visits	Measure of physician activity	Unrelated to complexity of the care provided in the visit (e.g., an acute visit for a sinus infection vs. a comprehensive wellness exam)
Patient panel size	Measure of total potential patient care provided over a period of time based on average patient utilization	Does not adjust for age, chronicity, or under- or overutilization
wRVUs	A standardized method measuring the physician work effort against a base unit	Does not account for differences in payer type and therefore resulting net revenue

Figure 9.2   Productivity metrics.

charges, net collections, patient visits, patient panel size, and work relative value units (wRVUs). There were advantages and disadvantages as incentives to each in the effort to promote physician productivity.

Gross charges were typically defined as professional (nontechnical) charges for the patient care services individually provided by the physician. This measure was an indicator of overall activity levels but was impacted by the fee schedule utilized; therefore there may not have been a consistent relationship with the actual physician work effort, revenue, or related practice expense.

Net collections were typically defined as collections from patients and insurance companies for an individual physician's personally provided patient care. This measure was complicated by inconsistent collection results from physician to physician as well as the differences in reimbursement between various payers. Capitation and other managed care methodologies made collections a more complex and a less direct incentive for physicians. Also compensation models based on collections did not account for the practice expense necessary to provide the service.

Patient visits were often used as a measure of productivity, sometimes in combination with other measures. However, the financial and clinical value of a single patient visit could vary significantly according to the specialty of the physician and the resulting current procedural terminology (CPT) code. Patient visits also did not take into account the practice operational expenses. The value of a physician visit was also highly dependent on a physician's documentation and coding accuracy.

Patient panel size became an important measure when capitated insurance plans increased in popularity, but had the disadvantage of having a limited connection to the actual volume of patient care provided, revenue received, or practice expenses in caring for a group of patients. Patient panel size could also serve to incentivize a physician to limit the care provided because the actual volume of direct care provided was not considered. During this time, many physicians had unreasonably large panel sizes and tended to alter their practice style to handle medical issues by telephone as well as using consultants to provide care they did not want to provide. This model rewarded physicians for having large panels of patients, but with no sophisticated data, it was not possible to evaluate the quality of care or properly incentivize preventative services. This may have actually increased the total cost of care.

Work relative value units (wRVUs) utilized as a component in compensation formulas was the first attempt at a standardized method to measure the work effort expended by an individual physician in providing direct care to patients. Prior to the resource-based relative value scale (RBRVS) system, medicare paid for physician services using "usual, customary, and reasonable" rate-setting methods. Created in the late 1980s, the RBRVS system included values for the work, practice, and malpractice expense for each CPT code. By excluding the relative value components related to overhead and malpractice expenses related to a specific procedure in compensation models, wRVUs allowed for the ability to value the physician's individual effort (time, technical skill, mental effort, and judgment) in a more consistent manner across the various services, procedures, and specialty areas. However, as with gross charges, patient visits, and patient panel size, wRVUs did not reflect the resulting revenue or accompanying expense within the practice. Shifts in the payer mix within a physician's panel or in a single practice could cause significant variability in the overall financial results (Figure 9.2).

Compensation models often used one or a combination of the measures outlined above. Expense allocation methodologies included equal allocations that assumed practice expense was fixed on a per provider basis, allocations applied to the revenue generated by each physician that assumed practice expense was variable and combinations of both fixed and variable allocations. Depending on the methodology chosen, expense allocation could result in great variability in the resulting pay and incentives among a group of physicians (Figure 9.3).

What has been missing in most compensation plans is a compensation model that includes compensation risk and rewards related to *value*. As payers began to develop and evolve existing reimbursement models to include incentives and their own quality ratings physician compensation models that did not include comparable measures became out of sync once again with the potential revenue of a practice. In fact, many progressive organizations began including elements of value in their compensation models early on, in an attempt to begin influencing physician behavior in these important areas.

Expense items	Fixed expense	Variable expense
Expense for office space	If all physicians use the same amount of space	If a physician requires more or fewer exam or procedure rooms
Staff cost for wages and benefits	If the focus is on core staffing for management, reception, and medical assistance	If a physician requires higher or lower levels of support from one or more category of staff (e.g., two medical assistants or nurses rather than one)

Figure 9.3 Expense metrics.

Quality Programs, Metrics, and Measures

Historically, insurance companies established their own quality measures and often times they tended to be more focused on cost than true quality. In 2007, one insurance company, for example, suggested a quality measure called a "split tab" prescription in an attempt to decrease total pharmaceutical cost. Generic drug utilization is similarly focused more on cost than on the efficacy of certain medications. Quality measures that are suggested by insurance companies need to be evaluated to determine if they are both appropriate and achievable.

As physician organizations begin to incorporate quality incentives into their compensation programs, there are a number of measures to consider. It is generally recommended to begin with a manageable number of quality measures (perhaps 2–5 measures) with the potential of a 10%–15% +/– effect on earnings. As actual revenue based on quality incentives from payers increases, the weight of quality within a compensation formula should increase correspondingly.

The elements for initial consideration include participation in NCQA patient-centered medical home (PCMH) recognition, meaningful use participation incentives derived from the CMS value-based incentive programs, physician quality reporting systems (PQRS), utilization of evidence-based guidelines for patient care, emerging value-based reimbursements, participation in care management programs, case rate, and bundled payment programs and shared savings (Figure 9.4).

Patient-Centered Medical Homes

One movement focused on improvement of the quality and efficiency of patient care began in the late 1960s by the American Academy of Pediatrics. In 1978, the World Health Organization further outlined the basic tenants of the medical home and the role that primary care physicians (PCPs) needed to play. Some physicians have adopted these tenants of practice, supporting the goals of achieving patient-centered care. The core features of PCMH initiatives are having an identified personal physician, PCP, within a physician directed medical practice where a "whole person" focus is established to provide care in a coordinated fashion with enhanced access and promotion of measureable quality and safety goals and initiatives. Principles of PCMH focus on coordination of care by PCP and his/her care team with the goal of prevention, improved management of chronic conditions and a decrease in hospitalization rates and

Emerging quality elements and programs
Patient-centered medical home
Meaningful use
Value-based incentive measures (CMS)
Participation in PQRS reporting
Utilization of evidence-based guidelines
Value-based reimbursements
Care management programs
Case rate reimbursements
Bundled payment programs
Shared savings programs

Figure 9.4   Quality metrics.

unnecessary or duplicative specialty and ancillary services. It was hoped that private payers would be willing to either pay an additional stipend per member per month or increased fee-for-service reimbursement levels to those practices with PCMH recognition. Unfortunately, only a few payers have been willing to do this in certain markets. While the payers have been generally supportive of PCMH they have not been willing to reach into their pockets to reward the effort. In some markets, payers require PCMH recognition for inclusion in a narrow network or other incentive programs (Figures 9.5 and 9.6).

CMS Medicare Value-Based Initiatives

The center for medicare and medicaid innovation (CMS) has been a source of new payment models, many as the result of the Patient Protection and Affordable Care Act (PPACA). CMS introduced incentives for physicians to adopt and use EMR technology and to use those systems in a prescribed, effective way (meaningful use), PQRS, and the value base payment modifier (VBPM).

Meaningful Use

Initially, meaningful use provided financial bonuses to physicians over a five year period if they could demonstrate adoption of EMR technology and proper utilization of the system and an attestation to that proper use. In 2015,

The standards
Enhance access and continuity
Identify and manage patient populations
Plan and manage care
Provide self-care and community support
Track and coordinate care
Measure and improve performance

Figure 9.5 Key elements in patient-centered medical care.

Must-pass elements
Access during office hours
Use data for population management
Provide care management
Support self-care processes
Track referrals and follow up
Implement continuous quality improvement

Figure 9.6 Must-pass elements for patient-centered medical care.

physicians who had not adopted EMR technology or were unable to attest to meaningful use have seen reduced payments for their traditional Medicare patients of 1% that will increase to 2% in 2016, and 3% in 2017 (Figure 9.7).

Meaningful use incentives through Medicaid*	
	Starting any year 2011 through 2016
Year 1	$21,250
Year 2	$8500
Year 3	$8500
Year 4	$8500
Year 5	$8500
Year 6	$8500
Total	$63,750
*>30% Medicaid or >20% and is a pediatrician.	

Meaningful use through CMS	Starting in 2011	Starting in 2012	Starting in 2013	Starting in 2014
2011	$18,000			
2012	$12,000	$18,000		
2013*	$7840	$11,760	$14,700	
2014**	$3920	$7840	$11,760	$11,760
2015	$1960	$3920	$7840	$7840
2016		$1960	$3920	$3920
Total maximum possible	$43,720	$43,480	$38,220	$23,520

*Sequestration reduced payments by 2% in 2013.
**Last year to begin participation.

Figure 9.7 Meaningful use incentives through CMS.

Failure to use EMR reductions in CMS payments		
Failure to adopt		
2015	−1% payment adjustment	All Medicare payments
2016	−2% payment adjustment	All Medicare payments
2017	−3% payment adjustment	All Medicare payments
2018	−4% payment adjustment	All Medicare payments
2019	−5% payment adjustment	All Medicare payments

Physician Quality Reporting System

The PQRS is a medicare quality reporting system that promotes the submission of quality data from providers in order to report on quality across large populations. Reporting of PQRS specialty-specific measures was initially voluntary, but later resulted in a reward of additional reimbursement by CMS. As of 2015, those physicians not reporting PQRS measures appropriate to their specialty lose 1.5% of their Medicare reimbursement and will lose 2% as of 2016 (Figure 9.8).

Reporting year	Payment in 2015	Payment in 2016
2014*	−1.5% effect	−2% effect

*Reporting requirements vary between individual and group practices but the payment effect is the same.

Figure 9.8 PQRS payment adjustments.

Value-Based Payment Modifier

Large physician group practices (100+) had the opportunity for additional medicare reimbursement under the value-based payment modifier (VBPM) program starting in 2015 based on care provided in 2013. The VBPM will apply to all the physicians regardless of group size starting in 2017. All eligible professionals who have not successfully reported PQRS measures in 2015 will be assessed a 2%–4% VBPM reduction.

Quality tiering will result in a +/− adjustment based on two composite scores—quality and cost. The cost measures that will be used for quality tiering include the total per capita cost (Part A and Part B Medicare charges) and the total per capita costs for beneficiaries with specified chronic conditions. Group cost measures are adjusted by specialty. As with hospital models for value-based payments, the program is intended to be budget neutral (Figure 9.9).

Value-Based Reimbursement

Increasingly, payers have attempted to shift reimbursement from volume (fee-or-service—payment for each service provided but without any connection to the result of the care) to value. Value has been defined by payers as a combination of the quality of care and outcomes determined by defined quality metrics along with a reduction in the overall cost of care. While payment for services provided continues to be based on fee for service payment, total payment can increase (or decrease) depending on the outcome of performance measures. Incentive payments can be made on a bonus basis based on retrospective review of performance measures or in some cases may include a component of fee for service payment that is withheld pending achievement of those measures.

Performance metrics have been developed by both governmental and private payers. Most include certain expectations regarding the use of an electronic medical records (EMRs or EHRs) along with a focus on documentation

Year 1–2015 (based on 2013)	Low quality	Average quality	High quality
Low cost	+0	+2x	+4x
Average cost	−2x	+0	+2x
High cost	−4x	−2x	+0

Figure 9.9   Value-based payment modifier incentives.

of key preventative measures, such as immunizations, mammography, and colonoscopy, along with evidence of appropriate intervals of care and evaluation for chronic conditions such as diabetes and congestive obstructive pulmonary disease (COPD).

Increasingly, elements considered in value-based reimbursement models also include clinical outcomes data and patient satisfaction. Total cost of care or cost efficiency measures are also included in most progressive value-based models. In some cases, participation is based on a minimum threshold of achievement, as seen in the development of narrow networks. Narrow networks include only those providers who achieve the minimal standards set by an individual payer. In other networks, the payer includes many physicians but only rewards those meeting the established metrics.

Care Management Programs

Private insurance companies and now CMS have also provided incentive programs with payment to physicians on a per member per month basis to those PCPs willing to establish or participate in a care management program. Using either bachelor prepared or advanced practice nurses or in some cases medical assistants, physician practices agree to provide additional elements of preventative and chronic care management to those patients who meet certain defined criteria. In most cases, care management is provided at no cost to the patient. CMS's CCM program requires patients to be responsible for their copayment of the management fee (~$8/month in 2015). Care management includes preventative care reminders, phone and in-person visits with the care manager, and other methods of promoting patient compliance with established care plans.

Case Rates and Bundled Payments

In bundled payment or payment per case (case rates), physicians and facilities are paid a flat fee for an episode of care such as a surgery, or even for a specified time period for a chronic condition such as diabetes or COPD. These programs help align the financial incentives between the hospital, physicians, and between acute and post-acute facilities. Medicare is committed to rapidly increasing its value-based payments in the near future. These kinds of programs will help to facilitate that transition. The bundled payment programs cover the patients from a few days prior to admission to up to 90 days post admission, making the delivery system responsible for the cost of care and the cost of complications.

Shared Savings, Full Risk, and Accountable Care Organizations

A final method of rewarding physicians for high-quality and cost-efficient care of their patients has been established within accountable care and shared savings programs. In these programs, physicians have the opportunity to participate in a payer specific, predetermined percentage of any savings achieved over a defined time frame compared to an agreed upon prior period. However, in order to receive any shared savings, there is a need to achieve the established benchmarks for quality and patient satisfaction. In 2015, for instance, CMS requires attainment of minimum benchmarks and related total points in specific domains in order to quality for shared savings. Those who achieve savings, but who fail to meet the quality benchmarks, are not rewarded with these savings. Full risk programs, based on the total cost of care, are also being utilized and are increasing in adoption, much like the capitated programs of the 1990s but with metrics defining minimum quality standards to avoid inappropriate restriction of care that occurred in the past. These programs are generally considered transitional since the shared savings programs shift the savings out of the hospital and into the accountable care entity. Ultimately, the shared savings programs represent a zero-sum game that has a finite lifetime and must ultimately transition to different models.

Effect on Physician Compensation Models

With the myriad of new elements of revenue (and risk) affecting physicians and healthcare systems that extend beyond the traditional fee for service volume-based reimbursement methodologies of the past, new compensation models must evolve to provide proper incentives and distribution of revenue to those physicians who participate. Whether employed by a health system or through a private practice, current models of productivity-based compensation will no longer meet the needs of providing aligned incentives in the delivery of patient care.

The Need for and Elements of Change

In order to establish a new compensation model, the organization paying the physician must establish new principles for inclusion in their compensation model. These elements may include some or all of the following.

Selection of Specific Quality Metrics: Access

The best quality of care for a patient population cannot be achieved and sustained without sufficient patient access. Depending on the capacity of the practice a focus on access is key. The hours of availability, in addition to provision of care, at the times that meet the needs of working patients and students, is critical in assuring that the patient's need for care can be met. Physicians should be incentivized and/or required to provide a level of access beyond the traditional 9–5 weekday business hours.

Total hours of patient access need to be continually reassessed by focusing on PCPs' office-based care, leaving hospital care to trained and dedicated hospitalists. Physicians who transit from providing a combination of hospital and office-based care to office only practice can expect to see an increase in revenue of between 10% and 25% while enjoying an improved quality of life, which is increasingly attractive to younger physicians.

Care provided by dedicated hospitalists with an appropriate focus on quality metrics, including a reduction in readmissions, reduced length of stay, and improved patient experience can be a more efficient and effective process in the care of hospitalized patients due to their clinical focus and full time availability. Coupled with well-orchestrated transitions of care, a combination of office-based and hospitalist physicians can provide the maximum levels of access, quality, and experience to a population of patients.

Disease-Specific Care Management Guidelines

Once highly contested and laboriously discussed, the acceptance of standardized guidelines for the appropriate care of patients with certain conditions has improved significantly over the past decade. Improvements in the adoption of evidence-based guidelines have left little debate about the most appropriate intervals for care, preventative screenings, medication regimens, and ancillary testing. Any organization participating in value-based care must adopt defined care guidelines within their various specialty groups to assure that evidence-based care is being delivered.

Outcomes and Results

In the process of following evidence-based care guidelines, physicians must also receive and be rewarded for the improved outcomes that are achieved in their patient populations. Immunization rates, preventative testing, the ability to manage hemoglobin A1C, and blood pressure levels are examples of outcomes that can be measured and rewarded. While physicians will argue that they cannot assure patient compliance, they also underestimate their influence on patients in the area of preventative care. In reality, no programs expect full compliance. Physicians also have the right to refuse to continue to care for noncompliant patients which alone may change many patient's decisions about following their physician's advice.

Patient Experience

It is no longer an option for physicians to ignore the patient experience. Payers, including the federal government (through CMS) have made it clear that only those providers with acceptable levels of patient satisfaction will be allowed to receive rewards and/or participate in future reimbursement programs. While not widely adopted beyond large physician groups and healthcare aligned organizations, physician experience/patient satisfaction is a critical element of any compensation methodology. As physicians aggregate into larger and more sophisticated groups, standardized methods of patient satisfaction reporting are necessary and a focus on high benchmarks and continuous improvement is a key component.

Cost Efficiency and Utilization

Cost and utilization of care must also be included in the compensation methodology. Hospital, ancillary, and emergency room costs in addition to total cost of care must become a primary consideration in a physician's compensation. As PCPs are able to view the effect of their referrals to various specialties, and the resulting total cost of the care they refer, changes in referral patterns will result both in improving in-network alignment and rewarding the most cost efficient and effective specialists. The effect of changes in referral patterns alone with likely be a sufficient incentive to change the care patterns of specialists within your organization. Transparency and accuracy of data is a must in this process.

Examples of Weighting and Structure of Potential Compensation Models

Organizations will need to continue to blend traditional productivity-based reimbursement incentives with increasing levels of value-based incentives. It is recommended that organizations on 100% productivity models consider moving to a 10%–20% weight on a combination of quality metrics and patient satisfaction, with a gradual increase in total weight over time. It is also recommended that the specific metrics be developed with PCP and specialty physician input and that they be reviewed on an annual basis with the goal of setting both attainable goals as well as "stretch" goals that will evolve over time. In the beginning, a focus on one or two quality metrics should be targeted (e.g., diabetes management and preventative health screenings).

In net collections or net revenue-based models, a "withhold" model may be utilized to provide money to reward those who meet the defined goals of the organization, much like the value-based purchasing models applied to hospitals. While budget neutral to the physician organization, this method will shift a portion of net collections or net revenue from those underperforming on the agreed upon metrics to those who are meeting standards. Initially, 10% of total potential compensation should be a sufficient amount to gain the attention of physicians. Over time, the percentage of compensation attributed based on quality should increase by two or more fold (Figure 9.10).

As the reimbursement from third parties increases, the program matures and data improves, elements can be added to allow for the inclusion of shared savings, bundled payments, and case rates (Figures 9.11 and 9.12).

Base salary based on area fair market value (FMV)	$160,000	*Any level of bonus requires successful annual achievement of meaningful use and PCMH recognition			
10% withhold	($16,000)				
<75th percentile patient satisfaction	$0	5% available for achievement of ≥75th percentile patient satisfaction*	$8000	10% available for achievement of ≥90th percentile patient satisfaction*	$16,000
<Median achievement of quality metrics	$0	5% available for achievement of median quality metrics*	$8000	10% available for achievement of ≥75th percentile quality metrics*	$16,000
Resulting salary	$144,000		$160,000		$176,000

Figure 9.10 Basic value elements.

Base salary based on area fair market value (FMV)	$160,000	*Any level of bonus requires successful achievement of meaningful use and PCMH recognition			
10% withhold	($16,000)				
<80th percentile patient satisfaction	$0	5% available for achievement of ≥80th percentile patient satisfaction	$8000	10% available for achievement of ≥90th percentile patient satisfaction	$16,000
<75th percentile achievement of quality metrics	$0	5% available for achievement of 75th percentile quality metrics	$8000	10% available for achievement of ≥90th percentile quality metrics	$16,000
Access	$0	5% available for meeting >5 h/week after 6 PM and/or on weekends	$8000	10% available for meeting >8 h/week after 6 p.m. or on weekends	$16,000
PCP panel size	$0	5% available for achieving total panel over 12 months >2500*	$8000	10% available for achieving total panel over 12 months >3000*	$16,000
Resulting salary	$144,000		$176,000		$224,000

Figure 9.11 Expanded value elements.

Special Issues to Consider

Metrics for Specialty Physicians

Measures for patient satisfaction and access can also apply to specialists. Quality metrics are less robust for many specialists, but participation in case

Additional elements as payment incentives evolve					
Participation in bundled payment programs	$0	50% pro-rata share of bundled payments when elements above are met	$12,500	Full pro-rata share of bundled payments when elements above are met	$25,000
Participation in shared savings	$0	50% pro-rata share of shared savings payments when elements above are met	$10,000	Full pro-rata share of shared savings payments when elements above are met	$20,000
Resulting salary	$144,000		$206,500		$253,000

Figure 9.12   Payment methodology incentives.

rates and bundled payments can provide additional incentives. Measures can also be developed around communication and coordination of care with PCPs, actively participating in transitions of care, and reconciliation of medications. Specialty metrics often have to be specific to that specialty concentrating on specific diseases within that specialty. This is often difficult and time-consuming. It is best to target the high-volume specialists such as cardiologists, orthopedics, and others and focus on more global rewards for the lower volume specialties. Often some of the biggest rewards for a specialist are a steady source of consistent patient referrals from the PCPs who are incentivized to refer to efficient specialists with high levels of patient satisfaction and lower overall costs. This move to "keep it in the family" (the politically incorrect term is considered "keepage" vs. "leakage") can significantly improve the effectiveness and quality of care within a network of providers while incenting desired behaviors for all members of the care team.

Accommodation for Physicians Nearing Retirement or with In-Demand Subspecialty Skills

Participation in value-based reimbursement programs should be nonnegotiable. However, in some circumstances, physicians near retirement or with unique and limited subspecialty skills may need to be accommodated in order to achieve practice's or organization's goals. It is recommended that the accommodation come in the form of added assistance through ancillary medical or clerical staff rather than any reduction in the expectation for results. Organizations will need to carefully consider the minimum acceptable levels of achievement required for any individual physician with a degree of consistency and with adequate justification, in order to gain the broad support necessary to incent to remainder of the organization.

Incentives for Nonphysician Providers

An effective team-based incentive program should assist in the achievement of the organization's goals of providing quality- and cost-efficient care. Each organization in the process of establishing new compensation methods for physicians should carefully consider aligning incentives with advance practice nurses and physician assistants, as well as clinical, clerical, and management staff.

Advanced practice providers can be included in similar productivity and quality-based compensation models along with the physicians. However, often the needs and preferences of these advanced practice providers are better met through a combination of fixed salaries and benefits with the potential for bonuses based on organizational goals and metrics.

Experience has shown that a lack of alignment with the nonprovider staff can impede even the most sophisticated and well-crafted compensation models. Small levels of bonus potential (2%–4% of staff income) can provide sufficient incentive to drive improvement supported by the receptionists, medical assistants, and nurses on the front line.

Rewards for Leadership and Citizenship

No organization should underestimate the value of effective physician leadership. In a system focused on value-based care, physician leadership can drive positive change in a way not easily achieved by other administrative forces. Organizations should consider incentives for both formal leadership roles as well as for participation in physician and administrative meetings. Often payment of as little as $100 for participation in a regular meeting can achieve levels of attendance that meet the needs of organization's efforts to communicate their goals, objectives, and results over time. Consideration of hourly, monthly, or annual stipends for leadership and meeting attendance can improve alignment with the organizations' goals. Meetings are often a critical component of the communication necessary to educate and align physicians in a group.

Not only should an organization reward physician leadership, but also common to include part of the physician compensation under the heading of corporate alignment or corporate citizenship. This category can include certain corporate strategic goals that align with that physician or that

Types of citizenship incentives	
Monthly meeting attendance	$100/meeting
Formal leadership position	$2500/year
Mentoring new physicians	$2000/mentored physician
Participation in annual strategic planning meeting	$250/year
Seniority	X% increase in base salary

Figure 9.13 Citizenship and leadership metrics.

specialty can be listed to help better align the physicians with the strategic imperatives of the delivery model (Figure 9.13).

Compensation Models and Formulas: The Only Constant Is Change

With the evolution of healthcare reimbursement over the next decade, there must be continued adjustment and refinement to even the most robust compensation methodology. It is recommended that the compensation formula be reviewed by a team of administrative and physician leaders annually, taking into account changes in patient population, reimbursement, quality results, and patient satisfaction to allow for adjustment in the weights and measures included from year to year.

Physician participation in this process is necessary to engage those at the front line. An organization's ability to address physician's concerns and demonstrate a commitment to use of sound principles and metrics will allow for a sustainable model and an appropriate level of commitment to the organizational goals as they continue to evolve.

Bibliography

1. Doerr TD, Olson HB, Zimmerman DC. The accountable primary care model: Beyond medical home 2.0. *The American Journal of Accountable Care.* December 12, 2014; 54–61.
2. Milburn JB, Maurar M. Chapter 4. New reimbursement systems and value-based compensation incentives. In *Strategies for Value-Based Physician Compensation.* Englewood, Colorado: Medical Group Management Association, 2014.
3. Kerry BK. *Medicare's Value-based Physician Payment Modifier: Improving the Quality and Efficiency of Medical Care.* Princeton, New Jersey: Robert Wood Johnson Foundation. July 2012.

4. Physician Payment Reform Introduction. *VBP Physician Payment Reform Introduction.* http://www.nbch.org. Accessed 11/21/2014.
5. Value-Based Payment Modifier—Centers for Medicare and Medicaid Services. http://CMS.gov. Accessed 11/21/2014.
6. Fred Pennic. http://hitconsultant.net/2014/05/29/6-most-common-value-based-payment-models. Accessed 11/21/2014.
7. Efficiency & Effectiveness. Developing a compensation model that encourages value-based care. *Cost and Quality Academy Journal.* October 2014.
8. Expand Primary Care Panel Size Through Systemization. *Patient Activation.* The Advisory Board Company. 2014.
9. The Patient Centered Medical Home. *History, Seven Core Features, Evidence and Transformational Change.* Washington, DC: Robert Graham Center. Center for Policy Studies in Family Medicine and Primary care.
10. Floyd P. Roadmap for Physician Compensation in a Value-Based World. http://Physicanleaders.org. September/October 2014. Accessed 7/6/2015.
11. Green LV et al. Primary care physician shortages could be eliminated through use of teams, nonphysicians, and electronic communication. *Health Affairs.* 2013; 32(1): 11–19.
12. Roblin DW et al. Use of midlevel practitioners to achieve labor cost savings in the primary care practice of an MCO. HSR: *Health Services Research.* 2004; 39(3): 607–626.
13. Hollingsworth JM et al. Specialty care and the patient-centered medical home. *Med Care.* 2011; 49: 4–9; Bureau of Labor Statistics Occupational Outlook Handbook www.bls.gov/ooh/, accessed September 27, 2013. Health Care Advisory Board interviews and analysis.

Chapter 10

Technology and Decision Support

Katie Carow

Contents

EHRs, HIEs, and Federal Repositories: How Are EMRs, HIEs, and Federal and State Date Repositories Aiding in the Improvement of Population Health?

Past

The intent of healthcare data collection, in the past, was concentrated on reimbursement, utilization monitoring, and regulatory oversight. Payors, provider associations, specialty-specific registries, and quality organizations were the first aggregators of healthcare data. This information was often supplied due to government mandates, but was not available for audit or dissemination to the general public. The level of public data transparency was traditionally higher for acute care inpatient services. However, in more recent years, this degree of transparency has expanded to include some outpatient and ambulatory surgical procedures, home care, and skilled nursing services.

The primary reason for the increase in the quantity and quality of electronic healthcare information is to aid in achieving the goals of the Triple Aim (cost reduction, quality improvement, and increasing access to care). The impetus for this change was the passage of the American Recovery and Reinvestment Act (ARRA)/Health Information Technology for Economic and Clinical Health (HITECH) Act in February 2009. This was an effort to promote the adoption and meaningful use (MU) of health information technology across the industry. Grants and funds were designated that encouraged the automation of health information at the individual provider, hospital, system, state, regional, and national levels.

Through passage of the HITECH Act, incentives and penalties were outlined for the adoption of Electronic Health Records (EHRs) and adherence to MU criteria. (Meaningful use is defined as using certified EHR technology to improve quality, safety, efficiency; reduce health disparities; engage patients and family, improve care coordination, and population and public health).[1] These incentives and penalties encouraged hospitals and physicians to adopt EHRs at a rapid rate since the maximum financial support for adoption, was only available for hospitals and providers attesting to participate by 2012. Further encouraging adoption, were the looming financial penalties. These penalties would be incurred by providers participating in the Medicare and Medicaid programs, who did not transition to EHRs by 2015.

In 2010 and 2011, the Office of the National Coordinator for Health Information Technology (ONC) designated grant funding to encourage the collection and exchange of health information at both the regional- and state-levels. The state and regional processes were parallel to the national interoperability initiatives that were implemented. As a result of these initiatives, 56 organizations which included states, territories, and qualified state designated entities, were awarded funds to increase connectivity and enable the transmission of patient-centered data to improve the quality and efficiency of care.[1,31]

Additional state initiatives being championed by both the All Payor Claims Database (APCD) Council and the National Association of Healthcare Data Organizations are the implementation of an all-payor claims database. Twelve states already collect all-payor data, six states are currently in the implementation phase, and seventeen have indicated a strong interest in adopting all-payor data.[2]

At the same time, Regional Health Improvement Collaboratives (RHICs), under the national Network for Regional Healthcare Improvement, are in the process of documenting best practices and recommending processes and standards, based upon detailed "big data" analysis and best practices.

At the national level, the Agency for Healthcare Research and Quality (AHRQ) has been funding research, data collection, and dissemination of evidence and evidence-based tools to provide guidelines on care delivery. The ultimate goal is to achieve higher quality and cost reductions. Most of AHRQ's activities, in the past, have been focused on hospitals, but with care transitioning to other delivery settings, their research is also expanding.[3] One other aggregator of clinical data includes the Patient-Centered Clinical Research Network (PCORnet). These are organizations comprised of multiple clinical data research networks to study the trajectory of chronic diseases and identify therapies that benefit the most from them.

All of these initiatives at the individual, micro, and macro levels of the healthcare delivery system are concurrently driving the U.S. Healthcare System toward more data-driven evidence-based care delivery. How this magnitude of knowledge will be applied to enhance care is currently in pilot and early innovator stages of adoption.

Present

Claims data and EHRs are currently the largest source of healthcare information available driving population health clinical decisions. The degree to which this information is available and accessible varies based on the type of hospital and financial situation. Because of the state and Federal incentives offered to and assessed against providers, EHR installations accelerated. However, the majority of organizations are not consistently using the data to drive clinical decisions and improve population health...yet.

The organizations that have lagged in their adoption of EHRs were critical access, rural independent, and financially challenged hospitals in addition to Federally Qualified Health Centers (FQHCs). However, this has improved dramatically. In 2013, 78% of the office-based physicians reported that they adopted some type of EHR system.[4] In 2012, 79.3% of FQHCs reported using EHRs in all their sites, in comparison to 50.7% in 2010[5], 89% of Critical Access Hospitals reported that they are using an EHR.[6]

Although the percentage of organizations installing EHRs is increasing, the challenge continues to be how many organizations can attest to MU and actually begin to use the data to drive care decisions. The proportion of FQHCs that was ready for Stage 1 MU more than doubled from 2010 to 2012 at 36.7%, but this remains far lower than the 79.3% who reported having an EHR.[5] As of July 2013, 61% of Critical Access Hospitals had attested to Stage 1 MU, compared to 89% of Critical Access Hospitals reporting they had an EHR. About half of all physicians, 48% had an EHR system with advanced functionalities in 2013, which was double the adoption rate in 2009.[4] Although the increases are impressive, there is still room for continued adoption and application of the information to drive care decisions.

Three of the more innovative organizations in terms of their adoption and use of Health IT and "big data" are the Veterans Health Administration (VHA), Cleveland Clinic, and Mayo Clinic. They are culling and aggregating data from disparate sources, including EHRs, and are using this information to drive clinical care. Some hospitals are accomplishing this within their own organizations, and others are forming commercialized partnerships to help accomplish their goals.

The VHA is one example of an advanced Health IT organization that is managing their patient population independently. The VHA EHR system has clinical reminders and alerts, with bar code technology to validate patients' drug unit dosages, and electronic access to laboratory and radiology findings. To further capitalize on the EHR information gathered, the VHA also constructed a Corporate Data Warehouse that consolidates 60 domains of clinical and operational data including demographics, lab results, outpatient pharmacy medications, vital signs, and immunizations. This information is upgraded every four hours for near-time analysis and reporting. For acute inpatients, the VHA uses the data to identify at-risk populations for hospitalization or death by analyzing demographics, inpatient and outpatient diagnoses, vital signs, medications, lab results, and prior use of health services. For outpatients, primary care practice information has been loaded into the Corporate Data Warehouse, which allows for improved post-hospitalization discharge follow-up and reduced hospitalizations for low acuity conditions. The VHA also has the ability to monitor care along the continuum within their system. Patients are assigned a Care Assessment Score which highlights to providers those patients in their panel needing a care plan, so appropriate referrals can be made to VHA sites using geospatial maps near the patient's work or home. Even more ambitious, the VHA is enrolling veterans in a genomics longitudinal study. This will be the largest government study of this type, requiring volumes of structured, as well as unstructured data, such as clinical progress notes, texts, and e-mails.[34]

Both the Cleveland Clinic and the Mayo Clinic have decided to work with external companies to achieve their population health goals. The Cleveland Clinic partners with Explorys, a spin-off company founded by its CMO and the co-founders of Everstream, to aggregate, analyze, and apply predictive analytics to drive care. Through the partnership, the Cleveland Clinic is able to integrate clinical data, identify at-risk populations, measure the cost of care, and determine the breakeven for pay-for-performance contracts. Historically, most hospitals used claims data to manage the revenue cycle, but the Cleveland Clinic is now using "big data" analytics to inform doctors and allied health professionals on care delivery decisions. Over a half million Cleveland Clinic patients have access to a Personal Health Record which allows for viewing of appointments and test results, reviewing of physician notes, and refilling prescriptions. In order to provide this level of intelligence, Cleveland Clinic followed a multistep approach to data aggregation, which involved identifying all of the sources of data, gathering out-of-network claims from payors, and merging this with information from non-affiliated physicians. Explorys was able to provide the IT support to make this a reality by compiling the data and providing a sophisticated search engine. Because Explorys contracts with many healthcare entities, they are also able to provide comparative benchmark data using information from a multitude of hospitals. The aggregated data gives providers at the Cleveland Clinic the ability to identify patients at a macro level, so that the at-risk populations in need of preventative services, who are not currently utilizing the Cleveland Clinic, can be contacted to maintain their health.[7]

In 2013, The Mayo Clinic and Optum, a subsidiary of UnitedHealth Group, decided to found Optum Labs to improve the value of healthcare by accelerating innovation and translation, using emerging infrastructure and data resources to determine treatment efficacy, cost effectiveness and outcomes, and tapping the expertise of diverse industry stakeholders to address critical innovation issues in the healthcare industry. The backbone of the Optum Labs database is patient-level claims data from 150 million individuals, over 10 years, merged with consumer and physician data, health risk appraisals, demographics, and mortality data. This database includes additional information such as plan enrollment details, medical and pharmaceutical claims, lab results, and notes that are abstracted and normalized from EHRs. This level of information is significant because it allows Optum Labs' 21 collaborating partners (as of July 2015) to develop research agendas and select research and methodological studies aimed at developing new scientific approaches to healthcare at the practitioner and patient level. The application of this knowledge allows the Mayo Clinic to study the collective outcomes of many patients and apply the best individualized treatment when multiple chronic conditions exist. Based on this magnitude of research and practical clinical application, Mayo Clinic is able to inform policy decisions and national and international initiatives.[8]

These three organizations illustrate the most advanced applications of EHR systems being utilized in hospitals and systems, today. However, the level of change extends far beyond the hospital walls, looking to public health, education, and societal issues at a national level.

Future

The amount of healthcare data that will be transparently available going forward is voluminous. Collaborators, associations, and the Federal government are all working toward the common goal of interoperable, aggregated, and uniform data sets to study and improve population health. Regardless if work will be completed through several groups, or through one centralized agency, care will be delivered based on analytical and qualitative data with cost to cure considerations. The end result will be evidence-based strategies to maintain wellness, encourage prevention of disease in at-risk populations, and direct treatments provided based on outcomes and costs. The Office of the National Coordinator for Health Information Technology (ONC) has illustrated the flow of information and resulting knowledge (Figure 10.1).

In order to achieve this goal, various collaborative entities have emerged who are attempting to standardize all healthcare data aggregated, to enable collective analysis and drive national, but also possibly international care

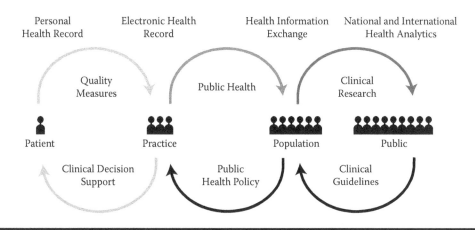

Figure 10.1   Information flow of healthcare data. (From The Office of the National Coordinator for Health Information Technology, Connecting Health and Care for the Nation: A Shared Nationwide Interoperability Roadmap, Federal Government Report, 2015.)

decisions. The organization that appears to have the most significant Federal support is HealtheWay with their eHealth Exchange and Carequality initiatives. The mission of the organization is to reduce barriers to interoperability and enable the trusted exchange of health information across the nation through public and private collaboration. The ultimate goal is to build consensus on policies and standards to minimize barriers to interoperability and provide services that enable health information exchange networks to interoperate.[9]

A second major interoperability initiative that has national vendor support is the CommonWell Health Alliance, which announced its formation at the HIMSS 2013 National Conference. The mission of the CommonWell Health Alliance is to create a vendor-neutral platform that breaks down the technological and process barriers, which currently inhibit the exchange of health data. The Alliance is focused on creating a national infrastructure with common standards and policies for data exchange that all of its members, and other technology companies, adopt.

Once national interoperability of data and aggregation is achieved, organizations such as the National Institutes of Health (NIH), PCORI, AHRQ, and CancerLinQ will possess enhanced capabilities to analyze population health trends, identify successful preventative measures and high efficacy treatments, estimate possible outcomes and the associated costs, and improve care delivery. The NIH Collaboratory will capitalize on interoperability even further to develop evidence based on clinical trial designs to evaluate current practices and inform future care. PCORI, an additional national collaborative, will be able to fund more comparative effectiveness research originating from disparate EHRs and other data sources, and also incorporate information from patient-powered research networks related to specific conditions. The AHRQ utilizes evidence to improve the safety, quality, accessibility, and affordability of care, with efforts being placed on increasing adoption. A final example of what the future capabilities could be are being developed through the American Society of Clinical Oncology (ASCO) CancerLinQ. This organization will have the ability to aggregate and analyze information originating from academic cancer centers, in addition to community-based entities nationally, to define the care being delivered, benchmark quality metrics, improve patient outcomes, and provide real-time clinical decision support for patient care.[10]

It is through the study of healthcare analytics, using statistics and actuarial support, merged with clinical expertise, that healthcare will be improved and cost reduced.

Middleware/Connection Technologies: How Is Middleware Being Used to Facilitate the Exchange of Information and Improve Interoperability between Different Systems? Is Middleware a Midterm Solution?

Middleware, as defined by Webster's dictionary, is the "Software that mediates between an application program and a network. It manages the interaction between disparate applications across the heterogeneous computing platforms." Currently, healthcare organizations are struggling with the exchange and integration of information. This can be attributed to two factors: a significant increase in the volume of data that is electronically collected through EHRs, payor claims, demographic data, and governmental registries; and the explosion of technologies that are available to monitor patient's health on-site, at healthcare facilities, and remotely. This has resulted in an overflow of information, but is useless in the absence of synthesized guidance without middleware technology. Silos are formed with high-tech systems and devices that do not effectively communicate with each other and do not enhance the holistic care of a patient.

There are multiple situations that would prove to be beneficial to the patient if technological devices were interoperable and the flow of information (tests results, medical history, current medicines, and health status) were possible (Figure 10.2).

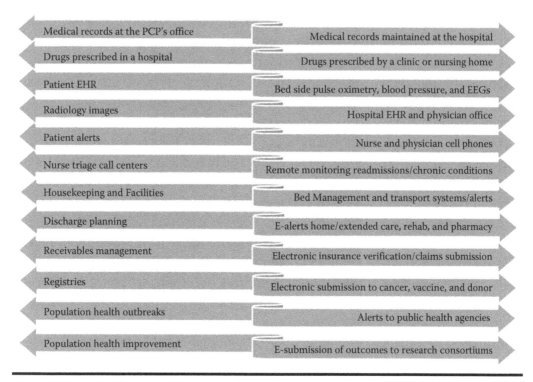

Figure 10.2   Challenges of interoperability in healthcare.

Some information is currently interoperable, but the difficulty is the degree of interoperability is inconsistent among and within organizations. The cause of the interoperability is the legacy systems in place that are now being merged. Recent requirements to meet MU, the development of Health Insurance Exchanges (HIEs) and the need to transfer financial information using X12 standards are accelerating the pace toward interoperability. Because of this, more emphasis is being placed on standards-based representation of information and communication.[11] Without seamless integration, it opens the door to safety and quality errors, minimizes cost reductions due to duplication of efforts, and prevents care delivery in off-site locations. Less than one-third of healthcare entities have integrated their EHR systems with even some of their medical devices, according to the Healthcare Information and Management Systems Society. When that information is not transmitted electronically, it has to be manually entered into the EHR by nurses, taking them away from direct patient care and potentially leading to dangerous errors. It is estimated that improved interoperability between medical devices and EHRs would save the U.S. healthcare system $30 billion a year.[12] The inability to collectively aggregate information from the various systems, stymies progress toward population health improvement and collective research to determine best practices and preventative care.

One solution to the existing interoperability dilemma is the purchase of middleware that allows legacy systems to communicate with one another to be able to populate data warehouses. The middleware maps the fields in the legacy systems to the EHR or data warehouse. Currently, most middleware focuses on enabling communication at the request of applications, abstracting various pieces of information, at set times, such as historic weights and imaging scans to assess changes over time and aid in diagnosis. However, more robust middleware programs include systems that integrate data real time.[13]

The more advanced middleware systems are able to exchange data in a variety of formats. These include live data streams, with programmed alerts that notify caregivers of significant changes or life-threatening incidents. Additionally, today's complex middleware has the ability to provide different levels of security and access, meeting Health Insurance Portability and Accountability Act (HIPAA) standards, based upon who is querying the information. Sophisticated middleware systems have prioritization of information and transmission flexibility built into their capabilities, so that audio alerts can override on-going monitoring, smartphones receive text alerts, while family members receive e-mails. The systems can also integrate treatment/intervention results, provider notes and feedback, on-going physiological results, and environmental conditions.

There are several providers currently offering middleware technologies: Orion Healthcare, Oracle Fusion, Emdeon, Surescripts, Zoeticx, Intersystems, Edifecs, Health Language Inc., Intelligent Medical Objects, RTI Connext, ECRI, Covisint, Vision Share, and DICOM Grid, to name a few. Each company specializes in different aspects of connectivity. There is no single middleware source for connecting all devices, or this chapter would be unnecessary! Each middleware company has varied expertise from EHR unification; deidentification of patient information to allow for secure movement of images and test results; conversion of biometric alerts to smartphone messaging; transmission of standard documents between Medicare and commercial payors, pharmacies, and providers; enabling translation services from free text to automated vocabularies; and data analysis using critical thinking functions. There are a limitless number of functions that middleware can serve to enhance data transmission.

However, it is not always realized that the applications, infrastructure, and resources underlying applications must be configured, in addition to being interoperable with external entities, such as HIEs, payors, the government, and Regional Health Information Exchanges (RHIC), too. Some experts say certain manufacturers of EHR systems and medical devices tend to limit interoperability, because there is no profit in making their systems interoperable; and device makers that want to make their products interoperable have to design them to interact with multiple EHR systems instead of using a uniform standard. Hospitals also indicate that they must purchase middleware software to connect patient monitoring systems, wireless utility systems, and infusion pumps to internal EHRs. But the use of middleware is pricey. Some estimate that it costs up to $10,000 per bed in one-time costs for medical device integration, which does not even account for the maintenance costs.[12]

A few experts believe middleware is a short-term Band-Aid until a permanent solution is developed. Aaron Goldmuntz, Vice President of Business Development for the Center for Medical Interoperability, said he expects that the adoption of standards would reduce the need for middleware and eventually eliminate it. However, he noted that middleware companies currently play a significant role in bridging the gaps of interoperability due to the number of legacy devices still in operation."[14] There is also a question if HIEs, which function as regional aggregators of data, will be sustainable in the long term, too, both due to the expiration of stimulus funds that seeded the startups and the decline in the need for HIEs as more systems are seamlessly integrated. The purchase of middleware to maximize the functionality of other technologies, results in an incremental price and adds a layer of complexity to existing networks and systems. If national initiatives encouraging the adoption of standards and aggregation of healthcare data are passed, the need for middleware will diminish.

Only time will tell if middleware will be necessary in the future. However, the ONC has recently published a document to outline a 10-year plan to achieve national interoperability. Outlined below are the key long-term strategies (Figure 10.3).

In the short-term, the ONC has set goals to accomplish the following:

1. Establish a governance framework for interoperability that includes "overarching rules of the road," involving both the public and private sectors' implementation and operational-level issues, and a method for recognition and accountability for the organizations that comply with the rules.
2. Improve technical standards and implementation guidance for common clinical data set transmissions.
3. Advance policies and grants to create incentives to use common technical standards for clinical HIT transmissions.

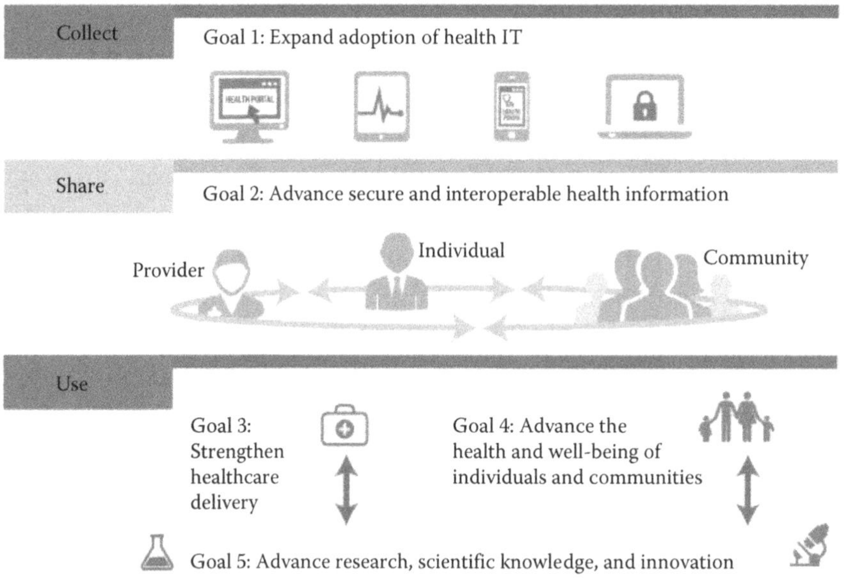

Figure 10.3   ONC 10-year long-term strategies. (From The Office of the National Coordinator for Health Information Technology, Connecting Health and Care for the Nation: A Shared Nationwide Interoperability Roadmap, Federal Government Report, 2015.)

4. Clarify privacy and security regulations, such as HIPAA rules, that enable data interoperability with covered entities and business associates.[15]

It will be interesting to observe what will be accomplished. The ONC's successes or failures will ultimately determine the long-term viability and need for middleware services.

Consumerism Applications: How Will the Information Gathered Aid Patients in Staying Healthy and Accessing Care, and Physicians in Diagnosing Illnesses and Improving Consumer Satisfaction?

Throughout this chapter, the primary discussion has been related to the adoption and use of technology, but the reason why analytics are being gathered is for the well-being of the patient. Consumerism is a recent buzz word in the healthcare field, although it has been used in other industries for years. The primary meaning of consumerism in healthcare is a movement in which patients are involved in their own care decisions through a partnership with physicians. Consumerism encourages health information empowerment and a basic understanding of body functions, chronic disease, and disease prevention. It involves patient education, through clinicians, to increase patients' involvement in the decision-making process.

Patient involvement and engagement in care decisions has dramatically increased in the last decade. This has led to the development and use of health and wellness apps, formation of disease-specific websites, and patient-promoted research. The increased level of ownership in personal health is evident, even at the highest levels of government, with Michelle Obama's "Let's Move!" program focused on raising a healthier generation of kids.

One key method that patients monitor their health is through mobile devices. In early 2013, the Pew Foundation's Tracking for Health Study found that 69% of Americans track some form of health-related information and fully 21% of Americans use some form of digital device.[16] The phone apps being used most frequently are geared toward exercise, diet, and weight, as illustrated in the chart of Figure 10.4. According to the Robert Wood Johnson study, there is a significant age-based difference in the adoption of health tracking apps on cell phones, ranging from 18% of those aged 66+, versus 100% for those aged 18–25. The purpose for cell phone tracking is also very different. The rate of self-tracking for a health-related reason is 69% versus 14% for a medical reason.[17] The ranking of health and medical tracking apps loaded on cell phones are consistent with this—blood pressure, diabetes, and medication are reported less frequently than exercise and diet (see below). One reason for this rate of app adoption could be the age of the population using the app tracking. As mentioned previously, the users of health tracking apps are much younger, and therefore, healthier, so they would have little need for medical or chronic condition apps (Figure 10.4).

Another form of patient consumerism is the exchange of knowledge through websites. These target specific medical conditions or foster research. Three of the more well-known websites are 23andMe, PatientsLikeMe, and Crohnology. The 23andMe website allows interested parties to submit samples for genetic testing and supplement it with family history and demographics. Participants have the ability to select the desired level of anonymity in which their genetic data is shared with researchers.[18] PatientsLikeMe is a public company which collects chronic disease information and shares deidentified data with "pharmaceutical companies, medical device companies, nonprofits, and research institutions." Initially,

What kind of apps do you currently have on your phone?

Of respondents who use cell phone apps, ranked from highest to lowest

Personal health data applications

- Exercise
- Diet
- Weight loss
- Athletic activity
- Sleep

Self-tracking for health and wellness (much lower usage)

- Blood pressure monitoring
- Diabetes monitoring
- Medication compliance monitoring

Figure 10.4   Health apps utilization. (Adapted from Personal Data for the Public Good: New Opportunities to Enrich Understanding of Individual and Population Health, 2014. Health Data Exploration Project. CAL IT2, UC Irvine and UC San Diego. Supported by a grant from the Robert Wood Johnson Foundation.)

PatientsLikeMe was open to patients with Lou Gehrig's disease, but now, the site has expanded to over 2000 diseases and conditions ranging from auto-immune disorders to behavioral health.[18,33] Crohnology is a patient-powered research network that is focused on finding a cure for Crohn's disease and colitis. This website aggregates patient provided data, such as periods of treatment and relative wellness, by asking research questions and conducting studies, to determine the efficacy of what works for participating members.[19] Like many disease-based websites, the continued existence is dependent upon engaged members' participation and research and grants funding on-going operating expenses.

Some of the more consumer-driven population health solutions, with a wellness focus, are more esoteric. One example is the Quantified Self movement. The website tag line is "self-knowledge through numbers." The group holds international meetings, conferences, community forums, develops web content, and offers a self-tracking guide—measuring weight and monitoring diabetes through wearable devices. Supporters of the movement track their activity, diet, mood, and sleep. They hold group meetings and use Internet discussion boards to share experiences and compare findings.[20] Another unique resource, available through an app, is CitiSense. It monitors the environment to identify toxic locales resulting from pollution caused by fertilizers, power plants, and traffic congestion. The data is aggregated, analyzed, and plotted using geospatial maps, so individuals can change their exposure and behavior to impact their personal health. This will benefit patients with COPD, asthma, and a host of other respiratory diseases.[21]

Even more prevalent than personal health tracking tools and websites, are consumerism strategies being implemented by providers in partnership with their patients. UH Rainbow Care Network, a pediatric hospital in Cleveland, is working with their most complex chronic patients to decrease hospital admissions. They provide patients with a multidisciplinary assessment which includes primary care and specialty physicians, social workers, and dietitians. UH Rainbow Care Network also develops a follow-up plan with the family to enhance the at-home support network. This has resulted in a reduction of costs and length of stay. North Shore-Long Island Jewish is also working with their costly patients in high-risk categories, such as cardiac and orthopedics, in a fashion similar to UH Rainbow Care Network, by using integrated specialty services, post-acute and community-based care, and follow-up.[22]

Maintaining health and partnering with the indigent pose unique challenges. These stem from societal issues such as education, income, and access to care. Four organizations that have formulated unique solutions, resulting in higher patient engagement and cost management, are Oak Street Health in Chicago, Catholic Health Initiatives in Louisville, Montefiore in New York, and Fairview Health in Minnesota. Oak Street Health provides its patients with both medical and social services to Medicare and Medicaid dual-eligibles. They have patient panels that are a fourth of the average panel size (500–750 patients). Patients are cared for using a team-approach which includes a geriatrician, nurse, medical assistant, and care coordinator. Because of the small panel size, more time is spent with each patient. If the patient is diagnosed with a chronic condition they are offered comprehensive follow-up appointments within 48 hours of discharge. All of this is being done to insure that care plans are followed. Additional amenities offered at Oak Street Health, include on-site dental and pharmacy services, transportation to clinics, and community gathering places for educational sessions or socializing. These are made available to encourage consumer engagement.

Catholic Health Initiatives also has a primary care program with patient instructions on how to manage chronic conditions. Their patients are low income, similar to Oak Street Health, so they are provided transportation to clinics and given telephones for compliance monitoring. Eighty percent of those in the primary care practice are enrolled. The health improvements were remarkable. After nine months, there was a 30% decline in ED visits and a 50% reduction in inpatient usage. The pilot was a win for both parties. Patients indicated better physical and mental health[23] and the amount of uncompensated care was estimated at a 10%–15% reduction, if implemented system-wide.

Another program to improve health is being piloted at Montefiore Medical Center in the Bronx. There is a high prevalence of childhood obesity in the community. Area students were all given Fitbits and appear to be very engaged in reviewing the statistics and seeing the impact. Outcome results, however are unavailable, as of today.

Fairview Health Services, in Minnesota, concentrates their efforts on partnering with the 5% of patients with the highest-cost conditions. These include chronic obstructive pulmonary disease and congestive heart failure. The potential savings from aggressively managing this population more than justifies the expense incurred from more frequent checkups, self-monitoring equipment, care manager calls, and even home care visits.[22]

As mentioned in the prior examples, physicians and hospitals are becoming more astute at partnering with patients to manage their chronic conditions and diseases. However, the greatest impact can be realized by identifying and targeting the broader population who are currently healthy, but at-risk for future diseases. Data collection and analyses are essential to identify patients at risk. One difficulty, mentioned by several CMS Medicare Shared Savings Program (MSSP) and Accountable Care Organization (ACO) Pilot participants, is the significant lag in Medicare and Medicaid claims prohibiting the monitoring of readmissions and the at-risk population. St. Luke's Health Partners in Idaho is one example of a provider engaging the at-risk patient population. They are beginning to use their analytics platform to not only manage their most acute patients, but also identify patients who are starting to get sick, so that they can be targeted for specific preventative services.

The increase in patient involvement in their care decisions, hence consumerism, also positively impacts overall satisfaction. Patients prefer to have control over health decisions. According to a HealthLeaders Media Population Health Survey, two-thirds (66%), of healthcare organizations, expect to invest in patient engagement programs, improving access by encouraging patients to become more aware of their own health status and their role in maintaining good health. Almost as many (60%) expect to implement wellness-related public outreach programs.[23] One example of an organization that has restructured around patient engagement is North Shore-Long Island Jewish. They have formed Care Solutions, which provides care management services to all the system's value-based programs and integrated their call center functions with physician offices to accomplish its "service-right-now" promise. They also train their care managers in behavioral science skills to aid in developing patient trust, including how body language and word choices influence perceived trust.[22]

In whatever mode patients choose to monitor their health, it will be necessary for society as a whole to implement plans for population health improvement. It would be short-sighted to assume that only healthcare organizations impact overall health. Extraneous influencers include physical and social environments, economic conditions, education, individual actions, and governmental policies. It is through the education of patients, and sharing of available knowledge and resources, that society will move the needle on improving health and wellness.

Technology in the Home: What Are the Wellness, Remote Monitoring, Diagnoses, and Treatment Devices That Can Be Used in the Home?

Remote monitoring devices and home-based technologies are one of the next big waves of healthcare. This care delivery approach meets the Triple Aim goals of reducing the cost of care, increasing quality, and improving access, while providing a high level of patient satisfaction and convenience.

"According to the AARP Public Policy Institute, nearly 90 percent of people over the age 65 indicate they want to stay in their home as long as possible, and 80% in the same age bracket believe their current home is where they will always live."[24] In order to enable seniors to "age-in-place," safety, health, and wellness services will need to be offered on-site at their residences. For the working adult needing healthcare services, biometric and wearable monitoring devices can monitor patients on the job, at home, and on vacation, adding a level of convenience that was previously unavailable. One patient, who owns a metal refinishing business with her husband, was quoted in Modern Healthcare as saying, "'We are very busy, and sometimes with a (doctor's) appointment, you have to wait 45 minutes,' she said. By messaging her doctor with their readings, they don't have to take the time to go to the doctor's office and interrupt their work. When they have to speak with Mejia, the physician, they contact him through the clinic's web-based portal and get a quick response. 'If I think of something in the middle of the night, I can send him a message and he'll answer in the morning,' she said."[25]

There is also some evidence that demonstrates that better outcomes result when remote monitoring occurs. One study published in the *Journal of the American Geriatrics Society*, indicated that positive outcomes are higher from care provided in the home versus at a traditional acute care hospital, with 44% of patients indicating improved Activities of Daily Living two weeks after admission to the home, while only 21% of patients indicating a decline; only 25% of patients admitted to an acute care hospital indicated improved Activities of Daily Living two weeks after admission, and 31% indicated a decline. Similar results were shown with the Instrumental Activities of Daily Living outcomes.[26]

Last, the costs of using remote monitoring and diagnostic devices are nominal in comparison to emergency department visits, inpatient hospital stays, and readmissions. One device, called the Health Buddy Program, integrates a telehealth tool with care managers for chronically ill Medicare beneficiaries. The Health Buddy telehealth program, was associated with spending reductions of approximately, $312–$542 per person per quarter, as compared to those only treated in the clinic.[27] Another study published in Health Affairs mentions savings of 19% from treating Medicare Advantage and Medicaid patients in the home, versus in an acute care setting, for common diagnoses. The savings were derived from lower average lengths-of-stay and fewer lab and hospital-based diagnostic tests.[32]

The three primary purposes for remote care include prevention, diagnoses, and treatment. These are useful for both patients and providers. Patients can submit their health status through wearable devices, phone apps, the Internet, cloud-based applications, wireless devices, or video applications. Below are several of the health technologies being used today.

Wearable Devices

The most publicized wearable device is the Apple Watch. It is a fitness and sports tracker, measures heart rate, sedentary time, distance of exercise, intensity, and calories burned. This is followed by Fitbit Surge, which is marketed as the "ultimate fitness super watch." The capabilities include GPS tracking of distance, pace and elevation climbed, PurePulse Heart Rate, steps climbed, calories burned, and running and cardio workouts synched to smartphones and computers. The Pulse O_2, offered by Withings, measures heart rate, blood oxygen level, and sleep cycle. This wirelessly syncs to the iOS and Android devices. Two other interesting products in development include wearable tattoos developed by MC10, similar to surgical tape, that detect patient vitals; and Peek Retina, which can be clipped over the camera of a smartphone to allow health workers to see inside an eye and capture high-quality images to be sent to experts for diagnosis. This can detect eye illnesses that are 80% treatable and currently result in blindness in 39M people. Google Glass is another wearable device that is well-known, although this technology has not been embraced by clinicians due to interoperability, security, and charging requirements. Once these obstacles are overcome, acceptance may increase. Google Glass allows the clinician and the patient to have a face-to-face conversation, while securely streaming the audio and visual appointment information, so it can accurately be recorded in the patient's electronic medical record real-time. The clinician also has the capability to pull up historical information from the EHR and have the results delivered to the Google Glass device.

Smartphone Apps

In addition to the wearable devices, there are a plethora of healthcare apps being developed for smartphones. Currently, the functionality for most apps is limited and the adoption rate minimal. In a study conducted by the INS Institute, it was found that 43,000 health-related apps are available in the Apple iTunes store. However, only 16,275 apps are directly related to patient health and treatment. More than 90% reviewed scored <40 out of 100 for functionality. While 10,840 of the apps reviewed provide and display information, <50% are also able to provide instructions and only 20% can capture user-entered data. The adoption rate of the apps is minimal, with <50% of available healthcare apps being downloaded fewer than 500 times. Five of the Apple iTunes healthcare apps account for 15% of all downloads.[28]

There are several patient-driven apps that are frequently used. Fitbit offers an app that can be accessed through a computer or smartphone that allows you to track your running and hiking stats, map your routes, workouts, and diet using bar codes.[30] Azumio currently leads the diabetes app market with 17.8% market share, according to a new report from Research2Guidance. This can be synched to a computer or smartphone. Another app that is available is called the AgaMatrix Health Manager that tracks glucose, insulin, carbs, and weight all in one place and can be easily e-mailed. The app is compatible with Apple and Android devices and the Cloud. Withings offers a Wireless Blood Pressure Monitor that is compatible with smartphones. Another app, called Oto, offered by Cellscope, attaches to your cell phones to examine your child's ears and forward videos to a doctor for evaluation within two hours.

There are also apps that are geared toward the provider. These top apps are all subscription based. The top five grossing medical Apple iTunes apps as of May 2014 include Epocrates, Sanford Guide, Micromedex Drug

Reference, ASCCP Mobile, and Tarascon Pharmacopedia. Three of the top five apps provide pharmacogenic information. Epocrates delivers clinical information, including a provider directory, drug information, drug interaction checker, medical calculators, and news. Sanford Guide focuses on infectious disease providers. Subscribers obtain access to comprehensive, treatment-focused coverage of bacterial, fungal, mycobacterial, parasitic, viral infections, and HIV/AIDS. It also includes anti-infective drug information, prevention, and useful tables, tools, and calculators to assist with dosing. Micromedex Drug Reference Essentials is very similar to the Sanford Guide. It provides access to drug information at the point of care. ASCCP Mobile is a disease-based app. It provides consensus guidelines and treatments for Managing Abnormal Cervical Cancer Screening Tests and Cancer Precursors after responses to patient-related questions are provided. The last of the top five apps is Tarascon Pharmacopedia. This app contains information on thousands of drugs to help clinicians make better decisions at the point of care.[29]

Hand-Held Devices

There are also hand-held devices such as glucose monitors with WaveSense Technology under the names of PrestoPro, BG Star, and MyStar Extra. Withings is another manufacturer that offers a variety of in-home health products that are compatible with RunKeeper, MyFitnessPal, and LoseIt. Another hand-held device is the Smart Body Analyzer which measures weight, body composition, air quality, and heart rate. One of the newer hand-held devices that has created much interest is rHealth. In 2014, it won the Nokia SensingX Challenge, but has not yet been IRB approved. It is a portable handheld device that can diagnose hundreds of diseases using a single drop of blood. All that is needed is mapping to each of the biomarkers.

Remote Monitoring/Coaching/Education

ADT, traditionally a security provider, is also starting to offer remote monitoring devices focused on senior care. They not only have GPS location devices, but also fall detection pendants and a two-way communication button. This is backed-up with 24/7 support and emergency responders. Prevent, sold by Omada, is a digital therapeutic used to reduce the risk for type 2 diabetes, heart disease, and obesity. They combine personal health coaching with the web, mobile, and smart devices. Their services offer a combination of behavioral, social support, and technology services to achieve patient change. MyGetWellNetwork also provides coaching, but in the form of education, through discharge instructions, prescriptions, education videos, and clinical pathways related to AMI, cardiac arrhythmia, COPD, DVT, diabetes, heart failure, pediatric asthma, pneumonia, pulmonary embolism, and total hip and knee replacements.

Telehealth Services

There are also video services available to reach health experts via computer or phone. 2nd.MD is one such technology. It is an employer paid benefit that provides second opinions via video conferencing. One of the larger telemedicine and telehealth solutions is offered by Vidyo. This allows hospitals, research centers, and physician clinics in both urban, and even more critical, rural markets, to visually connect patients and healthcare professionals, for routine checkups, home health services, telestroke assessments, and surgical consults. At UH Rainbow Care, an emergency telemedicine kiosk was installed in inner-city Cleveland that is open until 11 PM. An attendant sees patients and consults with an on-call physician who remotely examines the patients with a stethoscope, otoscope, and blood pressure monitor. This has avoided many ED visits. They also provide some of UH Rainbow Care's sickest patients, who are difficult to transport round-the-clock, access to a multidisciplinary team via telephone and telemedicine. The patients are then given iPad Minis, which are used to provide telemedicine consultations.[22]

 Despite the significant benefits of remote monitoring and devices available, adoption has not peaked. Interoperability with EHRs and other care delivery systems, continues to improve, but there are still inconsistencies. Second, there is a lack of reimbursement from commercial and government payors for many of the monitoring devices. Although the convenience of the devices, and enhanced outcomes, may lead to high customer satisfaction, the cost for the device and the on-going monitoring is often billed to the patient, rather than the insurer. There are also security issues to address. Only some of the technologies, which require the transmission of Personal Health Information (PHI) are currently HIPPA-compliant. Most importantly, physicians and clinicians are unaware of the technologies that exist. When providers are alerted to new devices, they have no criteria on which to evaluate technologies for their effectiveness and ability to supplement face-to-face care. Until these issues are addressed, the adoption of remote monitoring and diagnostic devices may lag.

Bibliography

1. *EHR Incentives & Certification*. February 6. Accessed March 7, 2015. http://www.healthit.gov/providers-professionals/meaningful-use-definition-objectives.
2. Council, APCD. Copyright 2009–2015 UNH, the APCD Council, and NAHDO. *Interactive State Report Map*. Accessed March 7, 2015. http://www.apcdcouncil.org/state/map.
3. Feinstein KW. *Regional Health Improvement Collaboratives*. Pittsburgh, PA: Jewish Healthcare Foundation and Pittsburgh Regional Health Initiative, 2011.
4. Room, HHS Press. *More physicians and hospitals are using EHRs than before*. August 7, 2014. Accessed March 8, 2015. http://www.hhs.gov/news/press/pres/08/20140807a.html.
5. Furukawa M, Jones E. Adoption and use of electronic health records among federally qualified health centers grew substantially during 2010–2012. In *Health Affairs*, 1254–1261. Bethesda, MD: Project HOPE, 2014.
6. Gabriel MH, Furukawa MF, Jones EB, King J, Samy LK. *Progress and Challenges with the Implementation and Use of Electronic Health*. September 2013. Accessed March 8, 2015. http://www.healthit.gov/sites/default/files/cah-data_brief12.pdf.
7. Harris CM. Interview by enabling population management for clinically integrated networks—Modern Healthcare. *HIMSS 2014 Annual Conference*, Orlando, FL. Chief Information Officer and Chairman of the Information Technology Division at Cleveland Clinic.
8. Wallace P, Shah N, Dennen T, Crown W. Optum labs: Building a novel node in the learning health care system. In *Health Affairs*, 1187–1194. Bethesdaa, MD: Project HOPE, 2014.
9. Healtheway, Inc. 2015. *About HealtheWay*. Accessed March 8, 2015. http://healthewayinc.org/about-us/.
10. Howie L, Hirsch B, Locklear T, Abernethy AP. Assessing the value of patient-generated data to comparative effectiveness research. In *Health Affairs*. Bethesda, MD: Project HOPE, 2014, pp. 1220–1227.
11. Someshwar P. Interoperability: Not a non-issue. *Healthcare IT News*. June 13, 2013. Accessed March 9, 2015. http://www.healthcareitnews.com/blog/interoperability-not-non-issue?page = 0.
12. Lee J. Hospitals expected to press devicemakers, EHR vendors to make their products 'talk'. *Modern Healthcare*. November 23, 2013. Accessed March 10, 2015. http://www.modernhealthcare.com/article/20131123/MAGAZINE/311239982.
13. Bacon JS, Jean M. On middleware for emerging health services. *Journal of Internet Services and Applications* 2014; p. 8.

14. Greenspun H, Deloitte Center for Health Solutions, Deloitte LLP. Four actions to put health care on a path toward system-wide interoperability. *Deloitte.* February 12, 2015. Accessed July 22, 2015. http://blogs.deloitte.com/center-forhealthsolutions/2015/02/four-actions-to-put-health-care-on-a-path-toward-system-wide-interoperability.html#.VP-yxfnF8no.

15. The Office of the National Coordinator for Health Information Technology, Connecting Health and Care for the Nation: A Shared Nationwide Interoperability Roadmap, Federal Government Report, 2015.

16. Duggan M, Fox S. Tracking for health. *Pew Research CenterInternet, Science and Tech.* January 28, 2013. Accessed March 13, 2015. http://www.pewinternet.org/2013/01/28/tracking-for-health/.

17. Personal Data for the Public Good: New Opportunities to Enrich Understanding of Individual and Population Health, 2014. Health Data Exploration Project. CAL IT2, UC Irvine and UC San Diego. Supported by a grant from the Robert Wood Johnson Foundation.

18. 2015. *23andMe.* Accessed March 12, 2015. https://www.23andme.com/.

19. 2015. *Crohnology.* Accessed March 12, 2015. https://crohnology.com/.

20. n.d. *QS Quantified Self.* Accessed March 12, 2015. http://conference.quantified-self.com/.

21. Misleh C. *CitiSense.* August 27, 2010. Accessed March 13, 2015. https://sosa.ucsd.edu/confluence/display/CitiSensePublic/CitiSense.

22. Larkin H. Lessons for hospitals transitioning to population health management. *H&HN Hospitals & Health Networks*, December 9, 2014. www.hhnmag.com/Magazine/2014/Dec/fea-pophealth-population-health-care-lessons.

23. Ferris T, Frankowski A, Soencer G. *Population Health: Are You as Ready as You Think You are?* Intelligence Report, Brentwood, TN: HealthLeaders Media, 2014.

24. Farber N, Shinkle D, Lynott J, Fox-Grage W, Harrell R. *Aging in Place: A State Survey of Livability Policies and Practices.* This In Brief Research Report, Washington, DC: National Conference of State Legislatures with the AARP Public Policy Institute, 2011.

25. Conn J. Staying connected providers and patients increasingly relying on home-based monitoring. *Modern Healthcare*, January 18, 2014. www.modernhealthcare.com/article/20140118/Magazine/301189929.

26. Leff B, Burton L, Mader SL, Naughton B, Burl J, Greenough, III WB, Guido S, Steinwachs D. Comparison of functional outcomes associated with hospital at home care and traditional acute hospital care. *Journal of the American Geriatric Society* 2009; 57(2):273–278.

27. Baker LC, Johnson SJ, Macaulay D, Birnbaum H. Integrated telehealth and care management program for medicare beneficiaries with chronic disease linked. *Health Affairs* 2011; 30(9):1689–1697.

28. Goedert J. IMS health expands support for mobile medical apps. *Health Data Management.* December 13, 2013. Accessed March 15, 2015. http://www.healthdatamanagement.com/news/ims-health-expands-support-for-mobile-medical-apps-47002-1.html.

29. Dolan B. In-depth: Top 200 paid iPhone apps for medical professionals. *MobiHealth News*. May 19, 2014. Accessed March 15, 2015. http://mobihealth-news.com/32972/in-depth-top-200-paid-iphone-apps-for-medical-professionals/.

30. Comstock J. Prediction: 24 million will use diabetes apps by 2018. *MobiHealth News*. March 24, 2014. Accessed March 15, 2015. http://mobihealthnews.com/31313/prediction-24-million-will-use-diabetes-apps-by-2018/.

31. HealthIT.gov. *State Health Information Exchange*. March 14, 2014. Accessed March 7, 2015. http://www.healthit.gov/policy-researchers-implementers/state-health-information-exchange.

32. Cryer L, Shannon SB, Van Amsterdam M, Leff B. Costs for hospital at home' patients were 19 percent lower, with equal or better outcomes compared to similar inpatients. *Health Affairs* 2012; June: 1237–1243.

33. 2005–2015. *PatientsLikeMe*. Accessed March 12, 2015. http://www.patients-likeme.com/.

34. Fihn S, Francis J, Clancy C, Nielson C, Rumsfeld J, Cullen T, Bates J, Graham G. Insights from advanced analytics at the veterans health administration. In *Health Affairs*, 1203–1210. Bethesda, MD: Project HOPE, 2014.

35. Hardy J. AHRQ FY 2015 Budget details activities, effort needed to fulfill new mission. www.ahrq.gov. March 14, 2014. http://www.ahrq.gov/news/newsletters/e-newsletter/416.html. Accessed March 7, 2015.

Chapter 11

Patient Engagement

George Mayzell

Contents

Any time you mention accountability in healthcare, Accountable Care Organizations (ACOs) and other similar entities that shift the responsibility of quality and cost of care to physicians and physician organizations, you always hear the complaint, "what about the patient?" Most physicians feel it is unfair to be held accountable for quality, cost, and outcomes when patient behaviors, compliance, and engagement are not held to the same standard.

While this seems inherently unfair, the landscape is now changing. In fact, patient compliance, adherence, and cooperation generally follows the classic bell-shaped curve with some patients being compliant, some noncompliant, but most reside somewhere in the middle. Physicians tend to the focus on those few noncompliant patients. In a classic population health

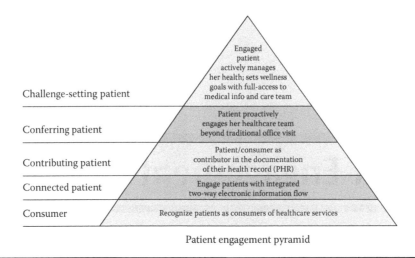

Figure 11.1   The Patient Engagement Pyramid, Hello Health Blog, August 8, 2014.

model, where the population is large, the few noncompliant patients do not skew the data in a significant way.

Consequently, there is much work is going on in the area of patient engagement. Better physician communication and improved patient health-care literacy should improve adherence and compliance (Figure 11.1).

Consumerism

The employers have historically decided traditional healthcare insurance. Since World War II, employers have been the major source of the funding of health insurance benefits. Employer-financed healthcare often means the employer selected the payer and the general benefit structure giving the members few choices among differing benefit structures. The increasing cost of healthcare premiums and the increasing competition of businesses, especially on an international basis, have driven employers to demand more economical models of providing healthcare to their employees. To date, there have been a few major changes that have provided effective solutions to decrease overall cost to these employers.

One of these changes is the advent of consumer-directed healthcare and/ or high deductible health plans. In this benefit structure, deductibles can range from one thousand to several thousands of dollars, so this shifts the cost to the employee/patient. This means free market considerations drive decision making and the patient is becoming a more involved consumer.

Price transparency has contributed the shift to model. Patients are now becoming true consumers, shopping for the best price and value in healthcare, and asking more questions about price. Consumers are also beginning to compare quality as well as price, in their decision making.

In the following section, we will divide the patient engagement activities into patient-centered activities; payer and health plan models, public health and public policy initiatives, and employer-based initiatives.

The second major change is the advent of both private and public healthcare insurance exchanges. Many employers (Walgreens being a poster child) are changing the model from a "defined benefit" plan to a "defined contribution" plan. In this model, employers are contributing a certain dollar amount to their employees (or family) and requiring them to go to private exchanges and select their own healthcare plan. These employers are glad to get out of the healthcare delivery business while still providing healthcare coverage for their employees.

From the employee's point of view, they must become the engaged consumers of healthcare since they are now selecting their own insurance coverage and benefit plan structures. We are moving from a business-to-business model to a business-to-consumer model. Many of these employees are selecting plans with high deductibles to reduce the overall premium. The research has clearly shown that when consumers are given the choice, they will select the least expensive plans, which often have higher deductibles, copays, and coinsurance. In this new model of consumerism, these employees are becoming very involved in the healthcare decision making process, since they are now directly paying the bill. This is being called the "retailization" of healthcare and is directly contributing to increased member engagement.

Attribution

As we move through new engagement models a big piece is the assignment of patients to a healthcare delivery system and physician provider. Currently, the model of connectivity is called "attribution." Patients are matched to their primary caregivers as part of a patient population. There are many different methodologies that may be used to do this; however, most of the models are based on various criteria. These include: the most recent visits, the number of visits, preventive health visits (or G code visits), and primary care physicians.

There is typically a mathematical model for attribution that links these patients to the physician that is providing the most relevant care. In many models, this is a primary care physician; however, in some models specialist attribution is also allowed. Some models may include physician extenders such as nurse practitioners and physician assistants to have "attributed" members.

Attribution becomes a critical factor to building aligned populations for population health management. Many delivery systems are specifically focusing, not only building a large volume of attributed members, but also making sure the right members are attributed to right physicians. This aggregated group of attributed members becomes the population, which can then be "managed" via new payment models and measurement of quality outcomes. In the future of healthcare delivery, many feel that the delivery system that has the most attributed members will be the most successful. One of the greatest challenges is that it is contingent on patients actually seeing their physician to "tag" them as connected. A key part of new engagement model is how we align patients that have not had a physician visit during the attributed period of time. These are often the patients that may only see their physician for acute episodes or may not see them at all, or may only see them every few years. In order for the financial models to work, these patients must be attributed to providers as well. These are future patients and you want them aligned to your delivery system prior to needing healthcare. This is one of the reasons why engagement of this low risk group becomes critical.

Next, we will divide the patient engagement activities into patient-centered activities, payer and health plan models, and employer models, public health and public policy initiatives, and employer-based initiatives.

Patient Engagement

In the traditional healthcare delivery system, patients have often not been active participant in their care, rather than a leader in directing their own healthcare. In the current model, payers, network referrals, and network steerage have not incentivized the patient for making healthier decisions. With the new benefit designs we are seeing in the market and with the changes in healthcare payment reform, this is rapidly changing. The patient is now becoming fiscally responsible for their own healthcare, and more importantly for their own health (Figure 11.2).

The Unengaged Patient

Healthcare providers want patients to take a more active role in their own care because it leads to lower costs and better outcomes. A review of 31 national surveys suggests it has been an elusive goal.

50%	60%	30%	61%
Medicare patients who usually don't bring a list of questions to doctors' appointments	Adults who don't tell health professionals they have drug allergies unless specifically asked	Adults who have never compared a medication they received from a pharmacist against their doctor's order	Americans who don't maintain their own medical record (paper or electronic)

Source: Center for Advancing Health, 2010

Figure 11.2 From the 2010 report "Snapshot of People's Engagement in their Healthcare." (From the Center for Advancing Health, 2010, http://www.cfah.org. © 2015. All rights reserved. With permission.)

As we consider increasing deductibles for patients and since consumer directed health plans and high deductible benefit programs are becoming more of the norm, the patient has a significant financial incentive to make good economic and healthcare decisions.

Additionally, with the evolution of healthcare insurance exchanges, healthcare is becoming much more retail driven. Historically, employers selected the insurer and the employee would have a few alternatives to choose from.

Large companies are now moving to "defined contribution" models where they are providing their employees a defined amount of money and the employees are directed to public or private exchanges to acquire their healthcare coverage. In this situation, the consumer is now making a "retail decision" on which type of coverage to purchase.

As a result, the future cost of healthcare will significantly be borne by individuals.

We are seeing a transition from healthcare's traditional business-to-business model to an emerging consumer and consumer driven model, or business to consumer model.

> We all grew up in the industry calling them patients. Then we made them wait and hope they are patient. Call them consumers or customers and you will see them through a new lens. This new perspective will change your organization.

Steve Lefar
CEO SG2

In this future model, we must engage the patient in a very different way. As we stratify patients into different groups, the engagement model is dependent on which groups they fall into.

In the high-risk patient category, engagement is through care management. This model is about sharing data and one-on-one communication between the patient (and in some cases, family members) and the patient care coordinator. This may include clinical care coordination but also can include dealing with the socioeconomic needs and high-risk behaviors. The bond can often be very intimate in that a mutual dependency is built over time. This evolving relationship can be a collaborative one built over time through effective communication (Figure 11.3).

In the medium-risk category are patients with chronic diseases. This is a clinical model using nurses practicing at the "top of their license" and others to help control and mitigate the risk of these chronic diseases. This includes strategies such as managing hemoglobin A-1 C in diabetics and blood pressure in hypertensive. These medium-risk categories are complex because many of these patients have multiple comorbidities. Historically, these patients were managed with specific disease management programs, however, that was typically only focused on one disease. The relationship with the care manager is often indirect and through the physician's office and their nursing staff and often focused on healthcare literacy and the sharing of information. It is often about making sure critical tests are completed and results shared with the appropriate parties. The patient engagement here is critical.

The next categories are much more challenging. These categories are where the "rubber meets the road" in terms of population health

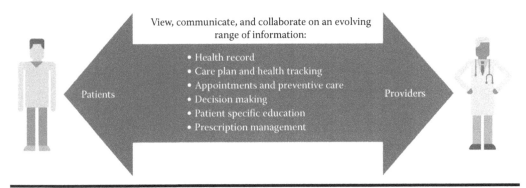

View, communicate, and collaborate on an evolving range of information:

- Health record
- Care plan and health tracking
- Appointments and preventive care
- Decision making
- Patient specific education
- Prescription management

Patients   Providers

Figure 11.3 Athena Health, 5 Elements of a Successful Patient Engagement Strategy, February 2014. (From http://www.pewinternet.org/fact-sheets/mobile-technology-fact-sheet/. With permission.)

management. The prior categories have most often been part of care management in the payer-based model. Most payers have struggled with engagement of this group of patients since it is more about wellness and prevention. Traditionally, health plans were not compensated for focusing on this population, so there was little focus. These include "rising risk" and "low risk" patients. In this group of patients, it is more about managing risk factors, identifying the determinants of risk, and other population-focused metrics. These include things like obesity, proper diet, exercise, smoking cessation, and other classic public health and population health initiatives. This group of patients is focused on behavioral change and makes up the very broad part of the pyramid of population health. It is almost impossible for a care manager to deal with patients on an individual basis in this category, so the focus is on general healthcare literacy, education, and behavior change at a group level. It is often through physician practices and a community focus and is one example of where the "medical neighborhood" can be the solution.

As stated previously, it is the "low risk" and "rising risk" populations that are the most challenging. Traditionally, these patients and the engagement of these groups, are where much of the research is ongoing (Figure 11.4).

One great example of this is the new rebranding of Walgreens, which is now marketing itself as the "the corner of happy and healthy." They are now focused on prevention, immunizations, and other strategies that focus on health, and not just healthcare. As an example, they recently discontinued the sale of tobacco products from their stores in an effort to promote health behavior (Figures 11.5 and 11.6).

Theories of Behavior Change

One of the most important areas of patient engagement is getting patients to focus on their own risky behaviors especially smoking, obesity, exercise, and compliance with prescribed therapies that can impact their overall health. This trans theoretical model was developed by James Prochaska at the University of Rhode Island.[16]

One of the prominent behavioral change models is called the Transtheoretical Model of Behavior change or TPM. TPM is concentrated in six stages of change and 10 processes of change. Only 20% of the population at risk is actively prepared to make appropriate changes at any given time.

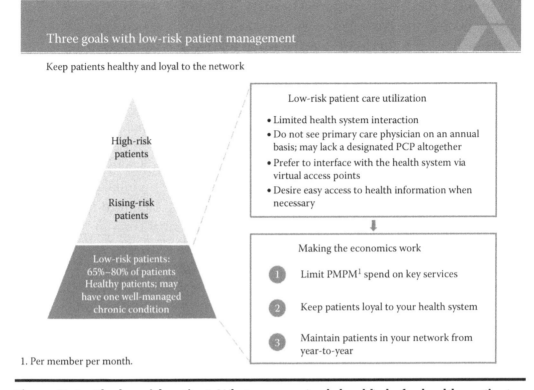

Figure 11.4   The low-risk patient. What you can (and should) do for healthy patients. (From the Advisory Board Company. © 2013. All rights reserved. With permission.)

The stages of changes are as follows:

Precontemplation: The patients in this stage are not considering change and no positive action is planned over the next six months.

Contemplation: In this stage, patients intend to change in the next six months. They are aware of some of the pros and cons of their behavior and are focused on the pros. This is often labeled as procrastination.

Preparation: Patients plan to take action over the next 30 days and there is a plan in place.

Action: This is the stage where overt change is taking place.

Maintenance: The focus here is on continued compliance and prevention of relapses. This can last from six months to five years.

Termination: This is when there is no longer a risk of relapse. The new behaviors have become routine.

We must focus on the population's needs and distribution of each specific stage of behavior. If patients are not in the contemplation stage, there

Making the math work

Engaging low-risk patients with portals, easy access

PCP activity	Weekly task breakdown under 4500 panel size	Weekly task breakdown under biannual low-risk patient visits[1]
Low-risk patient visits	23 h	9 h
Rising-risk patient visits	17 h	17 h
High-risk patient visits	7 h	7 h
Administrative, other tasks	21 h	15 h
Total	68 h/week	48 h/week

Strategy in brief: Biannual PCP visits for low-risk patients

• Encouraging biannual visits and electronic access point utilization for low-risk patients decreases PCP workload by 21 h per week, over 1000 h per year

• This strategy, supported by clinical evidence, affords the PCP a manageable workload under an increased panel size of 4500 patients

1. Assumes visits which last 22.3 minutes each; 15 minutes for low-risk patients; 3% high-risk, 27% rising-risk, 70% low-risk population; 4 visits per year among high-risk patients, 2 per year among rising-risk, and .57 per year among low-risk.

Figure 11.5   Engaging the low-risk patient. What you can (and should) do for healthy patients. (From the Advisory Board Company. © 2013. All rights reserved. With permission.)

is little hope of active change in the next six months. Only a few patients are actually ready for the "action" stage and interested in making a change (from precontemplation to contemplation). The "pros" of making a significant change must increase approximately twice as much as the "cons" of change. We must focus on the reasons for change, as well as reducing the barriers to change.

Physician Relationship and Influence

According to a 2003 physician survey, the physician/patient relationship is a trusted relationship which makes it a powerful influencer. A physician is trusted more than a spiritual advisor, coworker, or pharmacist, and only slightly less than family.[18] This relationship is a powerful force for change.

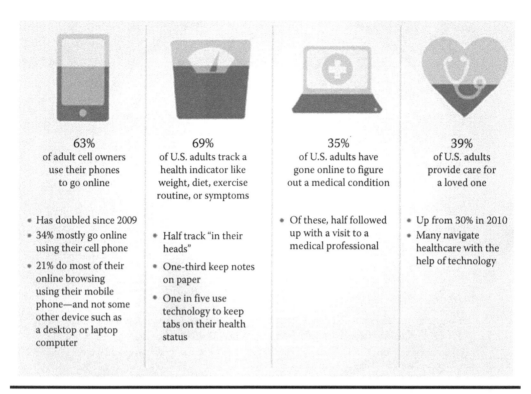

Figure 11.6   Athena Health—5 elements of a successful patient engagement strategy, based on Pew research data. (From www.pewinternet.org. With permission.)

Even a brief, less than five-minute conversation with a physician can cause quit rates (for cigarettes) of up to 10%.[9,15] Another study showed that the most important variable in predicting whether women would have a mammogram was whether the doctor had previously discussed it with the patient.

There are many new studies that are attempting to help to measure where individuals are on the change scale and to determine where interventions may be focused directly on those poised to make a change in behavior. These communications can then be tailored to be more effective in producing the appropriate change. Outcomes are also focusing on changing more than one behavior at a time. These unhealthy behaviors can be at different stages at different times, and this is a difficult process.

Much more work is happening in these areas to understand what it takes and what incentives actually create change. As this continuing science unfolds, we all want to identify less costly resources to affect significant change. Our focused messaging on where patients are in their willingness to change is based on economic, educational, and many other social determinants (see Figure 11.7).

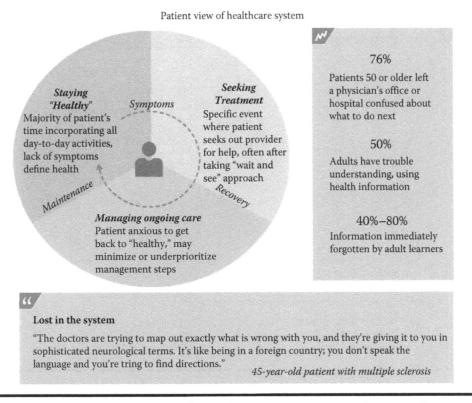

Patient view of healthcare system

Another way of looking at consumer incentives is to look at extrinsic rewards versus intrinsic rewards. Incentives such as cash, prizes, and positive and negative feedback are considered extrinsic rewards. Incentives such as personal recognition, competing with oneself or others, and personal benefit incentives would be considered intrinsic rewards.

Payer and Health Plan Models

Payers have attempted various approaches to get plan members and patient's attention. Health plans delivering the right message to the right person at the right time is critical, and these messages must be tailored to the socioeconomic status of the patient. Some are using a tool called the Patient Activation Measure or PAM, a 13-question survey developed at University of Oregon (http://SAURL.com/Hibbard).

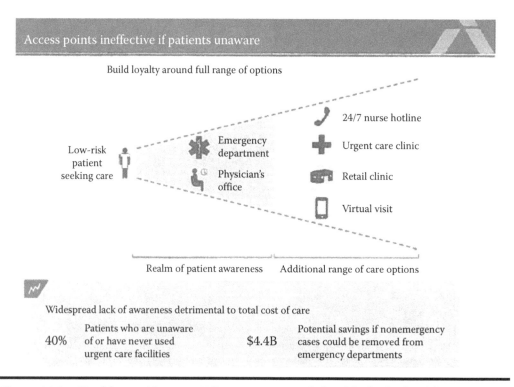

Figure 11.8 Healthcare Literacy: What you can (and should) do for healthy patients. (The Advisory Board Company. © 2013. All rights reserved. With permission.)

Other payers are using cash and quality and cost information to steer patients to high-quality, low-cost providers as well as identifying specific targeted procedures where the costs are extremely variable and quality is relatively consistent. With the broad variation in costs of a procedure, small cash rewards, deductibles, and outcomes information can radically change a patient's behavior.

In the payer world, there are several domains in which patient engagement takes place. There is customer service, wellness and prevention, and the relationship between patients and physicians. (Is this really the health plans?)

With the advent of high deductible plans, the patient must now spend several thousand dollars of their earnings on healthcare before the insurance coverage begins, (with the exception of well visits, annual screenings, etc.). High deductible insurance penetration has increased dramatically since their inception (Figure 11.8).[1]

Payers must focus on wellness and prevention programs, educating a target population, and the newest tactic, using social media to affect patient engagement. There can be a direct impact on utilization costs, with email, online games, and other similar activities.

Employer Models

Engagement at the employer level is becoming increasingly important. In today's employer environment, the employer is often the ultimate payer. This is true in a financial sense, but also may have an effect in the area of lost work time or lost productivity. Employers are often leading the charge in engaging their employees in healthy behaviors. This is often done in collaboration with payers. One of the main ways that employers are doing this is restructuring their benefit programs to encourage healthy behavior. This is often done by defining a list of expectations which are then documented and catalogued by the employee/employer. Once these expectations are met, then there can be a decrease in employee contribution to their healthcare coverage.

This has been done for several years in the area of tobacco use. In this scenario, payers have increased premium rates and employers have passed increased premiums on to their employees for this high-risk behavior. For a while, obesity was also included in this category, however, some legal challenges have affected this change. Attached is an example of some of the initiatives that employers have asked employees to consider in terms of biometric screening, etc. Another critical behavior change is identifying the appropriate information and analytics from the employer/beneficiary. In this scenario, health risk assessments are encouraged or required from the employer so that some of these high-risk behaviors can be adequately identified proactively managed (Figure 11.9).

Employer Programs

Work places are also becoming focal points for wellness activities, healthcare education with "lunch and learns," workplace clinics, and other activities. There can also be on-site physician offices in large workplaces, offering employees the opportunity to see a physician during work hours and not lose significant work productivity. There can also be workplace kiosks where the employee can interact with a physician through a virtual contact. Some models offer desktop communication technology. All of these are critical factors to keep employees engaged in work and functioning at maximum productivity. An additional approach that employers are using is "tag teaming" with either MCOs or other provider organizations to link the various care processes to the workplace environment. This might include screenings and/or ergonomics and other health education.

Hit Your Numbers	Points
Earn initial 50 points (Required)	
Health Assessment	15
Have a Biometrics Screening	15
If all 4 metrics are within range, no coaching required, you earned the points!	20
If any metrics are outside of range, points can still be achieved if you participate in telephonic coaching. Points will be earned when coaching is complete.	
TOTAL	**50**
You Pick	
Select *any* of the following activities to earn 50 points	
Up to date on annual PCP Visit	15
Up to date on Preventative Screenings (Age/Gender specific: Mammogram, Colonoscopy, Pap Smear)*	15
Participate in full marathon in 2015	30
Participate in half marathon in 2015	15
Participate in a 5k–10k in 2015	10
Attend/Listen to 2 AHS Wellness Seminars offered in 2015	10
WebMD Challenge	10
Daily Victory	10
My Health Assistant	10
Fitbit link + set/achieve one goal	10
Regular engagement in an organized workout program or ongoing class, at least 2 days a week; 3 consecutive months	5
Total	**50**
Grand Total	**100**

*We follow the preventive screening standards set by the U.S. Preventive Services Task Force (USPSTF) for frequency and age requirements for each screening. More information can be found in your WebMD portal.

We realize the concept of *Hit Your Numbers* is new and may sound daunting. Rest assured, we want everyone to achieve an incentive, so we've designed the program so everyone can achieve their incentive while also making effort to improve their health.

Remember, all your personal health information is kept confidential and is never shared with Adventist Health System. We only receive summary data regarding the employee population as a whole to help us design health and wellness benefits to meet the needs of our employees moving forward.

Figure 11.9   Employee incentive programs.

Public Health and Public Policy

Public health policy is about local or national policies that promote health. This can be such issues as laws and/or disclosures that the cigarette manufacturers must comply with. It may also include public service advertisements that are supported by television networks or other organizations. Initially, public policy and health have been focused on pollution, air and water supply, infectious diseases, and other basic healthcare needs. More recent trends have been working toward more proactive needs, such as childhood obesity and other societal risk behaviors.

A recent example is the recent Ebola challenges. Our country was not ready to respond to epidemics and pandemics and was quickly reminded of the cost and challenges of appropriately dealing with these kinds of issues.

Bibliography

1. Consumer driven health plans: Early evidence of potential impact on hospitals. *Health Affairs* 2006; 25(1): 174–185.
2. The Advisory Board. Competing on Patient Engagement. Forging a new competitive identity for a value-driven marketplace.
3. Sg2 Intelligence. Engaging the New Health Care Consumer.
4. H&HN. October 2012 www.hhmag.com Improving patient engagement.
5. The Advisory Board. Health Care Advisory Board. The consumer-oriented Ambulatory Network. Converting patient preferences into durable system advantage.
6. Leavitt Partners LLC. July 2014. Consumerism and the changing nature of health insurance products. Leavittpartners.com.
7. Merck. Medication Adherence. Working together to help achieve better treatment outcomes.
8. Burns J. Managed Care. June 2012. The Next Frontier Patient Engagement.
9. Pam 13; http://SAURL.com/Hibbard.
10. Prochaska et al. Evaluating a population-based recruitment approach and a stage-based expert system interventions for smoking cessation. Addiction behavior 2001; 26(4): 583–602.
11. Health Care Advisory Board, The Consumer-Oriented Ambulatory Network, Converting Patient Preference into Durable System Advantage.
12. HBI Cost and Quality Academy, Best Practices in Population and Disease Management, Engaging Patients to Ensure Adherence with Care Plans.
13. Healthcare Analytics Blog. Milliman MedInsight. Help Me, Help You—Patient Engagement and Care Coordination, posted by Barb Ward, July 12, 2013.

14. Athenahealth, Inc. Published February, 2014, athenahealth.com. Whitepapers/patient-engagement strategies.
15. GovernanceInstitute.com. Moving Forward. Winter 2013. Executive Summary.
16. Prochaska et al. counselor and stimulus control enhancements of a stage match expert system intervention for smokers and managed care setting. *Preventive Medicine* 2001; 32(1): 23–32.
17. Prochaska et al. Changing for good: the revolutionary program that explains the six stages of change and teaches you how to free yourself from bad habits. New York: W. Morrow; 1994. ISBN 0-688-11263-3.
18. Magee J. Realtionship-Based Health Care in the United States, UK, Canada, Germany, South Africa, and Japan. Presented at the World Medical Association "Patient Safety in Care Research." September 11, 2003.

Chapter 12

Population Health, Healthcare Disparities, and Policy

Edward M. Rafalski

Contents

As society seeks to improve the health of the population and eliminate disparity, trade-offs are made between investment in health and competing national interests such as defense, education, and infrastructure. In order to make rational decisions regarding the trade-offs, policy makers and providers alike need to come to some consensus regarding the nature of health investments. Are we investing in ever-larger healthcare systems or in systems of health? Are we interested in overall population health or the health of specific populations? If so, which one(s) and how will we choose them? In order to better understand the relationship between overall population health, health disparity, and the resulting policy implications reflecting the interdependence of each, there is a need to establish foundational terms and concepts.

Systems of Health versus Healthcare Systems

Primary, Secondary, and Tertiary Prevention

Prevention of disease is commonly structured in three stages: primary, secondary, and tertiary. Primary prevention is focused on avoiding disease altogether, generally by preventing disease development. Immunization, sanitation, and weight management/obesity prevention as a precursor to onset of chronic disease, such as diabetes, are all examples of primary prevention of disease. It is well established in the public health literature that the number of aggregate lives saved through immunization and sanitation far outweigh those saved though medical intervention. The same logic is now being applied to the underlying causes of disease, such as obesity, as a focus of resource allocation and emphasis by public health professionals. If we were to reduce the prevalence of chronic obesity we could reduce the overall incidence of related chronic diseases such as diabetes in the overall population, thereby saving lives and reducing diabetes-related expenditures.

Secondary prevention is focused on reducing illness onset, duration, or further transmission once infection has occurred, or in the case of cancer, a tumor has developed. Screening for disease, such as breast cancer mammography screening, is associated with secondary prevention. Screening for disease is perhaps the most effective means by which healthcare systems can identify those patients at greatest risk for developing a disease. Genetic mapping and family tree histories are two examples of additional screening methods that are being employed to determine which populations should be screened and for which disease types.

Tertiary prevention is focused on curing the illness once symptoms have appeared. It seeks to reduce complications, suffering, and long-term impairments and disabilities, for example, mastectomy for breast cancer.[1] This is where healthcare systems have historically focused their resources and where they have been financially rewarded for their efforts.

Healthcare Systems

Healthcare systems, which are the vehicle and formal organizational structure by which Western Medicine is delivered, particularly the version that is practiced in the United States, have been historically organized around secondary and tertiary prevention of disease. Healthcare is delivered by health systems and medical professionals intervening once the disease process has begun. This process is also described by some as providing direct medical services, caring for acute illness as well as the reactive management of disease.[2]

In life expectancy at birth, arguably a leading metric of the health of a population, the United States ranks 40th in the world with an expectancy of 79 years (equivalent to Cuba and Bermuda) while spending the largest proportion of its GDP, 17.9% in so doing, according to The World Bank.[3] The U.S. government's portion of the spend is currently ~8.3%.[4] This may be considered a crude return on investment calculation reflecting the return on overall population health as a proportion of societal resources expended. Arguably, there is room for improvement on the return. In contrast, India as the second most populous country in the world after China, government health spending represents 1.3% of GDP while life expectancy hovers at 66 years of age, well down the list of developed and developing nations. That level of expenditure puts India behind Afghanistan and Angola. China's government spends 3% of GDP on healthcare with life expectancy at 75 years. So, when comparing these three nations, each year of life expectancy in the United States reflects 0.105% of government GDP spend, 0.0197% in India, and 0.04% in China, respectively.

The systems of delivery that have been constructed in the United States, organizing themselves around the modern-day inpatient hospital, are inherently designed to conveniently enable intervention by physicians on patients when they are exhibiting signs and symptoms of disease that clinically warrant an intervention. Evidence-based medicine seeks to establish a formal scientific inquiry that is peer-reviewed and proven as an "accepted" intervention. However, significant variance in accepted interventions exists by region, system, and physician. This variance creates significant cost and outcome differences in the delivery of healthcare that have been well established by Gawande and others.[5,6] Further, the variance makes the overall system less efficient and more expensive with questionable return when cast in the light of life expectancy.

It has been well established that Americans consume a majority of medical resources in the last 2 years of life. The Institute for Healthcare Improvement has referenced the Dartmouth Health Atlas' Healthcare Intensity (HCI) index as a metric for this end of life consumption of resources applied to regions of the country.

> The HCI index is based on two variables: the number of days patients spent in the hospital and the number of physician encounters (visits) they experienced as inpatients. It is computed as the age–sex–race–illness standardized ratio of patient days and visits. For each variable, the ratio of a given hospital's utilization rate to the national average was calculated, and these two ratios were averaged to create the index. The study population includes beneficiaries with one of nine chronic conditions who were enrolled in traditional (fee-for-service) Medicare and died during the measurement period. To allow for 2 years of follow-back for all patients, the population is restricted to those whose age on the date of death was 67 to 99 years, and to those having full Part A and Part B entitlement throughout the last 2 years of life. Persons enrolled in managed care organizations were excluded from the analysis. For the hospital-specific analyses, patients had to be hospitalized for chronic illness at least once during their last 2 years of life to be included.[7]

For regional analyses, all patients diagnosed with a chronic illness were included. The index displays a significant amount of variation of expense when comparing regions of the country, suggesting that some states and their hospitals/health systems are more efficient than others when managing resources at the end of life (see Figure 12.1).

Hospital care intensity index, last two years of life, by component			
(Component: overall index; year: 2010; region levels: state)			
Alabama	0.91	Nevada	1.17
Alaska	0.66	New Hampshire	0.73
Arizona	0.97	New Jersey	1.48
Arkansas	0.88	New Mexico	0.68
California	1.17	New York	1.35
Colorado	0.72	North Carolina	0.80
Connecticut	1.03	North Dakota	0.63
Delaware	1.05	Ohio	0.95
District of Columbia	1.15	Oklahoma	0.86
Florida	1.20	Oregon	0.53
Georgia	0.89	Pennsylvania	1.09
Hawaii	0.96	Rhode Island	0.97
Idaho	0.48	South Carolina	0.88
Illinois	1.14	South Dakota	0.71
Indiana	0.88	Tennessee	0.94
Iowa	0.68	Texas	1.06
Kansas	0.82	Utah	0.48
Kentucky	1.02	Vermont	0.58
Louisiana	1.07	Virginia	0.91
Maine	0.68	Washington	0.62
Maryland	1.02	West Virginia	0.99
Massachusetts	0.97	Wisconsin	0.72
Michigan	1.05	Wyoming	0.64
Minnesota	0.68	National average	1.00
Mississippi	0.98	90th Percentile	1.17
Missouri	0.92	50th Percentile	0.91
Montana	0.57	10th Percentile	0.58
Nebraska	0.79		

Figure 12.1 Hospital care intensity index by state. (From Dartmouth Atlas, The Dartmouth Atlas of Healthcare, Hospital Care Intensity, 2014. Available at http://www.dartmouthatlas.org/data/table.aspx?ind=6. With permission.)

Systems of Health

Systems of health are organized around and focused on primary prevention. It is a process by which systems are constructed and organized to prevent disease. Waller has observed that constructing and organizing systems of health to prevent disease could be characterized as "health improvement" which includes "prevention and wellness" descriptors. This helps to address the factors of lifestyle behaviors, the physical environment, and social and economic factors influencing health, all of which are generally considered to be outside the realm of (traditional) care.[8] Others have referred to these characteristics as the leading determinants of health.[9] Determinants can include genetic predispositions, social circumstances, behavioral patterns, and medical care.

The Social Determinants of Health

The social, behavioral, and environmental determinants of health and health behaviors explain well over half, or 60%, of health outcomes (see Figure 12.2). These may be considered fundamental to primary prevention. Genetic predisposition accounts for 30%. Secondary and tertiary prevention, or medical care determinants, account for the balance, 10%, of health outcomes. Approximately 95% of the resources spent on health go to direct medical services in the United States, while 5% is allocated to population-wide

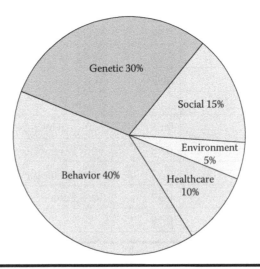

Figure 12.2   Leading determinants of health. (Adapted from McGinnis JM, Williams-Russo P, Knickman, JR., *Health Affairs*, 2002; 21: 78–93.)

approaches to health improvement. If health outcomes are to be improved, focusing the larger percentage on population-wide improvement may increase the probability of improvement and a higher return on investment as a percentage of GDP.

Genetic, Diagnosis, Zip, and Payer Codes

Stated another way, there are four codes that may be considered central to improving the health of a population through systems of health. The first is the genetic code—inherited genetic traits that predispose us to diseases such as cancers and heart disease. Affecting that code is the focus of a significant amount of research now that the human genome has been mapped. The second is the diagnosis code—the categorized clinical disposition of the patients once they have been diagnosed. Combinations of these codes inform interventions and clinical programming, particularly for patients with multiple chronic conditions such as obesity, diabetes, and heart disease. Third is the zip code—where a person lives may lead to disease formation. Areas with food deserts—low-income neighborhoods without access to fresh produce may redispose a population within that zip code to have poor choices in food consumption which then lead to early onset type II diabetes, for example. Last is the financial code—does the patient have health insurance and what is the benefit structure? While an increasing number of Americans are becoming insured through the Accountable Care Act and through Medicaid expansion, there are those that still lack coverage and access to regular ongoing care by a primary care physician which may lead to lack of compliance with screening for disease. As the Baby Boom generation, those born between 1945 and 1964, retire, Medicare is becoming an ever more sizeable and important payer of healthcare services. An efficient use of this program becomes all the more important from a Federal budgetary perspective requiring policy makers to potentially rethink approaches to increasing the value proposition of the program.

Population Health versus Health of Populations

Population Health

Population health is the paradigm by which healthcare systems organize to identify and target tailored interventions to specific segments of patients under their care. Recently, health systems have been focusing on key market segments to develop expertise in varying contracting models. Examples of these segments may include: Medicare (the Federal program for providing healthcare insurance for the elderly and disabled), patients at risk for readmission (patient readmission in an inpatient hospital facility, typically within 30 days of the previous patient admission/discharge) uninsured patients (patients lacking any type of healthcare coverage), and inappropriate emergency department users (patients accessing a hospital's emergency department multiple times during the course of a year for the same or related reasons).

Healthcare market reforms have been evolving to develop new methods of reimbursement for providers, both health system and physician. Traditionally, providers have been paid in a fee-for-service model in which payment is made in return for services rendered or procedures performed. In theory, the more interventions that are performed on the patient the more the provider makes in revenue. Examples of traditional fee-for-service payment models are Medicare and Medicaid (the States' administered program for the poor). Prospective payment (paying in advance for the care of a population cohort), also known as capitation, is one example of an evolution to another payment model. Health maintenance organizations (HMOs) pursued this model in the 1990s in an effort to curb cost and improve outcomes/quality. This was met with some consumer backlash due to the restrictive nature of insurance plans being offered. The efforts to move payment reform to this model at scale ultimately stalled. A second example, pay-for-performance (P4P), aligns reimbursement for healthcare delivery to outcome-based measures, such as clinical quality metrics. A third example is at-risk reimbursement. In this model, interventions, such as curbing unnecessary utilization of services, are designed to reduce healthcare costs. Savings are shared among the provider and the insurer. This is the most recent evolution of payment reform.

Regardless of which reimbursement model a healthcare provider pursues, which is typically a combination of multiple models, healthcare systems are already "at risk" for population health.[10] Uninsured patients not receiving care regularly from a primary care physician and developing multiple chronic health conditions place healthcare systems at a financial risk when they appear in an emergency room with an exacerbated health comorbidity that requires tertiary intervention—an intervention which is more expensive to deliver than a primary or secondary intervention. It is for this reason that there may be growing comfort and willingness in the healthcare industry among providers to begin the pursuit of at-risk financial arrangements with payers/the health insurance industry. There are some organizations that are further along in this evolution, including Kaiser Permanente, in which both the delivery and the insurance products being offered are fully integrated either through outright ownership, joint venture arrangements, or partnerships.

There are additional targeted populations defined by Accountable Care Organization (ACO) agreements. ACOs are groups of doctors, hospitals, and other healthcare providers, who come together voluntarily to give coordinated high-quality care to their Medicare patients. The goal of coordinated care is to ensure that patients, especially the chronically ill, get the right care at the right time, while avoiding unnecessary duplication of services and preventing medical errors. When an ACO succeeds in both delivering high-quality care and spending healthcare dollars more wisely, it will share in the savings it achieves for the Medicare program.[11] Anticipated care bundles/payments for these targeted populations include those for asthma management, prenatal care, and orthopedics. It is expected that Medicaid patients at risk for readmissions and high cost to treat chronic disease will also soon be a priority.

Health of Populations/Community Health

Improving the health of populations or community health, is focused on improving overall community health outcomes. Providers are typically not directly accountable for entire communities and their health outcomes, although this is increasingly becoming an IRS requirement under the Community Needs Assessment provision in the Form 990 required of non-profit healthcare providers. Through effective participation in broader health initiatives, providers may be able to collectively impact community health outcomes such as infant mortality.

For health systems, community health programming can be seen as a long-term population health strategy designed to keep high-risk people out of high-cost clinical service offerings and in medical homes focused on increasing patient compliance and engagement in primary prevention efforts. Medical homes have been in existence since the 1960s, at least in concept.[12] Key elements of the medical home include: patient access and scheduling, patient-centered care, continuity of care, and adoption of health information technology. All elements are designed to provide improved capabilities for treating patients in a more coordinated ongoing process.

What's Needed for Effective Population Health Management?

There are a number of key skill sets/functions that are crucial for effective population health management. Population health analytics, including: epidemiological, actuarial, geospatial, and statistical, are central to creating the knowledge base necessary to understand existing utilization patterns and opportunities for improvement. One example in geospatial analytics is that of hot-spotting community areas of opportunity for intervention/improvement strategies. Community-based hot-spotting initiatives in Camden and Memphis are examples of this skill set being applied to identify high-risk populations within larger geographic regions.[13]

Care coordination or care transitions across multiple care settings is another skill set that is required. Individualized community-based lay patient navigation, beyond the traditional social work role, is emerging as an effective intervention. This is evidenced by work in breast cancer prevention.[14,15]

Community-based resources, such as primary care access, patient self-management skills, and access to community resources to address patient-specific behavioral and social needs are all additional resources and skills needed to affect change in patient behavior and improve compliance.

Healthy People 2020 and the Definition of Disparity

The stated vision of Healthy People 2020 is a society in which all people live long, healthy lives. There are four overarching goals, which are to attain high-quality, longer lives free of preventable disease, disability, injury, and premature death; achieve health equity, eliminate disparities, and improve the health of all groups; create social and physical environments that promote good health for all; promote quality of life, healthy development, and healthy behaviors across all life stages. There are four foundational measures that serve as indicators of progress toward the 2020 goals: general health status, health-related quality of life and well-being, determinants of health, and disparities.[16]

Although the term "disparities" often is interpreted to mean racial or ethnic disparities, many dimensions of disparity exist in the United States, particularly in health. If a health outcome is seen in a greater or lesser extent between populations, there is disparity. Race or ethnicity, sex, sexual identity, age, disability, socioeconomic status, and geographic location all contribute to an individual's ability to achieve good health. Further, it is important to recognize the impact that social determinants have on health outcomes of specific populations. One methodology that is typically used to quantify disparities includes statistical testing, such as odds ratio or relative risk analysis, to determine the extent of the disparity when comparing two discrete populations, using an age-adjusting rate.

To better understand the context of disparities, it is important to understand characteristics that comprise the overall population. Some key overall descriptors include the following:

- In 2008, the U.S. population was estimated at 304 million.[17]
- In 2008, ~33%, or more than 100 million persons, identified themselves as belonging to a racial or ethnic minority population.[18]
- In 2008, 51%, or 154 million, were women.[19]
- In 2008, ~12%, or 36 million people, not living in nursing homes or other residential care facilities had a disability.[20] In 2008, an estimated 70.5 million persons lived in rural areas (23% of the population), while roughly 233.5 million lived in urban areas (77%).[21]
- In 2002, an estimated 4% of the U.S. population aged 18 to 44 years identified themselves as lesbian, gay, bisexual, or transgender.[22]

During the past two decades, one of Healthy People's overarching goals has focused on disparities. In Healthy People 2000, it was to reduce health disparities among Americans. In Healthy People 2010, it was to eliminate, not just reduce, health disparities. In Healthy People 2020, that goal was expanded even further: to achieve health equity, eliminate disparities, and improve the health of all groups.

Healthy People 2020 defines *health equity* as the "attainment of the highest level of health for all people. Achieving health equity requires valuing everyone equally with focused and ongoing societal efforts to address avoidable inequalities, historical and contemporary injustices, and the elimination of health and healthcare disparities."[23]

Healthy People 2020 defines a *health disparity* as "a particular type of health difference that is closely linked with social, economic, and environmental disadvantage. Health disparities adversely affect groups of people who have systematically experienced greater obstacles to health based on their racial or ethnic group; religion; socioeconomic status; gender; age; mental health; cognitive, sensory, or physical disability; sexual orientation or gender identity; geographic location; or other characteristics historically linked to discrimination or exclusion."[24]

Social Determinants

Over the years, efforts to eliminate disparities and achieve health equity have focused primarily on diseases or illnesses and on healthcare services. However, the absence of disease does not automatically equate to good health. According to the Department of Health and Human Services, powerful, complex relationships exist between health and biology, genetics, and individual behavior, and between health and health services, socioeconomic status, the physical environment, discrimination, racism, literacy levels, and legislative policies. These factors, which influence an individual's or population's health, are known as *determinants of health*. Others have referenced these as *"social" determinants of health*. Examples of social determinants may include the availability of and access to

- A high-quality education
- Nutritious food
- Decent and safe housing
- Affordable, reliable public transportation
- Culturally sensitive healthcare providers
- Health insurance
- Clean water and nonpolluted air

Throughout the next decade, Healthy People 2020 will assess health disparities in the U.S. population by tracking rates of illness, death, chronic conditions, behaviors, and other types of outcomes in relation to demographic factors including:

- Race and ethnicity
- Gender
- Sexual identity and orientation
- Disability status or special healthcare needs
- Geographic location (rural and urban)

Geographic Units of Analysis

Once determinants have been identified and segmented for disparity analysis, creating spatial units of analysis may be considered as a legitimate next step to uncovering variances in disparity by region. It has been observed that existing health data for large geographic areas mask important differences in how groups with heterogeneous population experience health.[25]

John Snow was the first to use a dot map to illustrate the cluster of cholera cases around a water pump in the Soho neighborhood of London in 1854. Snow used mapping to illustrate the connection between the quality of the water source and the cholera cases.[26] This type of microanalysis, combining the elements of epidemiology with that of mapping, led to modern geo-spatial analysis of disease—a key element of understanding differences in health outcomes among populations at the local level. This geographic analytical approach goes beyond that of metropolitan statistical area (MSA) or major city and down to the zip code, community area, neighborhood, block group, and census tract.

Local level data collection allows for the examination of health problems for specific groups at the community level, which is particularly relevant for large urban centers. The study of populations in smaller geographic areas can help to uncover the nature of health disparities and offer insight to shape targeted community-based interventions.[27] So, depending on the disparity being studied, simply reporting on a determinant at the national level may not be sufficient in expanding or understanding the disparity at a major urban, rural, city, community area, or neighborhood level. Further, depending on the type of intervention needed, the unit of analysis may direct the level of policy intervention needed; that is, federal, state, city, or community level.

Breast Cancer as a Case Study in Disparity

It has been established that there is a growing disparity in mortality from breast cancer in the United States when comparing Blacks to Whites. Orsi and others studied the phenomenon and found that disparities between non-Hispanic Black (NHB) and non-Hispanic White (NHW) populations widened for 6 of 15 health status indicators examined for the United States and in Chicago the majority of disparities widened in 11 of 15 indicators, 5 significantly. At the time, progress toward meeting Health People 2010 goal of eliminating disparities in the United States and Chicago remained bleak.[28] The study showed that from the period 1981 to the period 2007 the gap between NHB and NHWs widened from essentially being nonexistent to a gap of 62% (see Figure 12.3).

Whitman and others studied the racial disparity at the city level comparing results in the 25 largest cities in the United States. NHW and NHB rate

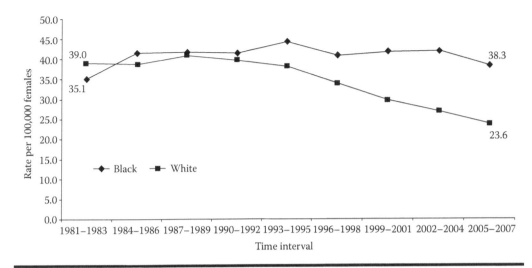

Figure 12.3 Black and white breast cancer mortality, Chicago, 1981–2007. (Data source: Illinois Department of Public Health Vital Statistics. Adapted from Sinai Urban Health Institute. With permission.)

ratios (RRs) were calculated, along with confidence intervals, as measures of the racial disparity. Almost all of the NHB rates were higher than the almost all the NHW rates. The authors used seven city-level (ecological) risk factors seeking correlates of the disparity including:

■ Population of city
■ % NHW
■ % NHB
■ Median household income
■ % below poverty
■ Gini index: measure of income inequality
■ Index of dissimilarity: measure of racial segregation

Among these seven ecological factors, only median household income and the index of dissimilarity were found to be significantly related to the RR.[29]

Updating the earlier study, Hunt and others studied the 50 largest U.S. cities, their race-specific breast cancer mortality rates and the corresponding RRs for each in 5-year intervals between 1990 and 2009 revealing large and growing disparities in Black:White cancer mortality in the United States and many of its largest cities.[30] Of the cities studied, 39 showed a Black:White disparity in the final time interval, 23 of which were statistically significant. Thirty-five cities saw an increase in the disparity from the first time interval

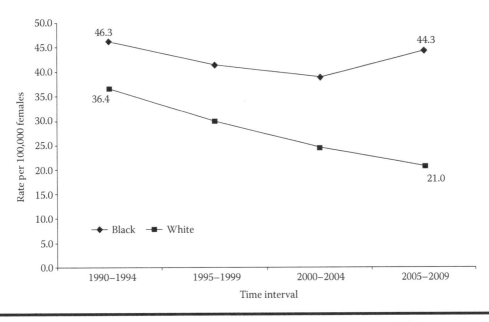

Figure 12.4   Black and white breast cancer mortality disparity, Memphis, 1990–2009. (Data source: Hunt BR, Whitman S, Hurlbert, MS, *Cancer Epidemiology*, April 2014; 38(2): 118–123. Adapted from Sinai Urban Health Institute. With permission.)

(1990–1994) to the last (2005–2009) and this was almost entirely because the White rate improved substantially, while the Black rate generally did not improve at all. Memphis led the nation in mortality disparity and the gap was in fact widening (see Figure 12.4).

It is not well understood why these disparities exist and what can be done to prevent them from widening. This is a growing and much needed area of research. As a function of Healthy People goals over the years, it is fair to say that, at least in breast cancer, little to no progress has been made since Healthy People 2000 goals were first established. In fact, disparities have worsened in many major cities, including Memphis, in the United States.

Environmental and Socioeconomic Factors

A key element of place as a determinant of health is the environment in which people live, referenced as one of three key population health determinant codes, the zip code, related to health outcomes. It has been well established in the area of asthma research, for example, that the home environment can have more to do with the onset of asthma in children than other determinants.[31] Further, it has been proven that interventions, such as case management of children with asthma, can have a positive effect on reducing school absenteeism and hospitalizations.[32] However, the work to intervene in place is arguably quite new with early results elusive and mixed.

Food Deserts

Food deserts, characterized by poor access to healthy and affordable food, may contribute to social and spatial disparities in diet and diet-related health outcomes. While the extent to which food deserts exist is debated worldwide, there are reviews that food deserts exist in the United States, where area-level deprivation compounds individual disadvantage.[33] The growth of fresh food markets throughout the country, many sponsored by healthcare organizations, has been one example of an intervention designed to address the lack of access to fresh produce in low-income areas within major metropolitan urban areas. There is a lack of conclusive evidence that this intervention has had any lasting effect on health.

Physical Activity Deserts

Environmental factors are suggested to play a major role in physical activity and other obesity-related behaviors. Lower socioeconomic status and high-minority block census groups have been shown to have reduced access to physical activity facilities, which in turn was associated with decreased physical activity and increased overweight patterns.[34] When considering primary prevention, this becomes a key issue in addressing the recent obesity epidemic which may be creating long-term disparities among younger generations of which we are currently unaware.

Pollution

The health effects of air pollution have been subjected to intense study in recent years. Exposure to pollutants such as airborne participate matter and ozone has been associated with increases in mortality and hospital admissions due to respiratory and cardiovascular disease. These effects have been found in short-term studies, which relate day-to-day variations in air pollution and health, and long-term studies, which have followed cohorts of exposed individuals over time. Effects have been seen at very low levels of exposure, and it is unclear whether a threshold concentration exists for particulate matter and ozone below which no effects on health are likely.[35]

Socioeconomic

When considering place in the context of health outcomes, the correlation of income and poor health outcomes, with income as a leading indicator of other social determinants of health, is well-established in the literature.[36,37] In fact, the Centers for Disease Control (CDC) have mapped the social determinants, along with poverty and health outcomes, thereby creating user-friendly visual displays that describe the patterns throughout the United States.

One of CDC's four overarching Health Protection Goals is "Healthy People in Healthy Places." This goal addresses the idea that the places where people live, work, learn, and play will protect and promote their health and safety, especially those people at greater risk of health disparities. Social determinants of health are factors in the social environment that contribute to or detract from the health of individuals and communities. These factors include but are not limited to the following:

■ Socioeconomic status
■ Transportation
■ Housing
■ Access to services
■ Discrimination by social grouping (e.g., race, gender, or class)
■ Social or environmental stressors

Social determinants of health have repeatedly been found to be associated with heart disease and stroke. These factors work either directly to affect the burden of heart disease and stroke and their risk factors, or indirectly, through their influence on health-promoting behaviors. With this in mind, maps of selected social determinants of health provide information to be used in tandem with other data sources to match heart disease and stroke prevention programs and policies to the needs of local populations. They also may generate hypotheses regarding the pathways between the social environment and health in general, and heart disease and stroke specifically.[38]

Interventions and policies designed to reduce poverty, dating back to President Johnson's "War on Poverty" in the 1960s, have proven sincere attempts with quantifiable results elusive at best.[39] Much is yet to be learned from this initial work of the last 50 years and arguably much is left to be done to address the issue of poverty as a leading indicator of health.

Ethics

Health Equity

Disagreements exist regarding the definition of the terms "disparity," "inequality," and "inequity." These disagreements center on which term to use, whether a judgment of what is avoidable and unfair is included, and how these judgments are made. Disparity acts as a signpost indicating that something is wrong. If a disparity is determined to be avoidable and unfair, then it is considered an inequity.

Health equity is the principle or goal that motivates efforts to eliminate disparities in health between groups of people who are economically or socially worse-off and their better-off counterparts. Health disparities are the metric by which we measure progress toward health equity.[40] The allocation of resources to address a disparity implies that the disparity is thought to be avoidable and unfair.[41]

This may perhaps form a conceptual foundation upon which to form health policy—society may choose to intervene in areas where inequities exist and are considered unacceptable. As measurement of health disparity continues to improve with advances in technology and data capture, such as the adoption of electronic medical records (EMRs), understanding where health disparities exist will become more easily documentable and understood. It is only recently that health systems have been capturing key data elements, such as race, as a normal course of business. We are only now beginning to understand the nature of health disparity and how the healthcare system can evolve into a system of health that takes into account inherent differences in health status and outcomes in a population.

Cost

Cost–Benefit or Effectiveness

It has been well established that the United States spends a greater proportion of its GDP on healthcare than any other country on earth, currently at 17.9%[42] (see Figure 12.5). Further, until very recently, it has continued to rise year after year. Yet, despite the significant investment in healthcare, the United States ranks last in virtually every measure of health status when compared to its developed country peers (see Figures 12.6 and 12.7).

Figure 12.5 Health expenditure (% of GDP). (Adapted from World Bank, http://data.worldbank.org/indicator/SH.XPD.TOTL.ZS/countries?display-map. With permission.)

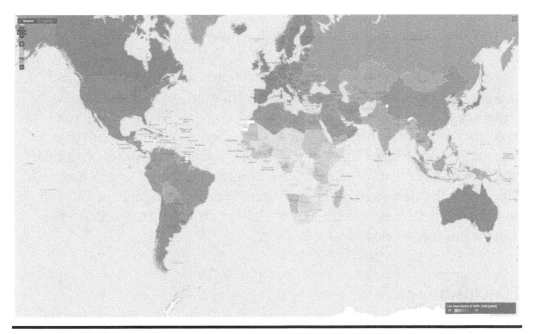

Figure 12.6 Life expectancy at birth, total (years). (Adapted from World Bank, http://data.worldbank.org/indicator/sp.PYN.LEOO.IN/countries?display-map. With permission.)

Health status rankings

Exhibit ES-1. Overall ranking

Country rankings
1.00–2.33
2.34–4.66
4.67–7.00

	AUS	CAN	GER	NETH	NZ	UK	US
Overall ranking (2010)	3	6	4	1	5	2	7
Quality care	4	7	5	2	1	3	6
Effective care	2	7	6	3	5	1	4
Safe care	6	5	3	1	4	2	7
Coordinated care	4	5	7	2	1	3	6
Patient-centered care	2	5	3	6	1	7	4
Access	6.5	5	3	1	4	2	6.5
Cost-related problem	6	3.5	3.5	2	5	1	7
Timeliness of care	6	7	2	1	3	4	5
Efficiency	2	6	5	3	4	1	7
Equity	4	5	3	1	6	2	7
Long, healthy, productive lives	1	2	3	4	5	6	7
Health expenditures/capita, 2007	$3357	$3895	$3588	$3837*	$2454	$2992	$7290

*Estimate. Expenditures shown in $US PPP (purchasing power parity).
Source: Calculated by the Commonwealth Fund based on 2007 international health policy survey; 2008 international health policy survey of sicker adults; 2009 international health policy survey of primary care physicians; commonwealth fund commission on a high performance health system national scorecard; and organization for economic cooperation and development, OECD health data, 2009 (Paris: OECD, Nov. 2009).

Figure 12.7   Health status rankings by country. (Adapted from the Commonwealth Fund, http://www.commonwealthfund.org/~/media/files/publications/fund-report/2014/jun/1755_davis_mirror_mirror_2014-pdf. With permission.)

Every dollar spent on healthcare is a resource that cannot be applied to other national needs such as defense, education, and infrastructure. These are rational trade-offs that are made. Cost–benefit analysis guides the researcher to ask whether the tradeoff made benefits society more than it costs. Cost–effectiveness analysis guides the researcher to ask whether the effects of an intervention of alternative programs led to an improvement. In either case, the data suggest that the United States is making less rational decisions with resources in the tradeoff of health when compared to peer countries in the developed world.

Conclusion

The burdens of an aging population and the rise of chronic disease are stressing healthcare resources and meeting today's challenges requires new models of care and new ways of thinking. Some have argued that healthcare needs to be "flipped." Providers should ask, "What matters to you?" as well as, "what's the matter?" This flip should inform everything to providers. It places the person, not the disease or the condition, at the center of improving health and healthcare. Flipping healthcare means flipping the balance of care from the hospital to the community; the balance of delivery from individual providers to care teams; the balance of power from the provider to the patient and family; the balance of costs from treatment to prevention and coproduction; and healthcare to health.[43] Embracing primary prevention, systems of health thinking, and population health with a focus on eliminating disparity may be considered a viable path to flipping healthcare and thereby improving the health value proposition offered currently in the United States.

Bibliography

1. Fleming ST. *Managerial Epidemiology, Concepts and Cases*. Chicago, IL: Health Administration Press; 2008.
2. Waller R. 2014 (a private conversation).
3. The World Bank. Health expenditure, total (% of GDP), 2014. Available at http://data.worldbank.org/indicator/SH.XPD.TOTL.ZS?order=wbapi_data_value_2012+wbapi_data_value+wbapi_data_value-last&sort=desc (accessed December 8, 2014).
4. Wall Street Journal. Sterilization deaths cast light on India's ailing public health system: For most of country's poor, underfunded and hard-to-access public medical care is only option, 2014. Available at http://www.wsj.com/articles/sterilization-deaths-cast-light-on-indias-ailing-public-health-system-1418079781?KEYWORDS=india (accessed December 9, 2014).
5. Gawande A. The cost conundrum. New Yorker, 2009. Available at http://www.newyorker.com/reporting/2009/06/01/090601fa fact gawande.
6. Dartmouth Atlas, The Dartmouth Atlas of Health Care, Hospital Care Intensity, 2014. Available at http://www.dartmouthatlas.org/data/table.aspx?ind=6.
7. *Ibid.*
8. Waller R. Personal communication, April 17, 2014.
9. McGinnis JM, Williams-Russo P, Knickman, JR. The case for more active policy attention to health promotion. *Health Affairs*, 2002; 21: 78–93.
10. Healthcare Advisory Board, 2014.
11. Centers for Medicare and Medicaid Services. Accountable Care Organizations (ACO), 2014. What's an ACO? Available at https://www.cms.gov/Medicare/Medicare-Fee-for-Service-Payment/ACO/index.html?redirect=/aco/ (accessed December 3, 2014).
12. National Institutes of Health. Medical homes: Challenges in translating theory into practice. Available at http://www.ncbi.nlm.nih.gov/pmc/articles/PMC2790523/ (accessed December 11, 2014).

13. Cutts T, Rafalski E, Grant C, Marinescu R. Utilization of hot spotting to identify community needs and coordinate care for high-cost patients in Memphis, TN. *Journal of Geographic Information System (JGIS)* (February, 2014); 6(1): 23–29.

14. Clark JA et al. Patterns of task and network actions performed by navigators to facilitate cancer care. *Health Care Management Review* (April/June, 2014); 39(2): 90–101.

15. Hunt BR et al. Metrics for the systematic evaluation of community-based outreach. *Journal of Cancer Education* (December, 2013); 26(4): 633–638.

16. US Department of Health and Human Services Office of Disease Prevention and Health Promotion. Healthy People 2020, 2014. Available at https://www.healthypeople.gov/2020/About-Healthy-People (accessed October 1, 2014).

17. U.S. Census Bureau, American Fact Finder, United States. American Community Survey. American Community Survey 1-year estimates. ACS demographic and housing estimates, 2008. Available at http://factfinder.census.gov (accessed October 1, 2014).

18. *Ibid.*

19. *Ibid.*

20. U.S. Census Bureau, American Fact Finder, United States. American Community Survey. American Community Survey 1-year estimates. Selected social characteristics in the United States, 2008. Available at http://factfinder.census.gov (accessed October 1, 2014).

21. U.S. Census Bureau, American FactFinder. American Community Survey. 2008 American Community Survey 1-year estimates. B01003. Total population – universe: Total population. Available at http://factfinder.census.gov (accessed October 1, 2014).

22. Mayer KH, Bradford JB, Makadon HJ et al. Sexual and gender minority health: What we know and what needs to be done. *American Journal of Public Health* 2008; 98: 989–95, doi:10.2105/AJPH.2007.127811 (accessed October 1, 2014).

23. U.S. Department of Health and Human Services, Office of Minority Health. National Partnership for Action to End Health Disparities. The National Plan for Action Draft as of February 17, 2010. Chapter 1: Introduction. Available at http://www.minorityhealth.hhs.gov/npa/templates/browse. aspx?&lvl = 2&lvlid = 34 (accessed October 1, 2014).

24. U.S. Department of Health and Human Services. The Secretary's Advisory Committee on National Health Promotion and Disease Prevention Objectives for 2020. Phase I report: Recommendations for the framework and format of Healthy People 2020. Section IV. Advisory Committee findings and recommendations. Available at http://www.healthypeople.gov/hp2020/advisory/PhaseI/sec4.htm#_Toc211942917 (accessed October 1, 2014).

25. Northridge ME et al. Contribution of smoking to excess mortality in Harlem. *American Journal of Epidemiology* 1998; 147: 250–258.

26. Tufte ER *Visual Explanations: Images and Quantities, Evidence and Narrative.* Cheshire: Graphics Press; 1991.

27. Whitman SH *Urban Health: Combating Disparities with Local Data.* New York: Oxford University Press; 2011.

28. Oris J, Margellos-Anast H, Whitman S. Black–White health disparities in the United States and Chicago: A 15-year progress analysis. *American Journal of Public Health*, 2010; 100: 349–356.

29. Whitman S, Orsi J, Hurlburt M. The racial disparity in breast cancer mortality in the 25 largest cities in the United States. *Cancer Epidemiology*, 2012; 36(2): e147–e151.

30. Hunt BR, Whitman S, Hurlbert MS. Increasing Black:White disparities in breast cancer mortality in the 50 largest cities in the United States. *Cancer Epidemiology*, April, 2014; 38(2): 118–123.

31. Strachan DP, Carey IM. Home environment and severe asthma in adolescence: A population based case-control study. *British Medical Journal* (October, 1995); 311(7012): 1053–1056.

32. Levy M et al. The efficacy of asthma case management in an urban school district in reducing school absences and hospitalizations for asthma. *Journal of School Health* 2006; 76: 320–324.

33. Beaulac J, Kristjansson E, Cummins S. A systematic review of food deserts, 1966–2007. *Preventing Chronic Disease* 2009; 6(3): A105.

34. Gordon-Larsen P. Inequality in the built environment underlies key health disparities in physical activity and obesity, *Pediatrics* 2006; 117: 417–424.

35. Brunekreef B, Holgate ST. Air pollution and health. *The Lancet* 2002; 360: 1233–1242.

36. Kennedy B et al. Income distribution, socioeconomic status, and self-rated health in the United States: Multilevel analysis. *British Medical Journal* 1998; 317: 917–921.

37. Benzeval M, Taylor J, Judge K. Evidence on the relationship between low income and poor health: Is the government doing enough? *Fiscal Studies* 2000; 21: 375–399.

38. Centers for Disease Control. Social determinants of health maps, 2014. Available at http://www.cdc.gov/dhdsp/maps/social_determinants_maps.htm. (accessed December 11, 2014).

39. Bailey M, Duquette NJ. How Johnson fought the war on poverty: The economics and politics of funding at the office of economic opportunity. *The Journal of Economic History* 2014; 74: 637–638.

40. Braveman P. What is health equity: And how does a life-course approach take us further toward it? *Maternal Child Health Journal* 2014; 18: 366–372.

41. Carter-Pokras O, Baquet C. What is a health disparity? *Public Health Reports* 2002; 117: 426–434.

42. The World Bank. Health expenditure, total (% of GDP), 2014. Available at http://data.worldbank.org/indicator/SH.XPD.TOTL.ZS?order = wbapi_data_value_2012+wbapi_data_value+wbapi_data_value-last&sort=desc (accessed December 8, 2014).

43. Bisognano M. Flipping healthcare: An essay by Maureen Bisognano and Dan Schumers. *British Medical Journal* (October) 2014. Available at http://www.bmj.com/content/349/bmj.g5852 (accessed December 8, 2014).

Chapter 13

Case Studies

Contents

Case Study One: Adventist Health Network Begins Transition from Volume to Value

Kevin S. Attride

Decision to Transition to Value

Adventist Health Network (AHN) is a clinically integrated network comprised of over 800 employed and community physicians collaborating with Adventist Midwest Health, an integrated delivery network, consisting of four acute care hospitals, over a dozen ambulatory facilities, and urgent care network. AHN serves the population in the western suburbs of Chicago amidst a fragmented healthcare provider delivery system that is heavily entrenched in a fee-for-service environment. With dozens of physician networks and health systems, however, only one dominant payer, the Chicago market lacks innovations seen in other markets. Seven Chicago-area medical schools also ensure the region is saturated with physicians.

Recognizing the industry's focus on outcomes and shift to greater accountability, AHN, in collaboration with Adventist Midwest Health leadership, made the determination to begin building competencies for population health management in 2013. In addition to building the framework necessary to be successful in population health, the organization had to contract with payers to support the venture. If remaining on fee-for-service (volume based) contracts, the network would begin to deteriorate revenue without any financial gains in the shift to managing the population. Therefore, the network planned to transition to shared savings contracts with the intention to move toward professional and full risk (capitated) contracts after establishing a path to achieving successful outcomes.

Available Options

Within the under-65 population (commercial patients), the market's dominant payer was an obvious choice with approximately two-third of the population in the surrounding area, but they were unwilling to collaborate for a mutually beneficial endeavor to manage the population. Cigna, however, was willing to begin discussions around improving outcomes and managing costs in a collaborative partnership. Their Collaborative Care model had been successful in many other markets, and they were interested in launching one in the Chicago area. Though a small population, 7000 Cigna patients would provide a good learning environment to begin building population management competencies.

As for the over-65 population, contracting with the Centers for Medicare and Medicaid Services (CMS) became an obvious choice as Medicare Advantage, the managed care plans for Medicare-aged adults, lacked a large enough population to manage without taking unknown volatility due to the risk of small populations. CMS had already begun their Medicare Shared Savings Program which shares savings back with a network that has formed an accountable care organization (ACO), when quality thresholds are achieved and costs trending are throttled below historical benchmarks. AHN made a strategic decision to partner with Alexian Brothers Health System, who had just contracted with CMS to join the Medicare Shared Savings Program through a new entity called Alexian Brothers ACO. The population attributed to AHN physicians came to 22,000 Medicare patients.

Having secured ACOs for commercial and Medicare populations, AHN began building the framework that would be necessary to drive successful outcomes with quality metrics and cost reductions.

Building Framework and Resources

One of the first tasks became building a telephonic care coordination team to support physicians with complex patients and prevent patients with rising risks from elevating to greater severity. The team was able to estimate the approximate number of nurses and social workers needed to support the population. One nurse worked alongside Cigna patients to support the rising-risk population. Three nurses worked directly with both the rising risk and complex patients of the Medicare population. A social worker also provided psycho-social support to the entire network. While the group was smaller than the estimated projections, AHN was balancing effectiveness with the cost of staffing a fledgling program, in which processes, documentation, and reporting were all being developed. In a 6-month period, the care coordination team made significant strides toward well-defined processes and transitions of care both internally and with Adventist Midwest Health acute care facilities. They continue to meet with clinics to educate on care processes and build relationships. This has significantly built physician support and led to greater collaboration between the numerous patient-centered medical homes and care coordination team.

Physician engagement was another key factor in the success of the initiatives. Before finalizing the contracts, the administrative team educated providers on the vision for the ACOs and what it involved. Many physicians were willing to move forward, but there was a minority of skeptics who had trouble with the rationale of moving to value-based activities. Due to multiple factors, including deep entrenchment in fee-for-service, they were challenged with understanding how the future of healthcare delivery would affect them. While not completely resolved, their clinics and partners have moved forward recognizing the necessity of driving value in a changing environment. Physicians continue to be educated in the vision of the organization and with activities that make the initiatives successful. Though they were educated in larger group sessions, AHN has seen smaller interclinic group sessions to be most successful. Physician leaders, administrators, care coordinators, and quality coaches interface with the clinics to instruct and build collaboration.

Actionable information is the third leg of the stool. AHN found Cigna to deliver a rich set of reports that provided performance metrics across the ACO, clinic and physician specific details, as well as patient-level reporting that allowed the care coordination team to appropriately target the right patients at the right time. This information was leveraged to begin achieving results more quickly than the Medicare Shared Savings Program. A local reporting vendor was used to deliver all reports and submit the group's quality reporting. Though slower to provide similar information, the Medicare reports were used for the same purposes, but there were some barriers inherent to the CMS initiative that made it more challenging. Attribution, the process of tying patients to physicians without the expressed selection of a health maintenance organization (HMO) model, was a challenge in which Medicare patients that were seen only by specialists or once by a primary care physician within the past 18 months added patients not easily managed. Quality reporting called GPRO, the group practice reporting option for CMS' Physician Quality Reporting System, requires discrete data from the patient record, and is unlike private health plans that capture quality measures through claims. Chart audits and tracking patient charts across the care continuum made quality measurement much more difficult. These issues continue to be evaluated and improved but have made data reporting more challenging.

Status and Opportunities

As of the early 2015, AHN proved to be successful in a few areas. For the Cigna population, costs have decreased with a trend performance beating the market by 2.4%. Hospital readmissions and unnecessary emergency visits have been reduced. Inpatient and advanced imaging costs also beat the market. Measured quality has also improved. All major indicators beat market performance, including preventive screenings. Adolescent well-care beat the rest of Chicago by 20%.

Though reporting is more robust for Cigna, AHN has also seen gains in the Medicare Shared Savings Program. Quality has improved over the course of the year and the submission of the group's quality reporting was successful for the second straight year. Due to lack of incentivized plan benefit design, costs were more challenging to curb, however, AHN was successful at reducing the steady climb of year-over-year expenditure gains, inching closer to the positive territory necessary to receive shared savings.

While AHN continues to see measured improvement, the organization has recognized some opportunities along the way. Care coordination is a foundational element, and as such, should be ready before the contract is launched. It was also recognized that connecting the team with physicians earlier would have improved the rate of physician collaboration. The care processes took longer than expected to build, and nurses with the right approach to managing the population were more difficult to find. While compensation was within market ranges, it was recognized that payers typically hire the same nurses and usually paid them more than provider organizations. The best nurses take the approach of coordinating an inch deep and a mile wide. While many nurses carefully study all the patient details and "go deep," they are only able to connect with a few patients. The emphasis for this care coordination team was to ensure knowing only enough crucial details about each patient to maximize connections with as many patients as possible.

There were also opportunities in physician selection and engagement. All AHN clinics were allowed to join the ACOs. Though clinics across the network were used to quality improvement programs, cost control for the Medicare population was a new competency. It was estimated that hand-selecting physicians who were highly engaged would have demonstrated greater results. Educating and instructing this smaller group would have been easier and more geographically concentrated.

There were also opportunities with reporting. The reporting process is best accomplished before or at the very beginning of the initiative to maximize actionable reports early on and ensure all patients are represented and tied to physicians managing their own population. Ensuring that all reports are actionable is also necessary.

While the Cigna initiative has been quite successful, the challenges with the Medicare Shared Savings Program demonstrate the difficulty of moving from volume to value. Physician buy-in, an established care coordination team and framework, along with actionable reporting and interconnected IT systems to provide the necessary data are prerequisites for success; however, everything cannot be built ahead of time. The financial impact has to be weighed as well. Adventist Health Network continues to push toward value to achieve outcomes that beat market performance and enhance existing models to continually improve patient care.

Case Study Two: One ACO's Journey to Comprehensive, Connected, Continuous Care

Cliff T. Fullerton, Jean Sullivan, and Briget da Graca

Baylor Scott & White Quality Alliance (BSWQA) is the clinically integrated accountable care organization (ACO) owned by Baylor Scott & White Health (BSWH), a large nonprofit healthcare system in North and Central Texas. BSWQA was first envisioned in 2009, as a part of the Baylor Health Care System's roadmap for healthcare improvement. It was established in 2011 with the mission of delivering the highest quality, cost-effective, and coordinated care possible to the patients and communities served by the Baylor Health Care System.[1] In 2014, a year after Baylor Health Care System and Scott & White Health merged, BSWQA expanded into the Central Texas region, welcoming more than 1000 physicians in the Scott & White Clinics, as well as Hillcrest Family Health Center and Hillcrest Physician Service Group. BSWQA uses the population health infrastructure listed in Figure 13.1 to manage the care of identified patient populations, including the BSWH-North Texas division employee health plan and managed care contract agreements with commercial and Medicare payers, which collectively account for ~166,000 covered lives.

What is striking about BSWQA's experience is that it grew out of a long history of success in a fee-for-service environment, and in the context of

Accountable for care	• >4000 physicians • 46 hospitals • Post-acute care facilities • Other stakeholders across the continuum
Integrated health system	• Baylor Scott & White Health • HealthTexas Provider Network (affiliated medical group practice in North Texas and 2nd largest subsidiary of BSWH) • Retails clinics (Walgreens Health Clinics)
Care management	• Care coordination services (RN care managers, health coordinators, social workers) • Care teams (advanced practice providers) • Disease management • Preventive health services • >100 evidence-based protocols and metrics
Data analytics/ reporting	• Patient identification • Risk stratification • Predictive modeling • Workflow analysis
Electronic health record	• In-patient and ambulatory care electronic health records • Patient portal
Patient-centered medical homes (PCMHs)	• Incorporates largest network of NCQA-recognized PCMHs (>400 physicians)

Figure 13.1 Baylor Scott & White Quality Alliance Infrastructure. (Adapted from Baylor Scott & White Quality Alliance, Value Report, 2014.)

a ban on the corporate practice of medicine that limits the application of the employed-physician model and hospital ownership of physician practices that can otherwise provide much of the integration and coordination across the continuum of care that the ACOs seek to implement.

Leadership

BSWQA is overseen by a board of managers made up of physicians, executives, a representative from the BSWH board of trustees, and a member of the community. The physician members were selected from multiple medical staff communities to represent all parts of the BSWH system, including Health Texas Provider Network (HTPN), the affiliated medical group practice. An extensive physician-led committee structure was established to create policies, determine and evaluate membership criteria, monitor regulatory compliance and financial performance, and create disease

BQA Committee	Committee Function
Membership and standards	Create standards for membership and manage performance of all participants; NCQA-accepted credentialing of physicians and other providers, and standards for alliance with post-acute care providers and facilities
Best care/clinical integration	Multidisciplinary creation and monitoring of quality and efficiency of care paths across continuum of care; chronic disease management; and transitional care management. This committee has almost 25 specialty subcommittees, each responsible for specialty-specific processes
Compliance	Organizational adherence to regulatory requirements; assurance of rights and ethical care for patients served
Finance/ contracting	Monitor financial performance of organization; create and adjudicate reward distribution; approve managed care contracts
Information technology	Ensure electronic connectivity to support clinical integration and measure both quality and cost performance

Figure 13.2   BSWQA Committee Structure. (Previously published in Ballard DJ, Fleming NS, Allison JT, Convery PB, Luquire R, eds. *Achieving STEEEP Health Care*. Boca Raton, FL: CRC Press; 2013. Table 27-2. With permission.)

management and population management care delivery protocols and pathways (Figure 13.2).[1]

BSWQA leaders were drawn extensively from past and present leaders within BSWH and HTPN, meaning that they had in-depth knowledge of the system's operations, strengths, weaknesses, and challenges that would need to be met for BSWQA to succeed in its mission. The president of BSWQA, for example, is a past chairman of the Best Care Committee as well as member of the board of directors and executive committee of Health Texas Provider Network, as well as a practicing family physician with 40 years of experience.[3] The BSWQA chief administrative officer likewise has many years of leadership experience and holds an appointment as the chief administrative officer for HTPN.[3] The alignment that this overlap in leadership provides has been critical to integrating the priorities related to population health with the other initiatives and transformations occurring within the system. This reduces the needless duplication of effort and enables accommodation of competing priorities while simultaneously reinforcing a collaborative culture.

Building on What Was Already There

Launching an ACO is unlikely to ever be a simple task. However, BSWQA avoided many of the initial growing pains related to integration of the pieces within the system—for example, inadequate integration of enterprise systems, slow uptake of electronic health records in physician practices, and poor communication between ambulatory care, in-patient, and post-acute care[4]—by building outward from an already integrated system rather than trying to incorporate unrelated pieces. When BSWQA was first formed in 2011, it was predominantly made up of the Baylor Health Care System hospitals (including acute, specialty, and postacute care facilities) and physicians within HTPN. Some years previously, HTPN had rolled out an electronic health record system across all its practices, providing a unified patient record,[5] and an analogous initiative to roll out a uniform electronic medical record and computerized physician order entry system across all Baylor Health Care System hospitals was nearing completion. HTPN was also in the process of requiring all its primary care practices to obtain National Committee for Quality Assurance (NCQA) recognition as patient-centered medical homes (PCMHs)—a process which standardized many of the elements essential for the population health management ACOs target—and establishing an Ambulatory Care Coordination department, targeting patient care advocacy, hospital discharge transition and follow-up, preventative services, and disease management.[5] Furthermore, the Baylor Health Care System hospitals and HTPN had a long history of collaborating on initiatives to improve the quality of care provided to their patients, with leaders from both the medical group and the hospital system investing in each other's infrastructure and actively participating in each other's governance structures.[5] They also had a strong culture of data-driven improvement, with extensive resources for quality measurement and reporting in place.[6] These have been augmented through substantial investment in data analytic software that facilitates automated patient identification, workflow analysis, risk-stratification, and predictive modeling.

All these factors contributed to BSWQA's early success in establishing its ACO framework. And once that framework was established, it essentially created the template within which additional providers and entities were added to the ACO. For example, primary care physicians recruited into BSWQA from outside of HTPN are required to obtain PCMH recognition within 2 years, since this standard had already been established by the way BSWQA grew out of HTPN and the Baylor Health Care System.[1] With the merger in 2013 that formed BSWH, the structure BSWQA had built on the foundation of the strong integration between HTPN and Baylor Health Care System hospitals opened out to embrace the Scott & White hospitals, as well as more than 900 new physicians within the Scott & White clinics. Additional leaders were brought into BSWQA from the Scott & White physician and executive leaders—including the chairman of the Scott & White Clinics and the chief medical officer—so that the strengths of overlapping leadership between the ACO and its constituent providers carried over into the expanded network. They furthermore brought a wealth of experience and expertise in behavioral health, which benefits the network as a whole.

Covered Lives

When BSWQA was first envisioned, it was expected to participate in the Medicare Shared Savings Program (MSSP). A practical problem arose, however, in that MSSP required patient attribution to be based on the physician's tax identification (ID) number. Since some of the BSWQA physicians practiced in groups that shared a single tax ID for billing purposes and included physicians not participating in BSWQA, this would have put the ACO at risk for patients mostly seeing a physician who was not participating in BSWQA's clinical integration activities, risks, and rewards.[7,8] BSWQA therefore switched focus to privately managed care contracts that offer opportunities for shared savings. In 2014, BSWQA had five such contracts in place, one covering the BSWH-North Texas division employee health benefits, and Medicare Advantage contracts with Aetna, Humana, and the Scott & White Health plan.[2] In September 2014, Aetna and BSWQA launched the Aetna Whole Health[SM] product in North Texas, naming BSWQA physicians and facilities as the preferred network serving members in seven counties surrounding Dallas/Fort Worth. Two large area employers included this product in their open enrollment period, and >20,000 members enrolled.[2] In 2015, BSWQA added the BSWH-Central (previously Scott & White) employee health plan, and began participating in MSSP. This latter was achieved, despite the fact that tax ID numbers are still used for patient attribution, through the practical measure of limiting participation to primary care practices that do not include any non-BSWQA physicians. This includes all the HTPN primary care practices as well as seven independent BSWQA primary care physicians, which, as of January 1, 2015, cover ~63,000 lives within MSSP.

Shared Savings

To date, costs and savings data are available only for BSWQA's longest standing contract—that with the BSWH-North Employee health plan. During its first year (2013), the employee health plan's actual expenses were 7% below the budgeted expenses, with actual costs of $480.63 per member per month compared to the budgeted $516.22.[9] This 7% does not, however, reflect actual savings that can be attributed to the ACO, as the budgeted costs were calculated to account for both expected medical costs (based on historical spending) and BSWQA's repayment of moneys loaned for its establishment by other entities within the system. The ~$14 million resulting from this under-budget performance were distributed as shown in Figure 13.3.

For physicians to receive their shared savings payments, they had to meet both the criteria for membership in BSWQA and the quality metrics established for the BSWH-North Employee Health Plan contract (see Figure 13.4).

Quality metrics for this first year focused primarily on process measures. This was to account for the fact that meaningful changes in clinical

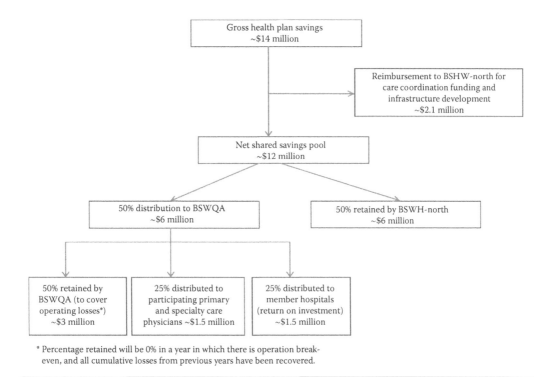

* Percentage retained will be 0% in a year in which there is operation break-even, and all cumulative losses from previous years have been recovered.

Figure 13.3 Allocation of savings from the 2013 BSWQA contract with the BSWH-North Employee Health Plan.

Criteria for BSWQA Membership[1]	Quality Metrics to Receive Shared Savings	
	Metric	Threshold
1. Pay fee to cover costs of credentialing and basic organization	1. Make three attempts to contact members discharged from inpatient stay (first attempt ≤4 days of discharge, last attempt ≤7 days of discharge).	95%
2. Submit quality and cost data	2. Increase members with annual provider wellness visit.	5% increase from previous year
3. Acquire an electronic health record	3. Annual HbA1c test for members diagnosed with diabetes mellitus.	90%, or 10% improvement from previous year
4. Log on to a secure website to view their quality and efficiency data ≥8 out of every 12 months	4. Annual LDL measurement for members diagnosed with diabetes mellitus.	90%, or 10% improvement from previous year
5. Agree to integrate clinical care with primary care and specialists jointly treating patients using agreed-upon, evidence-based care paths and protocols	5. Members diagnosed with diabetes mellitus have ≥2 office visits for diabetes annually.	90%, or 10% improvement from previous year
	6. Members diagnosed with chronic asthma are on controlled drugs, such as inhaled steroids, in addition to rescue medications.	70%, or 10% improvement from previous year
	7. Annual LDL measurement for members diagnosed with coronary artery disease.	90%, or 10% improvement from previous year
	8. Reduced readmission rate for members admitted to inpatient care for pneumonia, heart failure, or acute myocardial infarction.	5% improvement from previous year

Figure 13.4 Criteria to be met for participation in the shared savings in the BSWH-North Employee Health Plan contract (2013).

outcomes (e.g., HbA1c level for diabetes patients, or incidence of cardiovascular disease in patients diagnosed with hypertension) may take longer to achieve than a single calendar year. Additionally, data on process measure performance are readily available from existing data sources (e.g., claims and billing data, and electronic health record), whereas reliable, timely outcome data (including patient satisfaction and mortality data) are more difficult to obtain.[10–13] While obtaining such outcomes data will be important to measuring and maintaining quality of long-term care in BSWQA, at this stage of its evolution, establishing the framework for using quality metrics in distributing shared savings was of higher priority than wrestling with the challenges of obtaining reliable outcome data.

Challenges Overcome

BSWQA has expanded rapidly, and both its under-budget performance in the first year of the BSWH-North Employee Health Plan contract and the uptake of the Aetna Whole Health[SM] product are promising for future success. But while BSWQA had a strong foundation of leadership and commitment to quality to build on, a number of barriers had to be overcome to reach this stage in the journey.

A significant early challenge was recruiting sufficient numbers of both primary and specialty physicians serving a wide enough geographic area to ensure that they are able to deliver high-quality care to the patient population they serve across the continuum of care. This proved particularly challenging for specialties where one or two physician groups dominated the market, and so had little incentive to join an ACO to ensure they did not lose referral sources.[1] BSWQA assembled a network that met the requirements considered adequate to care for the population it serves before its first contract became active, but continues to recruit in specialties and areas where access can still be improved—for example, pediatrics and oncology.[1]

A second substantial challenge arose as more providers from outside HTPN—and therefore not on the common electronic health record implemented across HTPN—joined BSWQA.[1] A secure and feasible means of sharing clinical and performance data across disparate systems was needed. This is being accomplished through the implementation of a health information exchange, enabling the connection not only of disparate electronic health record systems, but also the integration of BSWQA's data analytics systems. This will allow simultaneous reporting of a patient's medical history, risk status, cost information, and other data relevant to population health management, enabling better-informed shared decision-making between patients and physicians at the point of care.[2]

Moving forward, it remains to be seen if the shared savings program will remain financially and operationally viable in the long term. While the early financial results are encouraging, it is too soon to tell whether the meaningful reductions in healthcare costs and gains in population health are being achieved. What BSWQA has achieved is the establishment of a strong framework, built on a history of close hospital–physician alignment and dedication to high-quality care, that should enable it to adapt as needed in its mission to provide accountable, evidence-based, cost-effective care to its communities.

Case Study Three: Launching Population Health Program in 12 Months

Marty Manning and Gary Wainer

Creating a population health management enterprise, a clinical integration program or an accountable care organization does not have to take multiple years or require your organization to incur hundreds of thousands of dollars in consulting fees. A basic familiarity with the common building blocks of these types of programs, combined with the right resources and strong project management, are the most essential ingredients needed for success. Over the past decade, the authors have built or assisted others in developing over a dozen such programs around the country. Here, they share an overview of essential program components they be incorporated into the rapid build of the Northwestern Medicine Physician Partners (NMPP) program.

There is an iconic Harvard Business Review article which posited that any business can be reduced to two basic elements—making the doughnuts and selling the doughnuts. The same holds true in developing a population health program, although we would depart slightly from that formula. For us, there are three critical elements: having a care delivery program (the "product"), having a network of physicians and other providers to participate in that program (the "delivery system"), and engaging with payers and others to bring patients to the program and pay for the costs of that program (the "customer").

Organizations seeking to build a program within a short time frame should develop a tactical plan outlining what they propose to do in each of these three areas. But perfection should not be allowed to become the enemy of the good. Population health management organizations, even mature ones, continue to evolve over time. Begin by developing a vision of where you want to be in, let us say, 5 years' time. With that end in mind, break down that vision into annual increments. Then develop an aggressive but manageable work plan to accomplish those annual increments.

Infrastructure Development (the "Product")

The infrastructure of a population health management program consists of both technology and human capital, and both must be assessed and considered in building out a care delivery platform.

Physician leadership is a critically important program component; one often looked at by the Federal Trade Commission in its assessment of clinical integration programs. Physician "sweat equity" is critical to the success of our organization. NMPP has a total of 58 governance seats on its Board and committees, only three of which are occupied by nonphysicians. NMPP began its human capital development by planning out the organizational and committee structures. The parent company designated a Board of Managers who would oversee the general strategic direction of the organization. The Board consists of 17 members, 16 of whom are physicians. The Board then approved the management team, consisting of a President, a Medical Director, a Director of Quality and Clinical Integration, a Director of Provider Relations, and a Director of Care Management.

The Board also created several committees whose structure mirrors that of the most successful organizations of this type across the country. The first committee that was activated was the Quality Improvement Committee. This committee, consisting of only member physicians, was charged with developing and monitoring performance of the measures used for charting improvements in care. Much of NMPP's first year's work has been to vet over 100 measures and working with its IT infrastructure to create disease and wellness registries, patient attribution methodologies, and risk stratification tools. The work plan for year two will include creating clinical pathways for best practices in delivering chronic and preventative care.

The Membership Committee, again comprised of all physician members, is charged with overseeing credentialing and membership processes. Membership is viewed as a privilege that carries with it obligations and requirements that exceed just credentialing criteria. Included in those additional criteria are being responsive to the Clinical Integration and Quality Programs, maintaining adequate technology in one's office, and participating in all contracts in which NMPP engages, among others.

The Committee meets all NCQA requirements for delegated credentialing and can rapidly credential new physicians into the organization because of its integration with the central verification office of the parent organization.

The Contracting Committee is charged with developing and approving NMPP's payer contracts, and for those HMO contracts for which NMPP is at risk, developing fee schedules.

The Utilization Management Committee monitors and has the goal of reducing variability in cost and ensuring appropriate utilization of services. Data such as ED usage, admissions for ambulatory sensitive conditions, and rates of tertiary facility use are all monitored. When outliers are identified, the committee works with the physician, or the system to correct the issue. While the UM Committee was a requirement for NMPP's participation in HMO contracts, the scope of the committee's activities will include oversight of performance on similar efficiency measures in NMPP's "value-based" contracts, such as the Medicare Shared Savings Program, Medicare Advantage, and commercial shared savings contracts.

NMPP's nurse care manager program, which is one of the core functions supporting all of its payer contracts, is staffed by RN's, and includes identification of the "high risk" patients and the development and tracking of care management plans for them. This team helps manage those patients through coordinating their care, identifying and closing gaps in care, and providing social and community resources to achieve better states of health.

Most population health management organizations do not have the luxury of single EMR or practice management system platform upon which to build their population health management IT capabilities. As a class of products, these population health IT systems leave much to be desired. They tend to be expensive and difficult to install, and few vendors offer tools that will provide for all of an organization's business needs in a single product. In our experience, the goal should be to determine your measures, use the technology one has, and plan to change out that platform in 3–5 years as products in this space mature. Anticipating that these systems will most likely be replaced in a few years, it might be advisable to structure vendor contracts on a "pay-as-you-go" basis to minimize abandonment costs as longer term solutions are developed. Startup organizations typically would not reach the "gold standard" in the first year or two of operations, so "perfection should not be allowed to become the enemy of the good."

NMPP was fortunate to have a single EMR platform for more than half its physicians. This unified platform allowed it to build a set of registries and communication tools to more effectively close gaps in care and coordinate care among physicians. NMPP has also been successful in building a process to bring in external data to provide a single unified data warehouse where entire population can be assessed and analyzed.

Provider Network ("Distribution System")

In putting together the provider network, there are typically two primary considerations: network adequacy and expectations of membership. An organization's requirements related to both will evolve over time as its program matures and becomes increasingly complex. *Network Adequacy* is a concept whose origins trace to the HMO world: does one's network has the minimum number of physicians in the right medical specialty and geographic areas to present itself to the market as a comprehensive network capable of serving the majority of needs of the patients that will collectively be their responsibility to care for? *Membership Requirements* will also evolve over time, but the intent is to codify what it means to be a "good citizen" or "member in good standing" in the network. Membership criteria go well beyond basic credentialing criteria. Credentialing criteria typically sets the minimum threshold for participation, to eliminate the 5% of applicants at the lower end of the bell-shaped curve. Membership criteria should be developed to be descriptive of what it means to be a part of a collaborative group of providers. These criteria should apply equally to employed physicians as well as those in private practice. NMPP's mantra has always been to be "employment-neutral"; in other words, from the point of view of the population health management program, it does not matter whether a physician is employed by the system or in an independent private practice. NMPP's concern is about the "interdependence" of all physician members.

One way NMPP was able to get a critical mass of physicians to become members of the program was to make membership a requirement for the physician to be in the network for the parent company's employee benefits plan. In fairly short order, NMPP was able to recruit physicians representing about 80% of the patient care activity of the healthcare system.

The development of NMPP's physician network began with the core group of system-employed physicians, who shared a common EMR platform. The employed physician had a pre-existing partial risk HMO contract, which was subsequently assigned to NMPP. As a part of that assignment, NMPP opened enrollment to private physicians in the community, enlarging the network from 260 to 550 physicians within 9 months.

The goals for physician enrollment were originally established using the network adequacy requirements of the HMO product, and needed to include significant numbers of primary care physicians. Additionally, NMPP's network had to include an appropriate network of specialists, subspecialists, and tertiary care services. Given NMPP's close relationship with two tertiary facilities (one an adult medicine center and other a pediatric hospital), as well as an already existing robust specialty roster at NMPP's home hospital was rapidly accomplished.

The initial NMPP membership requirements are that physicians be on staff at one of NMPP' score hospitals. The NMPP Membership Committee was designed to meet all of the NCQA requirements for payer credentialing. NMPP also received a state waiver allowing it to do re-credentialing every two years, in parallel with the hospital re-credentialing cycle, rather than on the 3-year cycle required of managed care organizations in Illinois. This substantially decreased the administrative burden for NMPP member physicians. Presently NMPP is delegated to do credentialing by all but one of its contracted payers, which allows it to move rapidly to include new members in its network. Having delegated credentialing has allowed NMPP to accelerate the solidification of its provider network.

Acquiring Patients to Manage ("Customers")

NMPP, like other start up organizations, had two ready sources of lives to manage: the participants in its parent corporation's own health benefits plans and the Medicare Shared Savings Program. Often, hospitals and healthcare systems are the largest single employer in their service area. Physicians are already providing care for the Medicare beneficiaries who would be attributed to your ACO, so they typically know these patients well. This is especially true of the patients who would benefit most from the kinds of things ACOs typically do, like manage patients in a disease registry and operate nurse care manager programs.

By building NMPP's initial program around these two captive audiences, it was able to quickly get to a "critical mass" sufficient to build and test program infrastructure, like physician results reporting and its nurse care manager programs, and engage physicians in governance activities of the program.

The NMPP participating provider agreement (PPA) allows NMPP to act as the agent of the member physician in negotiating group contracts with payers. As such, NMPP was able to expand its HMO presence and rapidly enter into the Medicare Shared Savings Program as an ACO and the Illinois Medicaid Accountable Care Entity, and to contract with the parent organization for care management for their employees. This rapid deployment allowed NMPP to attain 40,000 "managed lives" in less than an year's time.

Startup organizations should bear in mind that it is never too early to begin a dialogue with area payer organizations, even as they are just beginning to develop their programs. Talking with payers about your aspirations provides an important opportunity to gauge payer interest or resistance, and adjust plans accordingly early on. In talking with these payers, take an inventory of the "value-based" programs they offer, request and review the "standard" contracts they have for these programs, and collect a list of the measures these programs track. Knowing what measures the payers have selected can help inform your own measures selection process down the road. This is also a good time to begin discussing what kinds of data you will need to operate your program, and gauge the willingness of payers to allow data sharing to support your program objectives. In our experience, it can be exasperating getting data, even on your own employees from one's own TPA/payer.

Case Study Four: An Interprofessional Approach to Improving Care Coordination: The Transition Clinic at Rush University Medical Center

Vidya Chakravarthy, Regina McClenton, and Christopher M. Nolan (Primary authors); Robyn L. Golden and Anthony J. Perry (Secondary authors)

Background

Rush University Medical Center is 664-bed academic medical center located in Chicago, Illinois. Rush is nationally recognized for much of its work, and has a mission "to provide the best healthcare for the individuals and diverse communities we serve through the integration of outstanding patient care, education, research and community partnerships." The mission was recently updated to specifically emphasize "community partnerships," a focal point for Rush given the transforming healthcare landscape. In recent years, Rush has actively created partnerships with community healthcare providers in order to improve continuity of care, reduce unnecessary readmissions, and foster warm handoffs to the primary care setting. In support of their newly adopted vision to become nationally recognized for transforming healthcare, Rush created a new interprofessional care model called the Transition Clinic in September 2013. The Transition Clinic is composed of a "transition team" which consists of a primary care physician, registered nurse, licensed clinical social worker, and patient care navigator. Together, led by the primary care physician, the team works with patients who are unable to secure a follow-up appointment within one week of discharge and assists these patients in developing a primary care relationship. Following the opening of the clinic, Rush learned that over 90% of patients scheduled in the clinic either did not have a primary care provider or had not seen one within the past year.

The Transition Clinic aims to support patients while their health returns to baseline, by bridging the gap between hospital discharge and primary care follow up. With the help of the transition team, the clinic works with the patient to identify knowledge and resource gaps, and empowers the patient to manage their health until the next follow-up appointment. The transition team assures that the majority of patients who complete a transition clinic appointment are transitioned to an appropriate medical home to establish a long-term primary care relationship. By better managing post-discharge care, increasing accessibility, and establishing primary care relationships, the Transition Clinic has helped reduce the overall institutional readmission rate for patients it has supported by 14%.

Case

Fred* walked into Rush's Emergency Department, not really sure where else to go. For the past two weeks he was experiencing general pain all over his body, weakness, and shortness of breath. He was only 36 years old, how could this be happening? The only health condition he could recall hearing about was that he had high blood pressure, but he was sure the doctor was exaggerating. What was the big deal if his blood pressure was slightly high? It would come down eventually, right? There was no need to buy all those expensive medications that his doctor told him to take when paying his rent and putting food on the table was far more important.

---

* Please note that all character names are fictional.

After waiting for a short period of time, Fred was called back to the examination room. The nurse greeted him and began to take his blood pressure. After the last puff of air escaped from the blood pressure cuff, the nurse read the pressure gauge and her eyebrows furrowed in concern. She took another reading and came up with the same number: 198/128. Fred was immediately admitted to the hospital for hypertensive urgency.

Shortly after getting settled in his hospital bed and speaking with multiple doctors, Fred had the pleasure of meeting Sarah, one of the inpatient case managers. She was very pleasant and asked him questions about his job, home life, and means of transportation. She seemed concerned, but Fred had lived this way for his whole life and did not see anything missing. Given his limited income, he spent his money only on what was immediately necessary.

When Dr. Cooper entered the room, she validated Sarah's concerns and did see something missing. Dr. Cooper noted that Fred did not have an established primary care physician. Since Fred's insurance was out-of-network, she worried that he would not have someone to regularly monitor his blood pressure and overall health. While writing her notes in Fred's chart, she remembered a presentation she recently heard about the Transition Clinic, a new interprofessional care model, which was designed to support patients like Fred. She immediately sent a message to the clinic through the electronic medical record asking that an appointment be scheduled for Fred soon after he was discharged.

Betty, the Transition Clinic patient care navigator, immediately received Dr. Cooper's message and scheduled Fred for an appointment in the clinic four days after discharge. Shortly after, Linda, the Transition Clinic social worker, found that Fred's appointment had been added to the upcoming clinic schedule. After thoroughly reviewing his chart, she saw that he had been discharged the day before and might need assistance with managing his medications and overall health. Linda immediately called Fred to identify his follow-up needs and to confirm his upcoming appointment. During this lengthy conversation, Fred told Linda that while he never wanted to feel that way again, he did not understand how his pain and shortness of breath were related to high blood pressure. Fred also did not understand why taking his medications mattered. Not to mention, even if it did matter, Fred did not even know how to find an affordable doctor.

Linda was an excellent listener and emphasized the importance of medication compliance and established primary care, both of which could help ensure that Fred did not end up in the Emergency Room again. She learned more about Fred's living arrangements and gaps in resources, and helped Fred successfully navigate (or find his way) through the complex healthcare system.

Linda worked tirelessly, with both Fred and the rest of the transition team, to help him locate a Federally Qualified Health Center (FQHC) that was both near his home and could best serve his healthcare needs. She also scheduled a new patient appointment and provided him with all the necessary information, including the doctor's name, clinic address, phone number, and directions—all in an easy-to-read format. Before meeting Linda and the transition team, Fred thought that having a regular doctor was a luxury for those who could afford it. He never knew that FQHC was an affordable healthcare option. With the right knowledge and resources, Fred learned that healthcare was indeed accessible—and for that, he thanked the Transition Clinic term.

Since his Transition Clinic experience, Fred has not returned to the Emergency Room or hospital. Instead, Fred has established a relationship with a new primary care provider who regularly monitors his blood pressure, and, as Linda promised, ensures that Fred will never again feel the way he did when he walked into Rush's Emergency Room.

Conclusion

There are too many people like Fred in the world, and as there is more national focus on addressing rising healthcare costs, reducing fragmented care, and preventing chronic disease, we all must do our part to improve the overall health of the population. Rush has not only invested in the Transition Clinic to help alleviate this need, but also numerous other programs in order to improve the health of its own patients, as well as those of the greater Chicago area. One of Rush's population health initiatives includes joining the Medical Home Network (MHN) Accountable Care Organization (ACO). The MHNACO is a provider-driven network made up of hospitals and FQHCs on the near west and south sides of Chicago, which aims to improve care coordination for their Medicaid patients. Rush also developed the Advanced Bridge Coordination (ABC) Program, which aims to reduce re-hospitalization by connecting patients to primary care services and assisting them with their healthcare needs.

These efforts are only a small representation of what Rush, and many other institutions, need to do in order to provide the best care for its vulnerable populations. In order to achieve a mission of providing "the best healthcare for the individuals and diverse communities we serve," we must work together to not only create access, but also provide continuous, compassionate, and coordinated care.

Case Study Five: Cigna Collaborative Care

Peter W. McCauley, Richard D. Salmon, and Harriet Wallsh

At Cigna, we have recognized and devoted a significant amount of time reflecting on the fact that the current U.S. healthcare system rewards physicians and facilities for the volume of care delivered rather than the value or the quality of the care received. This traditional care model has proven to lead to poor quality, higher costs, and lower patient satisfaction—it is estimated that poor quality and wasteful spending drives 30% of all U.S. healthcare costs.* Two key flaws in the current healthcare system are at the root of these avoidable costs. First, the current system rewards for the quantity of care delivered—not quality of the patient care outcomes achieved. Second, because healthcare delivery is fragmented, doctors often do not have the information they need to make the most effective, efficient decisions for their patients. Lack of insight about their patients' total healthcare experience, including gaps in care, history of recent hospitalizations, medications, and specialist care means they are often working with incomplete information.

Cigna has worked to fix those flaws, by creating a model that provides rewards for quality outcomes and gives healthcare professionals the information—and the support—they need to achieve those outcomes.

In 2008, we started our first Accountable Care Organization (ACO) arrangement, which Cigna calls Cigna Collaborative Care (CCC), with Dartmouth Hitchcock in New Hampshire. We now have well over 100 of these arrangements across the United States. Innovation has allowed Cigna to learn what success looks like and how best to support our collaborative groups as they drive toward that success.

We have carefully selected large physician groups that have embraced adherence to evidence-based medicine guidelines (EBM), adopted a reward-for-value financial model, committed to the use of physician extenders in the team concept of medical management, and have made capital investments in the delivery of care such as implementation of electronic medical records.

---

* Evidence-based care gaps. Pervasive, Research says, Health Leaders Media, January 28, 2011.

Our relationship with CCC groups begins with a diagnostic assessment of their performance on both efficiency of care (cost) and quality of care (outcomes) for a specific population of their Cigna patients (usually a minimum of 5000). This evaluation allows Cigna and the CCC group to agree on areas where they are performing well, and on areas where there is an opportunity for improvement. These areas of opportunity are captured in a document called a Key Focus Action Plan (KFAP). The KFAP serves as a roadmap to success, allowing us to work together in a collaborative manner over a defined time frame to reduce the cost of care while improving quality outcomes. As an example, one of our CCC groups in the Midwest, using the data we provided, noted that when compared to the market, they had a higher rate of Cigna patients visiting the emergency room for conditions like congestive heart failure and asthma. In order to address this issue, they increased primary care physician access. Specifically, their primary care physicians committed to maintaining eight additional office hours each week beyond their normal patient care office hours using extended evening hours and Saturday afternoon and Sunday morning office hours.

Once the KFAP is agreed to, we continually provide actionable, patient-specific information to help drive success. This includes claim data—such as gaps in care, recent hospitalizations, emergency room visits, and prescription utilization. This information is shared to point them to patients who have the greatest risk and the potential to drive high costs, so they know *who* and can determine *what* needs to be done to avert those costs and improve outcomes.

We meet every quarter with each CCC group to review cost and quality performance metrics to evaluate the group's progress toward goals of improvement from their starting point, as well as, goals of improvement compared to their local market peers. These quarterly meetings are bolstered by monthly operations meetings to support and maintain the operating infrastructure of the collaborative relationship.

Finally, we hold learning collaborative meetings on a quarterly basis, giving all our CCCs the opportunity to learn from each other and share best practices.

Cigna holds our CCC groups to high standards; however, we make significant contributions to the relationship to support their success. In addition to the areas discussed earlier, we also provide:

▪ *Clinical Resources*: We help physicians identify specific quality and medical cost performance improvement opportunities, and offer tips and suggestions to drive better outcomes.

- *Integration with Clinical Programs*: We make it easier for physicians to connect their patients with available Cigna health improvement programs such as case management and disease management, which help improve patient health outcomes.
- *Information shared with Embedded Care Coordinators*: With actionable, patient-specific data, we empower and train members of our collaborative partner's staff to serve as dedicated patient/customer care coordinators. These coordinators use data supplied by Cigna to plan and coordinate evidence-based care plans, and follow up to ensure those plans are being utilized.
- *Financial Incentives:* When the CCC group improves quality, reduces total medical cost, and has a cost trend lower than their local market peers, the CCC group receives a portion of the savings as a performance based reimbursement. Our data and informatics allow our CCC groups to tie this performance-based reimbursement directly to physician performance so that each member of the group has aligned incentives based on outcomes. This arrangement continues to facilitate alignment away from fee for service, and toward performance-based reimbursement. If quality does not improve, there is no performance-based reimbursement—no matter what the impact on medical cost trend.

Using this approach, we have seen success in lowering total medical cost and improving quality. Our published results indicate that CCC groups that have participated for two or more years have, on average, demonstrated 2% better than market average total medical cost and 2% better than market average quality, and trended 1.1% better than market total medical cost trend.

Examples of success include one group that implemented extended office hours, embedded care coordinator outreach and 24 h triage in 2013, resulting in emergency room visits per thousand decreasing 17% compared to 2012, avoidable emergency room visits per thousand decreasing 15% compared to 2012, and high emergency room visits per thousand decreasing by 30% compared to 2012.

One group focused on mammograms and diabetic eye exams and performed 5% better than market in breast cancer screenings and 9% better than market on diabetic retinopathy screenings. After implementing a new patient education program about urgent care availability, another group achieved 26% lower emergency room avoidable visits per thousand, and delivered a 15% lower than market total emergency room spend with a trend that is better than the market.

We established Cigna Collaborative Care with large physician groups where 20% of high risk Cigna patients receive care. We are now expanding our approach to include specialists who account for 57% of total medical cost spend, hospitals where 25% of at-risk Cigna customers receive care each year, and small physician groups where 40% of at risk Cigna customers seek treatment. We have learned a great deal over the last 7 years and believe we are well positioned for future success. We are proud of our published results and validation from external parties like the KLAS 2014 Payer ACO Capabilities Research Report released in November 2014, which indicates that Cigna remains the national leader in the number of ACOs and a leader in the type of support we provide to our collaborative partners including robust data (Figure 13.5).

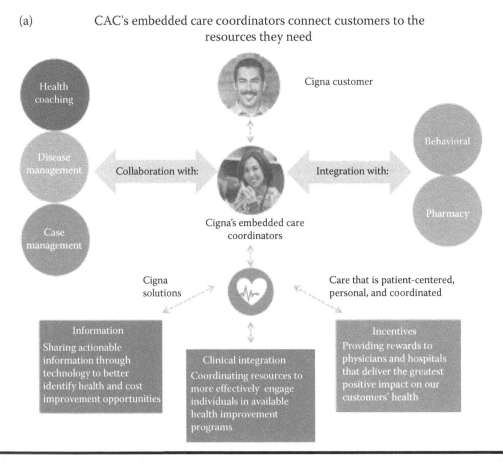

Figure 13.5 Cigna collaborative care.   *(Continued)*

(b)   Collaborative accountable care financial model

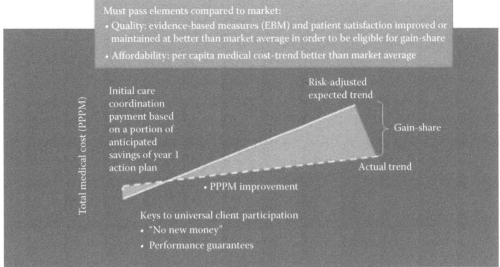

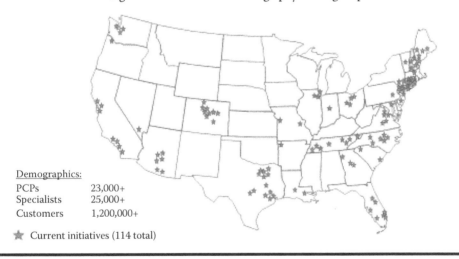

Cigna collaborative care—large physician groups

Demographics:
PCPs   23,000+
Specialists   25,000+
Customers   1,200,000+

⭐ Current initiatives (114 total)

Figure 13.5 (*Continued*)   Cigna collaborative care.

Case Study Six: Patient-Centered Medical Home (PCMH)

Catherine Dimou, Abigail Boyer, and Terrence Murphy

Rush Health

In order to establish a framework for practice-based care management, our organization chose to implement patient-centered medical home (PCMH)

capabilities in seven practices. Using the PCMH constructs, we hoped to better manage chronic care and reduce waste from over-utilization of services. Two pilot practices were identified for embedded nurse-care managers who would assist with patient management. Risk stratification based on chronic co-morbidities was used to identify patients for intervention.

A population management registry was developed that identifies patients with poorly controlled chronic conditions and high utilization patterns. Two practices were identified for case management services using an embedded nurse-care manager. Using an internally developed model to identify appropriate patients, care managers outreach patients to enroll them in care coordination services.

- Chronic conditions identified include: Diabetes, asthma, hypertension, and hyperlipidemia.
- In 2014, 210 patients have been managed of a total patient base of 395 in these practices (or of a total of 515 identified).

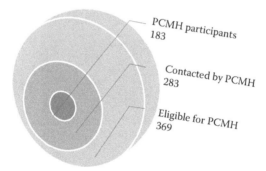

After enrollment, patients meet with a care manager face to face in provider offices or by phone for follow-up care. The care manager is responsible for creating a "previsit planning" document for the provider's review prior to the patient's scheduled visit. The previsit plan gives a summary of the patient's overall health, reviews established goals and most recent lab results, and reminds providers to order needed labs, screenings, and immunizations. The care manager is available to attend the upcoming appointment with the patient to facilitate effective communication between provider and patient. In between visits, the care manager checks in on the patient via phone or email to ensure that the patient is adhering to their treatment plan and any stumbling blocks are addressed. All care managers, have access to condition-specific pathways that outline best practices for optimal care.

These guidelines discuss topics such as health maintenance, diet and exercise, medication adherence, and self-monitoring adherence.

Outcomes: The cohort of actively managed PCMH patients ($n = 178$) has fewer ER visits, fewer inpatient admissions, and more frequent office use than a comparison cohort ($n = 102$) of patients' meeting eligibility criteria for inclusion in the program, but who declined participation.

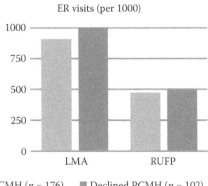

ER visits (per 1000)

■ PCMH ($n = 176$)   ■ Declined PCMH ($n = 102$)

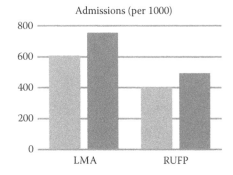

Admissions (per 1000)

■ PCMH ($n = 176$)   ■ Declined PCMH ($n = 102$)

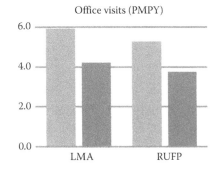

Office visits (PMPY)

■ PCMH ($n = 176$)   ■ Declined PCMH ($n = 102$)

PCMH's primary target population is uncontrolled diabetics (A1c >= 8.0). Relative to the comparison cohort, PCMH patients have experienced a decrease in average A1c, achieving significant progress toward A1c control.

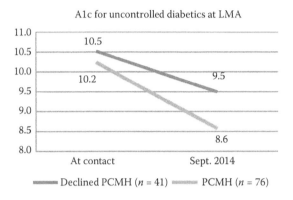

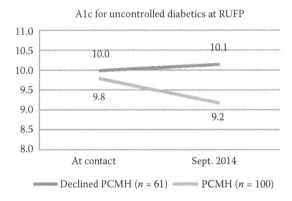

Over a 2-year period, patients have shown consistent improvement in the utilization of ED and in patient stays with an increase in outpatient visits. In addition, there has been an improvement in glycemic control in the care-managed population.

Bibliography

1. Couch CE, Winter FD, Jr., Roberts WL. Engaging STEEEP care through an accountable care organization. In: Ballard DJ, Fleming NS, Allison JT, Convery PB, Luquire R, eds. *Achieving STEEEP Health Care*. Boca Raton, FL: CRC Press; 2013: 217–226.
2. Baylor Scott & White Quality Alliance, Value Report, 2014.
3. Baylor Scott & White Quality Alliance. Leadership. http://www.baylorquality-alliance.com/leadership/Pages/leadership.aspx. Accessed January 19, 2015.

4. Terry K. Health IT: The glue for accountable care organizations. Four big systems show how they're using EHRs, connectivity, and data warehouses to drive ACOs. *Healthcare Information*. May 2011; 28(5): 16, 18, 20 passim.

5. Couch CE, Winter FD, Jr., Roberts WL. Driving STEEEP care across a physician provider network. In: Ballard DJ, Fleming NS, Allison JT, Convery PB, Luquire R, eds. *Achieving STEEEP Health Care*. Boca Raton, FL: CRC Press; 2013: 99–112.

6. Kennerly D, Valdes M, Nicewander DA, Green RT. STEEEP analytics. In: Ballard DJ, Fleming NS, Allison JT, Convery PB, Luquire R, eds. *Achieving STEEEP Health Care*. Boca Raton, FL: CRC Press; 2013: 75–80.

7. Couch CE. Why Baylor Health Care System would like to file for Medicare Shared Savings accountable care organization designation but cannot. *Mayo Clinic Proceedings*. Aug 2012; 87(8): 723–726.

8. ABIM Foundation. Choosing Wisely®. http://www.choosingwisely.org/. Accessed May 15, 2013.

9. Baylor Scott & White Quality Alliance. Baylor Scott & White Quality Alliance (BSWQA) First Year Results Point to Future Success in Population Health Management. BID HTPN_2167 8.142014.

10. Mant J. Process versus outcome indicators in the assessment of quality of health care. *International Journal for Quality in Health Care*. Dec 2001; 13(6): 475–480.

11. Furrow BR, Greaney TL, Johnson SH, Jost TS, Schwarts RL. *Introduction to Health Law and Policy. The Law of Health Care Organization and Financing*. St. Paul, MN: Thomson West; 2008: 1–95.

12. Berenson RA, Provonost PJ, Krumholz HM. Achieving the potential of health care performance measures. *Timely Analysis of Health Policy Issues* 2013. http://www.rwjf.org/content/dam/farm/reports/reports/2013/rwjf406195. Accessed February 4, 2014.

13. da Graca B, Filardo G, Nicewander D. Consequences for healthcare quality and research of the exclusion of records from the Death Master File. *Circulation: Cardiovascular Quality and Outcomes*. Jan 1, 2013; 6(1): 124–128.

Chapter 14

The Future of Healthcare Delivery

George Mayzell

Contents

I hope that by now I have convinced you that the current delivery system of the healthcare model is not sustainable. We know that it is inefficient, expensive, reactive (not proactive), and, in many cases, not evidence based. We know that it leads to significant disparities in healthcare and inefficient use of healthcare dollars and resources. We know that change must happen in order for us to be a competitive country with great healthcare, efficient productivity (industry), and a happy and "well" population.

As we discussed, our current system rewards volume "at all costs." It is clear that we must pay for healthcare differently, and most people believe that the trend from volume to value is already underway. We must reward outcomes and efficiency, and we must get utilize patient engagement to achieve these outcomes. If we look at Figure 14.1, we can see what this future model is expected to look like.

The challenge here is not so much where we are going but how fast we are going to get there. We talk about this as the two healthcare curves. The first curve is our current system curve, which we have desperately been

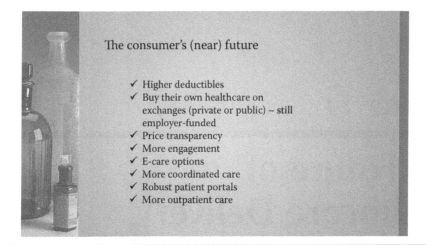

The consumer's (near) future

✓ Higher deductibles
✓ Buy their own healthcare on exchanges (private or public) – still employer-funded
✓ Price transparency
✓ More engagement
✓ E-care options
✓ More coordinated care
✓ Robust patient portals
✓ More outpatient care

Figure 14.1 Future customers.

trying to bend and modify for many years. This curve is based on unit cost and volume of care. While we might have been somewhat successful, most of the success has been aimed at mitigating the trend. We have simply slowed the increase. The second curve is a different curve, and this is the value-based payment curve (a population health curve). We must change the payment model and the delivery system to get to the second curve. This curve is based on creating value which includes cost and quality. The challenges, at least for the foreseeable future, will be living in the space between the two curves. This can be like having a foot on the dock and a foot in a canoe. This middle space is difficult to navigate. Much like the 1980s, where in a practice, a portion of patients were paid via capitation and a portion of patients were paid via fee-for-service. The delivery models are very different and it is very difficult to have two different delivery models in the same healthcare system (Figure 14.2). It is impossible to know how long this middle space will last, but it is highly likely that it will go on for some time. Most believe that the fee-for-service model, while slowly decreasing, will not be going away anytime soon. Things such as concierge care and a cash marketplace survive. The healthcare industry is very large with a lot of vested interests, making changing this quite difficult.

As we try to imagine what the new model will have to look like, here is a list of attributes that are critical:

■ Individual accountability
■ Aligned payments

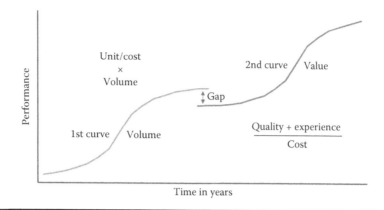

Figure 14.2 Volume to value. (Adapted from Navigant Executive Summary: Our Point of View Regarding Alignment and Performance Effectiveness, October 2014.)

- Transitions of care and communication
- Data at the individual level and at the population level
- A focus on prevention and early intervention
- A move from a sick system to a wellness system
- "Decision support" for evidence-based care in the delivery site
- Transparent pricing and healthcare information
- Physician leadership

Many of our current trends will continue. We will see continued consolidation of the industry with increasingly integrated delivery systems focusing on both vertical and horizontal integration. This is a critical functionality to get to an efficient model healthcare delivery. Rather than each entity making a profit for services, the new seamless delivery system will gain significant efficiencies. In business, we usually consider "the rule of threes," and I think that will be true in healthcare. Usually there are mergers and closings till there are three major competitors left in each geography. The greater challenge in healthcare is that often benefit structures will have to be looked at from a national basis to meet employer's needs. This will require a more national focus on healthcare delivery.

One of the interesting pieces in this future puzzle will have to be what the payer's role is in this new world. The payers will be vertically integrated into the delivery system so the financial management is directly inside the delivery system. Some health plans are starting to work on this model while others are being either bought by delivery systems or are buying delivery systems. It is also hard to know what role the government will play. Many feel that we are slowly crawling to a single-payer system.

Reimbursement will move from volume to value, and we can expect to see more bundling of services. In our current models, patients get bills from the hospital, lab, x-ray, physicians, radiologists, and others for the same service. In the future, the patient will get one bill for a procedure or episode of care, and the reimbursement will have to go back to the individual players separately. This will be seamless to the patient. It is also likely that we will go through a period of reference pricing where a set price is dictated for a set procedure diagnoses. In this reimbursement system, anything above that set price will need to be paid by the member. A critical piece of this new model will be the transparency that allows the patient to clearly understand the pricing model for care and service.

There will also be continued growth of healthcare exchanges, both the public exchanges and private exchanges. Recent legal challenges may change some of the rules around the public exchanges. However, most believe that the private exchanges will thrive and flourish as companies and employers go to defined contribution programs. In these programs, employers will pay a fixed fee for the employee and/or their family to get healthcare coverage and the employee left to make up any difference if they want a richer benefit plan. The member will also continue to have increasing and significant copayments and deductibles thus making the member accountable for the first dollar coverage. These high deductible plans or consumer directed healthcare helps lower premiums but also engages the customer in their healthcare spending. This "retailization" of healthcare will continue in an aggressive fashion (Figure 14.3).

In a Three- to Five-Year Timeframe

Here, we will see a continued move from a physician-centric model to a patient-centric model. Currently, much of the healthcare delivery model and is built around patients being "patient" with the care-delivery model. We hope that the waiting room will be no more as waiting is a waste for all. Healthcare will continue to move into the outpatient arena with a separation of inpatient care and hospitals. Hospitals will no longer be the center of the care universe, and integrated delivery systems will evolve with the continued consolidation of healthcare resources. Inpatient care will be

Population Health Metrics

Metric	Examples
Global	Health adjusted life expectancy Quality adjusted life expectancy Quality adjusted life year Years of healthy life
Health Status	Reported poor health Immunization rates Preventive health screens
Psychological Status	Psychological status scores Suicide rate Percentage with major depression
Function	Percentage of adults with disability Limited activity last 30 days Adults with obesity
Inequality	Geographic variation in age and mortality Mortality rates by sex, ethnicity, etc. Life expectancy by sex, ethnicity, etc.
Access	Percentage of population insured Percentage of population with a PCP
Social Deter	Average education level Tobacco use rates
Cost	Total cost of healthcare per person Cost last 60 days of life Cost acute vs. prevention

Figure 14.3   Different metrics for population health. (Adapted from Parrish RG. *Measuring Population Health Outcomes,* **July 2010; 7(4) and Health People 2020, 2013.)**

managed primarily by hospitalists, both general hospitalists and specialist hospitalists.

As patients get more demanding and expect more service, physicians and clinics will have to evolve into new delivery models. This will push connectivity with retail health clinics and others, which will continue to proliferate.

If (when) Walmart and others aggressively gets in the healthcare delivery business, this could be "destructive innovation." There will be increasing point of care testing and home-based testing where the patient/consumer has more control of the healthcare. Retail clinics will continue to grow and integrate into other medical neighborhoods, and these retail clinics will be in all sorts of retail establishments and link through electronic media to integrated delivery systems.

Robust telehealth will provide information, healthcare visits, and ongoing medical follow-up. These systems will be able to track patients at home for chronic diseases by helping the patient monitor blood sugars, blood pressure, cardiac rhythms, pulmonary function testing, and skin lesions (via camera). There would be more apps available for smart phones as well as smart watches which help an individual keep track of their own health. Physician extenders and community health workers will continue to be more involved in healthcare as a way of providing access in the community and less expensive healthcare delivery. True community medical neighborhoods will evolve in which patients will be tied into community resources, churches and religious organizations, and other nontraditional resources.

Also in this three- to five-year timeframe, there will need to be significant IT advances. Currently, most systems have many different electronic medical-record (EMR) systems many of which do not interface with each other. There are also very few active healthcare information exchanges or HIEs. We will see EMRs with increasing middleware to let the systems talk to each other. The ability to get patient information seamlessly across the system will prove to be a huge competitive advantage. In addition, systems will have to start talking to each other across geographies and alliances.

Another critical change in healthcare will have to be a revamping of the legal system with significant tort reform. While this issue has been argued for many years about its true financial impact, the increasing stress on the system for both the delivers of healthcare and the patients is significant. A fair and equitable tort reform system will have to be created.

New models will unfold for integration of nontraditional patients, that is, those patients who are "well" or have not seen healthcare providers. This connectivity with otherwise healthy individuals, will focus on preventive care and appropriate behavior changes, and will start to unfold

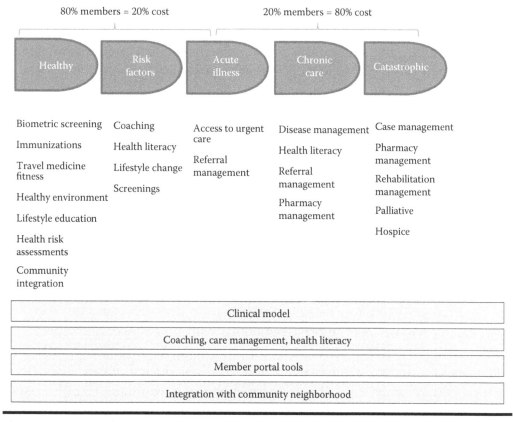

80% members = 20% cost   20% members = 80% cost

Healthy   Risk factors   Acute illness   Chronic care   Catastrophic

Biometric screening	Coaching	Access to urgent care	Disease management	Case management
Immunizations	Health literacy	Referral management	Health literacy	Pharmacy management
Travel medicine fitness	Lifestyle change		Referral management	Rehabilitation management
Healthy environment	Screenings		Pharmacy management	Palliative
Lifestyle education				Hospice
Health risk assessments				
Community integration				

Clinical model

Coaching, care management, health literacy

Member portal tools

Integration with community neighborhood

Figure 14.4   Population Health. (Adapted from the Fabius population health model. Courtesy of Ray Fabius.)

as financial models evolve to support this. The also be new nonphysician individuals that we need a part of the new healthcare delivery models (Figure 14.4).

In the Five- to Ten-Year Timeframe

Consumers will have a much more dominant role and be much more active in their own healthcare. Additional disruptive technologies will occur with patients' being able to self-manage much of their healthcare at home because they will have the ability to communicate seamlessly with their healthcare providers and interpret healthcare information using decision-support tools.

One fundamental governmental issue which will have to be resolved is the decision whether healthcare is a right or privilege. As the ACA legal battle sorts itself out, some of this will be elucidated. This right or privilege question or in other words will tax payers foot some of the healthcare bill for those who can afford it will be fundamental to how the future of healthcare delivery shapes up.

There will be more consolidation with nationwide networks developing. There will be a strong integration between the retail players, such as Walgreens, Walmart, and similar businesses, and the more classic delivery systems. One interesting potential future is that the new healthcare models may actually be driven by these retail giants rather than the current healthcare delivery models. Some of these retail titans could easily alter the course and final delivery system of healthcare. Technology will connect the systems seamlessly. There will be complete pricing transparency, and payments will now be bundled so that if the patient gets an MRI with contrast, there will not be separate billing for the MRI, the physician over read, and the contrast. Pricing will be much more competitive with this transparency, and patients will now shop for services with full pricing knowledge as well as outcomes knowledge. We may even face reference pricing, where prices for each procedure or episode of care is fixed by the government or other payers. If the price is over this fixed reimbursement, the patient must absorb the difference.

Physicians and other healthcare providers will be part of systems and will be fully employed by the systems. These systems will include a team-based approach to care with RNs, physician assistants, and nurse practitioners as well as other healthcare providers all working under the same roof. There will be continued consolidation and there will be a few large national systems as well as some large local providers.

Payment to the systems will be value-based and outcomes-based and no longer focus simply on activity. Consumers will be incentivized and involved in their own healthcare with clear financial as well as healthcare incentives to control their healthcare spend expenditures and their own health.

There will be a much broader focus on "health" as opposed to healthcare and much more activity on prevention and wellness rather than focusing on "sick" care. There will be a broadly accepted care process for both palliative and hospice (and advanced directives), and patient wishes will be broadly available either through cloud-based systems or through individual medical records that are carried with the patient like credit card.

Moreover, medical records will be much more transportable from delivery system to delivery system through a cloud-based technology or portable keychain or jump drive availability. This will be a sniffing evolution from our current Health Insurance Exchanges. There will be much more integration with community-based services and families, and churches and other community services.

Also in this timeframe, from a purely demographic point of view, we will have many more elderly individuals particularly in the old age group (over 85). Many of these care services will have to be carefully tailored for this age group, focusing on some of the geriatric models of functionality. In this age group, the focus is on feeling well and remaining high functioning, not only on life prolongation.

There will be much more emphasis on telemedicine and home health as technology evolves. Physicians will communicate with patients *via* telehealth electronic medicine. Many visits will be done *via* telemedicine.

EMRs will be interconnected and the standardized communication will be legally mandated so that medical information flows seamlessly wherever it is needed. In addition, decision-support information for evidence-based care, which will be continually expanding, will be integrated directly into the EMR so the differential diagnosis, treatment options, and evidence-based care will all be integrated directly into the electronic medical record and pharmaceutical modules.

On the medical side, new technologies will focus at the individual patient level, and personalized medications and care services will be the norm. Patients will be scanned gnomically, and medications that are focused at the personalized level will be made or delivered. Care delivery will be individualized using this information and computer-based modeling to deliver individualized care.

Summary

Many people agree on the direction that these changes should take and what they will look like. The biggest controversy in healthcare is how fast and how soon these changes will take place. There are many competing interests that have the ability to slow down much of the disruptive innovation. When all is said and done, it is plain old demand and supply economics that will drive these changes. We just can't afford to continue to pay for the rising costs of healthcare (Figure 14.5).

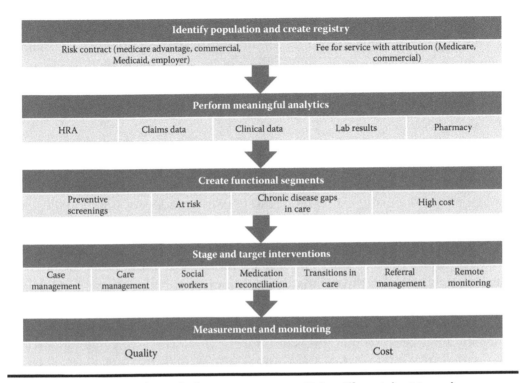

Figure 14.5   Science of population management. (Brian Silverstein, Managing Director, HC Wisdom, LLC.)

Bibliography

1. Nash DB, Reifsnyder J, Fabius RJL, Pracilio VP. *Population Health Creating a Culture of Wellness*. Jones & Bartlett Learning 2011. www.iblearning.com.
2. Kue Young T. *Population Health Concepts and Methods*. Second edition. Oxford University Press, Oxford, 2005, pp. 392.
3. Health Care Transformation: First Curve to Second Curve Markets. HRET. Prioritizing Population Health Interventions from Data Aggregation to Actionable Insights. 2013 The Advisory Board Company. Advisory.com
4. HRET. Trends in Hospital-based Population Health Infrastructure. December 2013.
5. Moving Forward. Winter 2013. Executive Summary.
6. IHA Illinois Hospital Association, Commitment to Transformation, Navigating the Journey to the "NewH," IHA Transforming Illinois Health Care Task Force 2014.
7. Health Care Advisory Board. The Consumer-Oriented Ambulatory Network, Converting Patient Preference into Durable System Advantage.
8. HBI Cost and Quality Academy. Best Practices in Population and Disease Management, Engaging Patients to Ensure Adherence with Care Plans.

9. Porter ME, Lee TH. The strategy that will fix health care. *Harvard Business Review*, October 2013; 91(10): 50–70.

10. The Advisory Board Company, Health Care Advisory Board, Care Transformation Center, The Scalable Population Health Enterprise, Generating Clinical and Financial Returns from Cost-Effective Care Management.

11. Bodenheimer T. Coordinating care—A perilous journey through the health care system. *New Engl J Med*. Health Policy Report. March 6, 2008; www.nejm.org.

12. Bush H. *Caring for the Costliest*. H&HN; November 2012. www.hhnmag.com.

13. Larkin H. *Population Health*. Embracing Risk.

14. GovernanceInstitute.com. *Moving Forward*. Winter 2013. Executive Summary.

15. Silverstein B. Managing Director, HC Wisdom, LLC.

16. Parrish RG. Preventing chronic disease, *Measuring Population Health Outcomes*, July 2010; 7(4).

17. The Fabius population health model. *Population Health: Creating Cultures of Wellness*; 2nd edition, Jones & Bartlett Learning.

Index